Drawing of the composer by Theodore Strawinsky, 1961

Igor Stravinsky

Igor Stravinsky

His life, works and views

Mikhail Druskin

translated by

Martin Cooper

Cambridge University Press

Cambridge

London   New York   New Rochelle
Melbourne   Sydney

Published by the Press Syndicate of the University of Cambridge
The Pitt Building, Trumpington Street, Cambridge CB2 1RP
32 East 57th Street, New York, NY 10022, USA
296 Beaconsfield Parade, Middle Park, Melbourne 3206, Australia

Originally published in Russian as *Igor Stravinsky –
lichnost', tvorchestvo, vzglyady* by Gosizdat (Sovetsky
Kompozitor) and © Gosizdat 1979

Now first published in English by Cambridge University Press
1983 as *Igor Stravinsky: his life, works and views*
English edition © Cambridge University Press 1983

Printed in Great Britain at
the University Press, Cambridge

Library of Congress catalogue card number: 82-1226

British Library Cataloguing in Publication Data
Druskin, Mikhail Semyonovich
Igor Stravinsky: his life, works and views
1. Stravinskïi, Igor   2. Composers – United
States – Biography
I. Title   II. Igor Stravinsky – lichnost',
tvorchestvo, vzglyady. *English*
783'.92'4   ML410.S932
ISBN 0 521 24590 7

Contents

Illustrations

Acknowledgments

The authors gratefully acknowledge the permission of the Trust Under the Will of Igor Stravinsky and of Robert Craft, to reprint in this book material from the books by Igor Stravinsky and Robert Craft entitled *Conversations with Igor Stravinsky*, © 1958, 1959 Igor Stravinsky; Memories and Commentaries © 1959, 1960 Igor Stravinsky; *Expositions and Developments*, © 1959, 1960, 1961, 1962 Igor Stravinsky; and *Dialogues*, © 1963 Igor Stravinsky, respectively (such books are available in the United States and Canada from the University of California Press, Berkeley, California 94720 and in Great Britain from Faber & Faber Publishers, 3 Queen Square, London WC1N 3AU); and from the books by Igor Stravinsky *Chronicles of My Life* © Igor Stravinsky, and *Poetics of Music* © 1947, 1975 President & Fellows of Harvard College.

Preface by Theodore Strawinsky

Among the countless books that have appeared about Stravinsky this is unquestionably one that deserves to be known to the wider public who cannot read it in the original. Mikhail Druskin is a distinguished musicologist, whose study of Stravinsky first appeared in Leningrad in 1974, followed by a German translation two years later. A second 'corrected and completed' edition was published in Leningrad in 1979; a French translation of it is in preparation; and English and American readers will, I feel sure, welcome the opportunity of becoming acquainted with Druskin's book in the present translation.

At the time of Stravinsky's death in 1971 there already existed a mass of works devoted to his music, to his aesthetics, and to his personality as containing the key to his development as an artist.[1] Some of these studies had a certain importance when they appeared, but since their subject was a living personality and a body of work that was still growing and evolving, they were as it were open-ended. The advantage enjoyed by Druskin's book (and others written, or at least completed, after Stravinsky's death) lies in the fact that it has now become possible to view the subject as a whole; and in making use of this advantage Druskin has shown altogether extraordinary qualities of sensibility, tact and psychological penetration. Furthermore Druskin is not only a musicologist – that is his profession – but also a profound and subtle student of human nature. This has enabled him to study Stravinsky's personality not only through his music but also as a human being, and one who responded with absolute immediacy to every aspect of human existence. It is in fact this human being that Druskin seeks in the composer, each helping to explain the other. On the other hand he has never allowed the admiration, the affection, even veneration that he feels for Stravinsky's music to detract one iota from his critical sense. It is this circumstance, I believe, that gives his opinions their authoritative character.

Druskin's analyses of Stravinsky's works, individually and as a whole, are unfailingly lucid, illuminated as it were from within. He examines each of the specific characteristics of Stravinsky's genius and has a firm grasp of the roots from which that music grew and developed over the years. This development was various, Protean, like that of his contemporary Picasso. Indeed, Picasso and Stravinsky are two personalities to whom among others – and doubtless more than to any others – our age owes its character. Nor is this parallel a fortuitous one, for Druskin also insists upon it. If we use the word 'Protean' of Stravinsky's evolution, it must be granted that logical minds will not fail to discover a number of apparent contradictions between its different phases. Were these in fact contradictions? They certainly acted as a stimulus first to the composer himself, who found himself repeatedly called upon to outdistance himself in order to find his new path, and then to students in search of the essence of his music. In Stravinsky's case his music meant his evolution. Then quite apart from such contradictions as these – and setting them in a still clearer light – there were the many paradoxical statements in which he delighted to express himself, whether verbally or in writing. These were given enormous publicity and disconcerted some even of his most fervent admirers, who found themselves suddenly confronted with a Stravinsky who was the opposite of the one they thought they knew. Here again Druskin is concerned to explain to his readers the actual truth embodied by the composer in his music and at the same time disguised in deliberate, often humorous paradoxes recalling those of G. K. Chesterton.

When it comes to the question of the Russian element in Stravinsky's music – something to which Druskin attaches major importance – his analysis goes to the true heart of the matter. Whereas the general public regards only Stravinsky's first period as 'Russian' (chiefly on account of the preponderance of Russian subjects) Druskin goes much further. He shows us the origins, the deep roots of Stravinsky's music, and tries to make us aware of the persistence of a Russian element in its very texture. In the early works this element was clear enough, but Druskin traces it right through the unhappily named 'neo-classical' works, where the track is not always easy to follow, and into the works of the last period, where it is often quite difficult. This was the period, after *The Rake's Progress*, when the 'Russian' composer who had become the chief figure in the neo-classical movement in twentieth-century music suddenly surprised the world by laying his art wide open to the serialism of the Second Viennese School, which he had always hitherto obstinately rejected. In fact Druskin demonstrates the persistent presence, against all appearances, of this Russian vein throughout the whole of Stravinsky's oeuvre.

Persistent though that element may have been, it was not the fundamental element of his aesthetics, which was – as Druskin shows

– his universal eclecticism. It is this that explains all the sudden changes and apparent breaks in his evolution as a composer, the last of which brought him, in serialism, a whole new area to exploit as a craftsman. I am quite prepared to admit that the Russian element persisted in the music of this last period, and indeed Druskin gives clear instances from *Requiem Canticles*, the chief work of these last years. It is only fair to say, moreover, that Stravinsky's nostalgia for Russia, which Druskin represents as having sharply increased during his last years in America, was then, as always, counterbalanced by another trait which was absolutely fundamental to his character and which was expressed in the wise words of C. F. Ramuz, who wrote 'You never were, and never could be a foreigner anywhere, for nowhere did you lack affinities with things, with life, you were nowhere separated from Being – and that is the greatest gift of all.' That indeed is how he was, with all his complexities, the man who is the subject of this book, the man who was my father. We were always close, both emotionally and intellectually, and we engaged in endless discussions of artistic, religious and philosophical problems. I was therefore delighted to find that Druskin's study includes, beside a true portrait of Stravinsky and an extremely apt analysis of his music, many illuminating observations on the position occupied by that music in what may be called the 'cultural substance' of the twentieth century.

Author's preface to second Russian edition

This book was completed in 1973 and first published in Russian in 1974; a German translation appeared in 1976. Having left the author's hands, the book led an independent existence. It had been planned for a number of years, and from the middle of the sixties fragments had appeared as articles in the Soviet and foreign Press. In the present edition (1979) a number of points have been clarified and some further information added. Otherwise the contents remain unchanged. It may, however, be as well to emphasise several ideas which form the basis of the book.

Stravinsky was one of the Russian composers who have exercised an enormous influence on contemporary music. Many different aspects of twentieth-century music are reflected in his works, but throughout his long life he remained a Russian artist, closely bound up with the traditions of Russian culture. This is one of the central themes of the book. At the same time Stravinsky cannot be understood without reference to twentieth-century Western culture and its many glaring contradictions. Like Valéry, T. S. Eliot, Picasso and Thomas Mann, Stravinsky sought to assimilate and to reflect in his music the whole artistic experience of the European past. The manifestation of this universalism in his music is a second fundamental theme.

If Stravinsky never ceased to attract the attention of the musical world, it was not only as an enormously gifted composer but also as a highly organised intellectual personality – a personality in which there were a number of paradoxes and contradictions. In order to penetrate the essential character of these contradictions, the author has attempted to present a more complete picture of Stravinsky's unique individuality, and this may be regarded as the third main idea of the book. As Goethe says –

> Wer den Dichter will verstehen
> Muss in Dichters Lande gehen

– in order, that is, to penetrate the 'poet's world' we must study not only his works but how he himself understood them and what he thought about himself, his contemporaries and his predecessors. In order to realise this ideal the author has made use of many quotations from Stravinsky's own pronouncements. These quotations are often embedded in the text, and their object is to direct the reader's attention to the personality of the composer and to the artistic and intellectual movements of his day. The quotations are interpreted critically and made the subject of discussion. In fact they serve as a natural reinforcement and corroboration of the author's theories.

It would of course be a mistake to equate Stravinsky's opinions with his musical legacy: his subjective interpretations of his own works may well differ from the estimates of objective critics. This is particularly true in the case of Stravinsky, whose artistic sympathies and antipathies were for many years – many decades, indeed – arbitrary and fluctuating. At the very height of his career he would on occasion make a parade of the wildest and most unexpected paradoxes. In this sense one could perhaps apply to him the witty observation of Somerset Maugham's:

The celebrated develop a technique to deal with the persons they come across. They show the world a mask, often an impressive one, but take care to conceal their real selves. They play the part that is expected of them and with practice learn to play it very well, but you are stupid if you think that this public performance of theirs corresponds with the man within.[1]

The quotations from Stravinsky's own words have been taken from six books written or edited by him at different periods and with different collaborators, who have left a certain imprint of their own upon the contents:

Chroniques de ma vie (Paris 1935–6; English translation as *Chronicle of my Life*, London 1936). This is an autobiographical narrative dictated by Stravinsky to V. F. Nouvel, for many years a collaborator with Serge Diaghilev. It goes up to 1934, a time when Stravinsky was proposing to stand for the Académie Française – hence in all probability the elaborately polite and occasionally even *mondain* tone.

Poétique musicale, with the collaboration of Pierre Souvchinsky and Alexis Roland-Manuel (Paris 1952; English translation by Arthur Knodel and Ingolf Dahl as *Poetics of Music*, Harvard University Press 1942, 4th edition 1977). This was based on lectures given at Harvard University 1939–40.

Four volumes of conversations, published under the joint authorship of Igor Stravinsky and Robert Craft:
Conversations with Stravinsky (London 1958)
Memories and Commentaries (London 1959)
Expositions and Developments (London 1959)

Dialogues and a Diary (London 1963)
Selections from these four books have been translated into Russian
and published in a single volume as *Dialogy* (Leningrad 1971).

The tone of the lectures which form the basis of *Poetics of Music* is
sharp and polemical, and the subject-matter alternates swiftly
between what is serious and important and what is superficial and
anecdotal. This unevenness of quality is easily explained by the
awkward position in which Stravinsky found himself during the first
year of his residence in the United States. Quite apart from that,
however, Stravinsky could hardly be expected to exhibit consistency
or to provide systematic substantiation in the exposition of his ideas
since, despite the undoubted sharpness of his intelligence and the
penetrating character of his observations, he never had any inclination for aesthetic speculation. What was characteristic of him was
an aphoristic way of talking, an explosive quality in the judgments
that he would often appear to deliver impromptu, though they may
well, in fact, have been premeditated. The charm of the conversations
with Robert Craft lies in the fact that here Stravinsky appears at his
ease and speaks freely, without restraint of any kind. Craft put the
questions and directed the course of these 'interviews', and it must be
admitted that it is not always easy to distinguish the voice of the man
steering the conversation from that of the man answering the
questions. However, for the most part Stravinsky's voice is clearly
distinguishable.

The many references to *Chronicle* and the various books containing Stravinsky's conversations with Robert Craft are inset in the text
and compared with the opinions and judgments of other major artists
of the twentieth century, thus emphasising Stravinsky's many and
various spiritual links with his contemporaries.

The present book consists of thirteen chapters including an
introduction and an epilogue. The skeleton of the book is formed by
three chapters ('The Russian element', 'World classics' and 'Torniamo all'antico . . .') in which the three stages of Stravinsky's
artistic development – the Russian period, the neo-classical and the
final period – are distinguished in the accepted manner. Interspersed
with these chapters are eight others which concentrate on the
theoretical aspects of the subject. The multiplicity of these angles of
vision establishes a system of cross-reference between the different
chapters of the book and gives rise to a kind of invertible counterpoint throughout the book.

1

Preliminary portrait

In writing about Stravinsky's personality it would plainly be an advantage to have spent a considerable amount of time in his company, to have observed him closely, to have followed – and indeed to have shared – his intense and often unexpected spiritual development, to have seen him regularly on working days and on special occasions, at his work table, in all the preliminary preparations for a first performance and at those performances themselves. It is a handicap not to have taken part in his private conversations or to have attended the many official receptions with which he was concerned, not to know at first hand his reading habits or the books he read, his daily interests, what he accepted and what he rejected in the milieu in which he lived, in urban civilisation generally, in the monuments of the cultural past, in nature. How invaluable to have had personal experience of how he arranged his working day, or how his ideas originated and of the course of their realisation; and what a privilege it would have been to have experienced personally the spontaneous ebullitions of such a highly and variously gifted personality, to have seen that remarkable temperament in effective action!

There is, however, a further difficulty in writing about the phenomenon of Stravinsky's personality and it lies in the fact that this personality was neither simple nor unambiguous. Although he was an artist of high intellectual development and strong purpose, his very subjective and fluctuating attitudes to life, to people and to art revealed the complexity and mercurial nature of his character. He himself said that the sonorous complex (in music) springs from the tension arising from the pull of polarised forces, and we may visualise the inner essence of his personality as a highly individual complex of just such opposed forces.

This tension was partly reflected in his personal appearance. Although small in build, he had the disproportionately large hands of an artisan which found a further contradiction in the small, noticeably elongated head. His facial features were harsh and angular – something particularly emphasised in Picasso's sketches of him – and he himself once jokingly observed that 'my music consists

1

entirely of bones'. A skeleton, of course, has many angles and intersecting lines and, to continue Stravinsky's own metaphor, we might say that his strongly knit frame was the exterior expression of the complex and apparently ill-regulated intersection of these lines. But in action – and Stravinsky was very impulsive by nature – these angles became smoother and softer, a harmony was revealed in the geometrical disproportions and a fundamental unity became apparent.

His eyes were immediately arresting – deepset, piercing, narrowly and intensely observant, as though intent on penetrating to the very heart of a subject. His way of holding himself, his 'carriage', betrayed both a *mondain* elegance and the casual ease of the artist; and this combination again gave the vague suggestion of some inner contradiction. How indeed are we to explain this touch of the *mondain* in an artist gifted – in Pushkin's words – 'with a sharp and cool intelligence', 'a swift and piercing eye'?

Compare, for example, the early Paris days of Stravinsky's contemporary, Picasso, in the *bateau-lavoir* haunted by Derain, Dufy, Braque, Léger, Apollinaire, Max Jacob. He, and the others, knew what it was to be really poor, and the pictures that he painted at that time contain many down-and-outs. Reputation and material comfort came to Picasso in time, but he was never attracted by aristocratic society. Or take a musician who stood at the opposite extreme to Stravinsky – Arnold Schoenberg, his senior by eight years, who knew real poverty not only in his early days but later too. He had a difficult life during which he naturally met many people but, business dealings apart, all of these shared his intellectual or artistic interests, and with his firm convictions and his egocentric tendencies he admitted only a few friends on an intimate footing. Or take another contemporary of Stravinsky's, Bela Bartók, a man who spent the greater part of his time with musicians and was more attracted by long expeditions studying folk-lore than by smart parties. Hindemith and Honegger were of course considerably younger than Stravinsky and developed in a different age and another milieu.

Stravinsky frequented the frivolous, 'social' world more than any composer of his own, or indeed of the younger, generation. He came into contact with the artistic world in the house of his father, a well-known singer of the Maryinsky Theatre, who entertained not only his colleagues but Stassov, Mussorgsky and Dostoevsky. Even as a child he was imbued with the whole phantasmagoria of the theatre, the freedom and insouciance of backstage life. As a young man he was a member of the highest circles of the artistic intelligentsia in

Petersburg, and took part in the 'Evenings of Contemporary Music' in which he played a leading role with A. P. Nurok and V. F. Nouvel. Through them he came into contact with contributors to the magazine *Mir Iskusstva* ('The World of Art') and with the man who set his personal seal on that paper, Serge Pavlovich Diaghilev. It was under Diaghilev's decisive influence and patronage that the young Stravinsky's dazzling career as a composer was established. On his mother's side Stravinsky was distantly related to Diaghilev. 'I need hardly say what an important part these two societies ["Evenings of Contemporary Music" and the "World of Art" group] played in my artistic and intellectual development and how they forwarded the growth of my creative powers.'[1]

It is not possible to sum up Diaghilev's personality in a single phrase. An aesthete of the greatest refinement, he possessed a faultless artistic taste, a keen flair for everything fresh or novel in the arts and a superb talent for organisation. During twenty years of intense activity up to his death in 1929 he triumphantly established Russian art in Western Europe, and the performances given by his 'Ballets Russes' stand out among the greatest events in the musical–theatrical history of the first decades of the twentieth century.

It was Diaghilev who revealed Stravinsky's genius to the world, and he took an enormous pride in his protégé, guarded him jealously and tried – unsuccessfully – to dominate him entirely as his own inalienable property. It was the clash of two wills, Diaghilev overbearing and intolerant of opposition and Stravinsky convinced of his own vocation; and the break between them described in *Conversations* was inevitable. This came later, however, and in the early years it was thanks to Diaghilev, though not without the assistance of another jealous patron, Debussy, that Stravinsky was quickly accepted by the aristocratic élite of Paris. He became a fashionable figure and was received in the smart salons of the day. There was Misia Sert, with her second husband Edwards, editor of *Le Matin*, and her brother Cipa Godebski, the friends of Ravel; and there was the Princesse Edmond de Polignac, who commissioned and performed new works by Fauré, Ravel, Satie, Falla and Poulenc as well as by Stravinsky. There was Gabrielle Chanel, of the great *couturier* house, one of Diaghilev's most generous supporters, the dancer Ida Rubinstein and the American arts-patron Elizabeth Sprague Coolidge, the last two of whom commissioned works by Stravinsky.

He developed close ties with many representatives of the other arts, with philosophers, physicists and theologians, and he met a number of important political figures. He gave interviews in which, he was later to relate, 'my words, my ideas and even the facts themselves were distorted to the point of unrecognisability',[2] but he went on giving them nevertheless, amazing his interviewers with his gift for repartee, the sharpness of his intelligence and the paradoxical character of his judgments. Has any other twentieth-century composer been considered worthy of such attention?

Stravinsky did not cultivate success artificially. Fame came to him unexpectedly at the age of twenty-eight with the performance of *Firebird* in Paris (1910) and was greatly increased three years later after the notorious first performance of *The Rite of Spring*. His name remained famous even after the Second World War, though the works that he wrote in the 1950's and 1960's did not enjoy the success of those that he wrote before 1930. At the end of his career the ovations that he received were due perhaps less to his music than to his personality, as the embodiment of a fame enjoyed while still living – something consisting in the last resort, as Rilke observed bitterly, of 'the sum of the misunderstandings that arise around the name of a famous artist'. As an old man he found it oppressive. 'A plague on eminence!',[3] he exclaimed on one occasion. And how tragic he sounds when he says

I was born out of due time in the sense that by temperament and talent I should have been more suited for the life of a small Bach, living in anonymity and composing regularly for an established service and for God. I did weather the world I was born to, weathered it well, you might say, and I have survived – though not uncorrupted – the hucksterism of publishers, music-festivals, recording companies and publicity – including my own.[4]

Behind the façade of *mondain* wit there lay concealed an intense intellectual life, and how these two extremes were combined in Stravinsky, how such totally opposed aspirations were compatible in a single character will always remain a mystery.

It may be said without fear of exaggeration that no contemporary expatriate composer could compare with Stravinsky in knowledge of the present-day world, whether it was in philosophy, religion, aesthetics, psychology, mathematics, or the history of art. Nor was he content to remain simply well informed, he wished to have a specialist's understanding of every subject, his own opinion on every problem and his own attitude to every point under discussion. Right into extreme old age he was an avid reader and always had a book in his hands. His library in Los Angeles contained something like 10,000 books, and in this indeed he resembled his father, who was also a passionate bibliophile. Reading answers a need for spiritual contact, and he was active and intense in both conversation and letter-writing. Until 1956, when his left leg was weakened by a stroke, he walked quickly and impatiently,[5] and his reactions were equally quick, whether it was to the remarks of his partner in a conversation or to the ideas of a writer, which he immediately seized upon and adapted to his own.

Work, however, was his main concern and he was indefatigable, never allowing himself a breathing space and able, if necessary, to continue eighteen hours on end. Robert Craft, who played a large part in Stravinsky's life after 1948 and was eventually to become his *alter ego*, bears witness to the fact that in 1957, when the composer was seventy-five, he worked ten hours a day – composing for four to five hours before lunch and orchestrating or transcribing for five to six hours after that. After 1923, however, Stravinsky took part in many concerts and therefore gave only approximately six months of the year to composition. He worked steadily and regularly every day – in his own words, 'like a man working office hours'. That, to use a figurative comparison, is the explanation of Stravinsky's hands, the hands of a 'craftsman'. Describing the process of composition he emphasised one particular feature: 'I insist on the word "pleasure", though some might find it too light-weight. It was the feeling I experienced in the actual process of working and in foreseeing the joy that every inspiration and every discovery would give me.'[6] Elsewhere he wrote that inspiration 'is found as a driving force in every human activity' but that 'this force is only brought into action by an effort, and that effort is work that brings inspiration'.[7]

Thus Stravinsky with his vocation as a 'sacrifice to Apollo' (to paraphrase Pushkin) and Stravinsky intent on being a figure in the public eye were one and the same person, an essentially contradictory individual. Although the whole tenor of his existence declared him to belong to 'this' world, he strove at the same time to rise not only above its frivolity, but above the conflicts of that other threatening age whose horizon was darkened by the storms of social revolution.

Why, then, do I insist on the contrasts in Stravinsky's personality? Picasso justly observed, 'It is not what an artist does that is important, but what he represents . . . It is Cézanne's disquiet that irresistibly attracts us, that we learn from; it is in Van Gogh's agonies that we find the true drama of humanity!' What is it indeed that attracts us in Stravinsky? Precisely this contrast of opposites between his spiritual and his emotional powers. I do not think that during the course of his sixty years' service to music – and his was a passionate service – his personality underwent such significant changes as his style of composition. On the contrary, I should say that his personality was finally shaped by the age of thirty, and that by then both the 'barbarian' and the 'aesthete' existed in him, the one possessed of an elemental power and the other concerned with modernising the styles of different epochs (including folk-music), while the stern 'ascetic' rejected artistic embellishment of any kind. These three features appeared in succession as dominating the three main periods of Stravinsky's career as a composer. Naturally, within those periods there were works which formed an exception to this general rule. Thus the *Octet* and *Symphonies of Wind Instruments* are 'ascetic', although Stravinsky was still in his Russian period when he wrote them; and the stylisation characteristic of the 'World of Art' movement is to be found in *Firebird* and *The Nightingale*, while the turbulent 'Scythian' element so characteristic of *The Rite of Spring* recurs in the last movements of *Symphony of Psalms* and *Symphony in Three Movements*, and is even perceptible in the opening section of *Requiem Canticles*, the composer's last significant work.

A rich stratification of this kind, rooted fundamentally in the polarisation of his emotional powers, is one of the attractions of Stravinsky's music: a listener who finds the works of any one individual period unsympathetic may be enthralled by works belonging to another. Furthermore, differences of individual taste may well account for different reactions to works that are chronologically close to each other. The impressions made, for instance, by *Petrushka* (1911) and *The Rite of Spring* (1913) or by *Les Noces* (1923) and *Pulcinella* (1920) are not comparable in character; and it is possible to be fond of *Symphony of Psalms* (1930) while rejecting *The Fairy's Kiss* (1928). There is an analogous correlation between *The Rake's Progress* (1951) and the *Septet* (1952), *The Flood* (1962) and *Threni* (1958). Yet beneath all these differences of manner we are aware of a single personality, a unity in complexity and a specifically Stravinskian vital sensibility, the manifestation of which changes with each new work. There are very few references to this in existing studies of Stravinsky. The study of an artist's sensibility, or temperament as it used to be called, is generally masked by questions of his attitudes and opinions. Such questions are of course very important for the understanding of his artistic aims, but they are by no means the whole story. In what light does the artist actually see the world, and what are the colours that he chooses from his palette – gloomy or serene, dark or light? One man's existence (though no one knows why) is full of joy, while another lives with perpetually furrowed brows. One man is naturally sociable, while another shuns society, and this not on account of his circumstances, his milieu, his education, or his political, philosophical, religious or ethical convictions. It is simply a matter of temperament, cast of mind and innate emotional characteristics. And I believe that these differences are quite as important as differences of artistic method in explaining Tchaikovsky's inability to understand or accept Brahms, Brahms's own rejection of Wagner, Picasso's of Matisse and Tolstoy's of Dostoevsky. It was precisely in the quality of his perception of life that Stravinsky differed from many of his contemporaries.

From Mahler onwards twentieth-century music has been marked by emotional suffering, by dramatic 'expression' and an obsession with the tragic. Arthur Honegger described the content of the first movement of his third ('Liturgique') symphony as 'the catastrophe in which we are living', and these words could stand on the title page of works by other composers, men seized by the same desire to represent the mounting impact of evil, dishonesty, violence and oppression. After the 1914–18 war a tragic note entered the works, even of the life-loving Ravel in *La Valse* and *Pianoforte Concerto for the Left Hand*; and similar things are to be found in the music of Hindemith (whose emotional sanity was frequently remarked by critics), not to speak of Schoenberg, Berg and Bartók.

The young Stravinsky made an electrifying effect by his youthful freshness when he first appeared on the musical scene. The triumphant popularity of *Fireworks* (1908), and still more of *Firebird* and *Petrushka*, was due to the festive nature of the music, its vitality and rhythmic impulse. In the twenties his musical language became more austere, more economical, even harsher, but it still preserved this festive character, despite a change in the organisation of the impulses behind it. This began somewhat earlier with the accentuation of the play-element in *Renard, The Soldier's Tale* and other works of the same kind (*Pribautki, Cat's Cradle Songs, Saucer Songs*, and *Three Stories for Children*); and there also intruded, in grotesque transformation, an element of dancing as a social activity (for example in *Ragtime*). The play-element was confirmed in *Les Noces* and its parallel in an altogether different style, *Pulcinella*.

In her interesting monograph on Picasso, N. Dmitrieva observes that at precisely this time, around 1910, artists became newly aware of the play-element – what Schiller[8] calls *der Spieltrieb* (the play instinct) in art. 'Man in general, and especially today, is not only *homo sapiens* or *homo faber* but also *homo ludens*, and this is not a weakness but a strength, a guarantee of his freedom.' The term *homo ludens* was first introduced by Johan Huizinga, who in a book with that title[9] wrote:

Play is not 'ordinary' or 'real' life. It is rather a stepping out of 'real' life . . . a voluntary activity . . . it is 'played out' within certain limits of time and space . . . The aim of play is itself . . . it is accompanied by feelings of tension, of joy, and of an awareness of an 'other' existence.

Homo ludens rejects all that is subjective and arbitrary: the pre-established rules that govern play regulate and give objective value to the formation and development of artistic images, and at the same time the play-principle, within its chosen framework of rules, assumes the freeing of the imagination, the freedom and unconstrainedness of the creative instinct.

One of the manifestations of this freedom is to be found in 'unexpectedness, deliberate eccentricity, a mocking inspiration and an inspired mockery', both (according to Dmitrieva) characteristics of Picasso and to an even higher degree of Stravinsky, in whose case they are combined with a national characteristic, as confirmed by Pushkin's shrewd observation that 'a distinctive feature of our national character is a kind of jovial slyness, a mocking and picturesque manner of expressing oneself'. This form of expression is an organic element in Stravinsky's personality, clearly manifested in the works based on Russian folk-texts up to and including *Les Noces*.

'Mocking inspiration', or 'inspired mockery', is an excellent definition of a whole group of Stravinsky's works, and indeed of a whole vein in his artistic personality which found expression in harlequinades and buffooneries, witty gestures and asides of all kinds. These characterise a series which begins with *Petrushka*, *Pulcinella*, *Mavra* and *The Soldier's Tale*, and is in a sense crowned by the exploitation of the tragic–comic role played by fate or destiny in the ballet *Jeu de cartes*, in *The Rake's Progress* and in the comic wrangling of Noah and his wife in *The Flood*.

It would be a mistake to suppose that this play-element is associated only with the grotesque or the comic. The impulse of Schiller's 'play-instinct' is more general and it is essentially ambivalent, as N. Dmitrieva shrewdly observes:[10]

The 'reality' created in play is, so to say, a double one: it is both genuine and spurious. This split, or contradiction, is in the widest sense of the word, 'humour'. Humour is an accompanying feature of play and does not interfere with its seriousness: it only ceases with the insights that play provides, and 'play reality' overcomes the consciousness of its own 'play' origin.

We shall return to these considerations when speaking of Stravinsky's works for the theatre. For the moment I wish to emphasise the fact that the feeling of 'festiveness' persists in Stravinsky's works, whether they are actually dominated by the play-element or whether that element is sublimated and transposed to another spiritual level, as for instance in *The Fairy's Kiss* on the one hand and *Symphony of Psalms, Capriccio, Persephone, Agon,* and *Canticum sacrum* on the other. An analogy with the apparent contradictions of this kind is provided by Anatole France's story, *Le Jongleur de Notre Dame* – the wandering minstrel who dances in religious ecstasy in front of the statue of the Blessed Virgin, his dance taking on a higher, ethical significance, and ceasing to be pure 'play'.

The element of play lies at the very heart of Stravinsky's music. Alexandre Tansman[11] was the first to draw attention to this, but he describes the different 'rules of the game' employed by Stravinsky, i.e. his use of different 'styles', and does not speak of the actual play-principle underlying all Stravinsky's music. Stravinsky in fact rejected crude social naturalism, emotional realism and the emotional hypertrophy of Expressionism, and aimed at objectivity and a supra-personal atmosphere. Thus the understanding of the 'rules of play' took a new form characterised by ritual, ceremonial features, something outside everyday existence, because, as Huizinga[12] points out, ritual is the highest spiritual expression of the play-principle, the accomplishment of an 'act'. Such an act may be 'joking', it may be grotesque, or it may be sacral in character, inspired by the age-old problems of existence which Stravinsky approaches on some occasions in the spirit of rejoicing and on others in the spirit of mourning or funeral, in which case the 'act' often has a note of tragedy.

Stravinsky's personality was permeated by this festival spirit and he was distinguished among his contemporaries by his joyful acceptance of an intelligent order in life. But this found no open emotional expression. Stravinsky's music is marked not so much by physical high spirits as by a quality of spiritual invigoration, and this is why, despite the energy that it radiates, there is always a note of confident tranquillity – the artistic ideal that he describes as 'dynamic calm'.[13] There are of course occasions on which 'play' becomes an artistic end in itself, when creative imagination and freshness of invention are replaced by craftsmanship. This is particularly noticeable during the critical decade between 1935 and 1945, when we find among his works pale copies of earlier discoveries which have become mannerisms; but there are not many instances of this.

Was Stravinsky exceptional in his apprehension of the world? There have of course been other twentieth-century composers whose works have been marked by this spontaneous, buoyant quality: Prokofiev immediately springs to mind. Bartók, Hindemith and the composers of 'Les Six' wrote many works in this vein, though in the last instance much of this was borrowed from Stravinsky himself. In fact his exalted handling of the festive element was something entirely his own, an integral, definitive characteristic of his artistic individuality.

Stravinsky had a predecessor in Debussy whose *L'Isle joyeuse* and *Fêtes* have this festive quality, though it does not mark by any means all of Debussy's music. Even so, it was this feature that attracted Stravinsky, who borrowed it and turned it to his own uses. He was not so close to Ravel, although the festive – in the commonly accepted use of the word – is more strongly expressed in Ravel's music than in Debussy's. Where Stravinsky differed from Ravel was in the fact that Ravel's music was more traditional in structure, decorative in outward appearance and strongly sensual in character. This was immediately alien to Stravinsky, who was instinctively repelled by the overtly sensual and still more by the erotic – hence his rejection of Wagner and still more markedly Richard Strauss, whose talent he mercilessly labelled as 'triumphant banality'.

In order to understand Stravinsky's aesthetic properly it is necessary to bear in mind that in his case the emotional element is always corrected, and sometimes even excessively controlled, by the intellectual, the rational. 'Art', he insists, 'demands of the artist before all else full consciousness.' The chief thing for the artist is 'to establish order and discipline on the purely sonorous plane to which I have always given preference over emotional elements', and, in greater detail, 'all order demands restraint, but it would be wrong to regard that as any impediment to liberty. On the contrary the "style" and restraint actually contribute to its development, and only prevent liberty from degenerating into licence . . . An artist's individuality stands out more clearly and in greater relief when he has to create within definite limits of a convention.'[14]

Order, discipline, consciousness – these are Stravinsky's favourite expressions, the fundamental priorities of his intelligence, his constant artistic premisses. Here we meet again the essence of the play-element. In Huizinga's words,[15] 'inside the play-ground an absolute and peculiar order reigns . . . play creates order, *is* order'.

Stravinsky liked to create within a strict, pre-ordained framework and the stricter this was, the more intense the heat of his inspiration.

'Let us understand each other', he wrote.[16] 'I am the first to acknowledge that daring is the motive impulse in our vast and marvellous activity, and for that very reason this impulse must not be hastily put to the service of disorder and coarse desires, the aim of which is to produce at all costs a sensation. I approve of daring: it knows no bounds, but there are also no bounds to the damage done by arbitrariness.' By musical poetics Stravinsky meant the study of how order is established in music. His aim was to assert 'the triumph of principle over the arbitrary, of order over randomness', and for a whole decade he repeated tirelessly, 'In all music there must be order, and I am for order.'

The disciplining of the will by the mind was a unique characteristic of Stravinsky's every activity and revealed his personality. It was clear not only in his music, his manner of behaving, his way of speaking and the habitual regularity of his daily life, but in the orderly arrangement on his desk of the coloured pencils, the Indian inks and everything that he needed while composing, including a device for drawing the stems of notes, invented by him and called a 'Stravigor', the composer holding the patent. All this was characteristic of him, not only in old age but much earlier. Ramuz, who collaborated with him in *The Soldier's Tale*, was a close friend of Stravinsky during the 1914–18 war, and he has told us that Stravinsky's work table resembled that of a surgeon rather than of a composer. The neatness and precision of his scores recalled those of a map, with every syllable, every note and every rest perfectly drawn.[17] Stravinsky himself used to joke about his passion for order and compared it to that of a gardener trimming his trees.

Stravinsky, we may suppose, would willingly have agreed with Pushkin's words that 'true taste consists in a feeling for proportion and balance'. Accurate awareness of the plan of the whole, its 'proportion and balance' in detail, unity of style – these are favourite expressions of Stravinsky's, and for this reason it is not surprising that he was interested in polyphony in its strict forms. This attraction began when he was eighteen and even earlier, when he began to study with Rimsky-Korsakov.

This first contact with the science of counterpoint opened up at once a far vaster and more fertile field in the domain of musical composition than anything that harmony could offer me. And so I set myself with heart and soul to the task of solving the many problems which it contains. This amused me tremendously, but it was only later that I realised to what an extent these exercises had helped to develop my judgment and my taste in music.[18]

Stravinsky's clear predilection for polyphony is very understandable, for here he found a method for constructing a web of musical sound strictly ordered and traditionally regulated. He referred to this on several occasions, as for instance in a remark published in November 1924 in the Polish journal *Muzyka*: 'Pure counterpoint seems to me the only material from which powerful and durable musical forms can be forged. Its place cannot be taken by the most refined harmony or the richest orchestration.' Fugue he spoke of as 'the perfect musical form . . . does not fugue presuppose the composer's submission to an established order?'[19] His frequent comparison of 'order' in music to metre, rhyme and rhythm in poetry is very characteristic. Speaking of his *Duo Concertante* he wrote, 'My object was to write a lyrical composition, a work of musical versification.'[20] The part played in poetry by rhyme, he believed, is played in music by repetitions in parallel phrases and passages in the development, while rhythmic firmness corresponds to poetic metre. For this reason he was later (1963) to maintain that he concerned himself with versifying in 'series' just as an artist of another kind might concern himself with versifying in angles or numbers.

There is, in fact, an interesting parallel between this and what Picasso said about the visual arts:[21] 'A picture is not prose, but poetry. It is painted in verses with plastic rhymes, and these rhymes are forms which harmonise with each other and are coordinated with other forms or with the space surrounding them.' In order to give his ideas a preciser form, Stravinsky compared himself with Schoenberg who actually said that he wished to express himself in musical prose, the reverse of *The Rake's Progress*, the model of a contemporary 'opera in verse'. Stravinsky actually spoke of *Erwartung* as 'an opera in prose'.[22]

However, do not let us go any further into that question; all that was necessary was to find an example of that concern with the idea of order in music which troubled him for decades and explains his deep study and adaptation of different stylistic manners, i.e. his appropriation of different 'orders' in the organisation of the material of music, his inclination to classicism and his rejection of those romantic excesses of which he found Wagner guilty. It also explains his disagreement in principle with the current ideas of Expressionism and particularly with those whom he calls modernists, dadaists or simply 'musical Teddy-boys', because they introduce arbitrariness, anarchy and disorder, and these, he believed, categorically contradict the true principle of art.

It would of course be a mistake to conclude from what has been said above that Stravinsky is simply a musical constructor prepared to confine his task to the simple ordering of sounds, that he tried to banish all picturesque interest from his music and that, in his personality, emotion was suppressed by intellect. In that case how are we to explain the elemental power, the explosive force which we meet in *The Rite of Spring*? Moreover echoes of that force may still be heard in the works of his middle, and even of his last period. What is the source of that immense rhythmic pressure and that ruthlessly expanding movement that was not lost even in the works written when he was over eighty?

Defending himself against those who were not satisfied by the polished reserve of many of his neo-classical works during the thirties, Stravinsky was very insistent on his sympathy with the Apollonian rather than the Dionysian element in music. 'There can be no doubt as to my choice between the two', he wrote, 'and if I appreciate so highly the value of classical ballet it is not simply a matter of taste on my part, but because I see exactly in it the perfect expression of the Apollonian principle.'[23] Nevertheless, when in 1948 his son Theodore wrote a small book in which he sketched his father's personal and artistic personality,[24] Stravinsky did not protest against the passage in which these two principles were said to be combined in some of his works, while in others one or the other principle predominated. Ten years later he acknowledged that, though he was an Apollonian artist by inclination, there were Dionysian features in his music.[25] It is hardly possible to find fault with this self-characterisation.

2

Petersburg

No twentieth-century composer travelled as much as Stravinsky, and it is remarkable that after the Second World War, when he was a really old man, his concert tours became even more ambitious than before, and he may indeed be said to have travelled round the world. As he grew older, his craving for new impressions seemed to increase rather than diminish. He continued travelling until he was eighty-eight.

Stravinsky was a frequent visitor to the great capital cities of the world and lived for long periods in Paris, in Los Angeles and in New York, but it is a strange fact that he never developed a feeling of close attachment to any of these, not even to Paris. He definitely disliked New York and spoke of it sarcastically. In his old age he did, it is true, show a certain preference for Venice, where he conducted the first performance of *The Rake's Progress* (1951) and *Canticum Sacrum* (1956), where *Threni* was given in 1958, and where he is in fact buried. On the other hand he never suggested, either in his books or in the innumerable interviews which he gave, that Venice was associated with any important moment in his artistic career.

The only exception to this list was Petersburg, where he spent some thirty years of his life, including his childhood and youth and his first years as a composer. He used to speak with an unwonted warmth of his native city, and the older he grew the more lyrical became the tone of his reminiscences. Those of us who witnessed his return there after half a century's absence are not likely to forget the joy of the occasion.

Stravinsky had left Petersburg at the age of twenty-eight in May 1910, and, returning for a short time in December to discuss with Benois and Diaghilev a number of questions relating to the Paris première of *Petrushka*, remarked 'and the town which only a few months before I had considered the most magnificent in the world now seemed to me depressingly small and provincial, as a child thinks of his bedroom door-handle as something large and significant and later is unable to connect the real object with his memories of it'. Probably, however, Stravinsky found evidence of the 'petty' and 'provincial' in other capitals later, and comparing them with Petersburg further illuminated the role that the city played in his imagination. He became acutely aware of this in his 'exile in another culture', as he called the three decades which he spent in the USA. At the end of his life he said that Petersburg was a city in which it was 'thrillingly interesting to live'. He was not speaking exclusively, or even primarily, about musical impressions, but more generally of the city's spiritual and intellectual culture and its unique character as a whole. It is obviously in this sense that we should understand Stravinsky's interesting remark that 'Petersburg is so much a part of my life that I am almost afraid to look further into myself lest I discover how much of me is still joined to it . . . it is dearer to me than any other city in the world.'[1]

What was it about Petersburg that so fascinated Stravinsky? The memories alluded to above date from 1962, when he was almost eighty, and what he saw in his mind's eye was an ochre city, which in this way reminded him of Rome. He emphasised, 'Italian not merely by imitation but by the direct work of such architects as Quarenghi and Rastrelli'.[2] He remembered fascinating walks down the Nevsky Prospekt, such favourite buildings as the Bourse, Smolny Cathedral, the Alexandrinsky Theatre, the Winter Palace, the Admiralty and of course the Maryinsky Theatre where his father sang.

Petersburg is indeed a city with a complex and many-sided history, and Russian writers and artists have often tried to communicate its essence, its 'soul', in the same way as Balzac, Zola, Maupassant and the Impressionist painters have done for Paris, or Dickens and Galsworthy for London. There is the fantastic, whimsical city, the Petersburg of Gogol's *Nose*, *The Overcoat* and *Nevsky Prospekt*, and the spectral, crepuscular Petersburg, cruel and tragic, scene of Dostoevsky's *Crime and Punishment* and André Bely's *Petersburg*. But there is also a quite different Petersburg, Pushkin's – the 'creation of Peter' with the mighty stream of the Neva, with its rearing Bronze Horseman, the Petersburg of beautiful architectural groupings, of piazzas or squares drawn as though with a pair of compasses, and 'prospects' straight as an arrow. Yuri Tynyanov has written of this very much in the spirit of Pushkin: 'The streets of Petersburg were designed before the houses, which do no more than fill out the street-lines; and the squares were designed before the streets and are therefore self-sufficient, independent of the houses and the streets which form them. The architectural unit of Petersburg is the square.'[3]

We shall not be far wrong, I think, in supposing that it was not only the intellectual atmosphere of Petersburg but the actual physical aspect of the city as it appeared to Pushkin – bright, solemn and spacious – that left this indelible mark on Stravinsky's memory. More than that, we find this image reflected in his music, overtly in the settings of *Petrushka* and *Mavra* and indirectly in other works. When Craft asked him 'has music ever been suggested to you by, or has a musical idea ever occurred to you from, a purely visual experience of movement, line or pattern?', Stravinsky answered unhesitatingly, 'Countless times!'[4]

Why then should we not assume that some aspects of Stravinsky's artistic methods were in fact influenced by his visual impressions of the city's majestic beauty? This may in fact be regarded as one of the manifestations of the Russian, Pushkin element in his music.

Petersburg is, I believe, unique in the wealth and variety of its eighteenth- and early nineteenth-century monuments and buildings. These are characterised by economy, by exquisite simplicity of ornament and by the combination of a freely sweeping general design with great precision in observing proportion, in correlating the basic geometric design, all features of city-planning. Are they not also very similar to characteristics of Stravinsky's music between 1920 and 1940 and in some cases much later, up to and including the 'domelike' construction of *Canticum Sacrum*? The word 'architecture' means the supreme art of construction, and it is in this art that Stravinsky proved himself a master, perfectly commanding the secret of building musical forms. He himself insisted that 'he attempted to build a new music on eighteenth-century classicism and using the construction principles of that classicism'.[5] He instinctively associated the graphic features of that style with the classical beauty and grandeur of Petersburg as celebrated by Pushkin.

This analogy of course by no means exhausts the sources of Stravinsky's neo-classicism, which was part of a broad cultural movement that attracted a large number of musicians and artists, among them two as different as Picasso and Hindemith, as we shall see later. We should bear in mind that Stravinsky himself observed that between 1910 and 1920 'the loss of Russia and its language, verbal as well as musical', caused a stylistic rupture in his music. And it was precisely at that time, when the Russian theme disappeared from his music (although Russian distinguishing marks continued to excite his musical imagination), that his persistent memories of Petersburg became sublimated and, transferred to a different artistic dimension, reappeared in the powerful sense of proportion and the strict regulation of musical forms in *Oedipus Rex* and *Symphony of Psalms*. Traces of this stylistic manner occur in later works such as *Orpheus* (1949) and even *Requiem Canticles* (1966), where the psalmodising of the chorus and the bell-like sonorities of the finale are typically Russian and seem, indeed, like transfigured echoes of the death scene in *Boris Godunov*.

Let us return to Stravinsky's own words: 'One could not better define the sensation produced by music than by saying that it is identical with that evoked by the interplay of architectural forms. Goethe thoroughly understood that when he called architecture petrified music.'[6] If indeed architecture is 'petrified music', is it not possible for building to become something that animates music, more especially in the works of a composer who identifies 'the sensation produced by music . . . with that evoked by the interplay of architectural forms'? Stravinsky spoke specifically of this. 'I have often considered that the fact of my birth and upbringing in a Neo-Italian – rather than in a purely Slavic or Oriental – city must be partly, and profoundly, responsible for the cultural direction of my later life.'[7] This description of the architectural character of Petersburg is one that we cannot accept. What Stravinsky calls 'Neo-Italian' is what we consider to be 'Russian Europeanism', an expression of B. Bursov's,[8] to which we shall return later. But in the present context it is something essentially different if we remember the composer's own words that the city was 'dearer to him than any other in the world'. He refers primarily to the classical style inseparable from the image of Petersburg as conditioning (though not of course exclusively) the direction not only of his artistic interests but his whole culture. No one who sets out to investigate Stravinsky's art should overlook this important acknowledgment of the composer's.

3

Pushkin

Let us now consider Stravinsky's declaration of his love of Pushkin, clearly stated and carefully fostered for decade after decade, during which he never ceased to be amazed by the poet's all-inclusive genius. During his visit to Leningrad (1962) he showed his delight when given a copy of the poet's death mask; and on that same occasion he observed very truly that 'no other country in the world has such a direct and intimate relationship to any of their poets as Russia has to Pushkin. Even for the Germans Goethe remains an Olympian figure.' Furthermore, those who were close to Stravinsky noticed that after his visit to Leningrad and Moscow he began enthusiastically re-reading Pushkin.

There are many further evidences of his devotion to the poet. He was delighted when he discovered that among the texts for *Les Noces* chosen from Kireevsky's collection there was possibly one by Pushkin.[1] Speaking of *Apollo Musagetes*, he said that 'the rhythm of the cello solo at No.41 in the Calliope variation, with the pizzicato accompaniment, is a Russian Alexandrine suggested to me by a couplet from Pushkin'.[2] He also recalled his conversations about Pushkin with André Gide, which had given him pleasure although he did not find Gide's personality sympathetic. Finally *Mavra* is dedicated to the memory of Pushkin, Glinka and Tchaikovsky. As far as the last two are concerned, he actually picked them out as representatives of the 'European' strain, as he saw it, in Russian music, though this was a tribute of grateful acknowledgment rather than of lasting devotion. Of the other figures in Russian cultural history he 'still considered Dostoevsky to be the greatest Russian writer after Pushkin',[3] but this seems a tribute of a general kind rather than an expression of deep personal feeling. In another way his attitude to Pushkin was prejudiced, but this was for special reasons which Stravinsky describes in detail in connection with *Mavra*. He was speaking of a visit to London with Diaghilev in the summer of 1921:

During this same London visit Diaghilev and I conceived another plan which I had very much at heart. What gave rise to it was our common love and admiration for our great poet Pushkin, who for foreigners alas! is but a name in an encyclopaedia, but whose genius in all its versatility and universality was not only particularly dear and precious to us, but represented a whole school of thought. By his nature, his mentality and his ideology Pushkin was the most perfect representative of that wonderful line which began with Peter the Great and has, by a fortunate alloy, united the most characteristically Russian elements with the spiritual riches of the West. Diaghilev unquestionably belonged to this line . . . and as for myself, I had always been aware that I had in me the germs of the same mentality only needing development, and I subsequently deliberately cultivated them.[4]

Here, in fact, we have a short formulation of the whole programme of Russian 'Europeanness', a sharply polemical statement directed against the aesthetic of the 'mighty handful' of the Russian nationalist composers. By his choice of Pushkin's *Little House at Kolomna*, Stravinsky said,

I asserted my attitude towards two trends of Russian thought . . . On the musical plane this poem of Pushkin's led me straight to Glinka and Tchaikovsky, and I resolutely took up my position beside them. I thus clearly defined my tastes and predilections, my opposition to the contrary aesthetic, and once more the good tradition established by these masters.[5]

Stravinsky's polemical accentuation of this antagonism between the two different attitudes among Russian thinkers demands special treatment, but here, in connection with Pushkin whom he quotes as a like-minded ally, I am concerned with something else – what, in fact, he understood by the 'good tradition', which he made it his aim to develop further. Did it really mean no more than 'the union of the most characteristically Russian elements with the spiritual riches of the West'? If so, it must be said that up to the time when he wrote the above passages, that is to say 1934, Stravinsky's music contained no more than isolated, uncoordinated traces of Russian elements and nothing of their characteristic essence. It is true that at different periods of his life, and right up to his death, he often said that the cast of his mind and the nature of his thinking remained Russian; but that is not what we are discussing here.

How then did he conceive the Pushkin tradition? Stravinsky was clearly not speaking his full mind or could not at that time fully explain himself. Let us try to do that for him, and for this we must turn to the works of Pushkin-scholars. Every unprejudiced reader must have been struck by a remarkable coincidence. All writers about Stravinsky comment on his Protean character, the puzzling alternation of styles in his music: and equally invariably critics, starting with Belinsky, have commented on the Protean character of Pushkin, particularly in speaking of his methods of creation. 'The might of a Proteus capable of appearing in every form and penetrating the spirit of different epochs' was Belinsky's description of this characteristic of Pushkin; and in 1832 P. Gnedich wrote in his message to the poet, 'Pushkin, Protean in thy supple language and the enchantment of thy singing!'

Turning to the studies of Soviet literary critics I should like to give some quotations. Here, for example, is G. A. Gukovsky: 'So once again we are faced by the problem of Pushkin's "Protean" character, the universal responsiveness that has astonished his descendants, that absence from his work of any unity of expression, already noted by Gogol . . . Even poems written by him in the same year are quite different in style.'[6] B. I. Bursov tells the same story: 'The Protean character of Pushkin has no parallel among the world's great writers, nor was this simply a natural trait of his genius: it was rather his greatest national characteristic', and later he speaks of 'the infinite multiplicity of his personality . . . the power of transformation or reincarnation that enabled him to present the wholly familiar in an entirely new light'.[7] And finally V. V. Vinogradov:

Pushkin's taste for parody was only an individual manifestation of the ability of his genius to make use of the most widely divergent styles for his own artistic purposes . . . A curious feature of Pushkin's work is the blending and novel reassembling of alien styles. The styles of writers not in themselves of any great range, but remarkable for a number of fine individual works, were elevated by Pushkin to a universal style that served as a model and ideal for every work of the same nature.[8]

Vinogradov presents an imposing list of writers whose styles served Pushkin as 'material for original creation', and these include Ovid, Shakespeare, Byron and Béranger as well as Trediakovsky, Lomonosov, Sumarokov and Derzhavin. He sums up his theory in a single sentence: 'Pushkin's creative thinking was a thinking in literary styles.'

No further quotation is necessary, for the idea which these authors express is clear. What we must now consider is whether it is legitimate to draw a parallel between the multi-faceted nature of Pushkin and the multiplicity of Stravinsky's stylistic 'manners'.

There can be no questioning the fact that 'thinking in artistic (or rather musical) styles' was a typical trait of Stravinsky's. He consciously selected different 'models', which he submitted to practical testing in his music, trying to penetrate their alien manner and to adapt it. He often used to say that we want to possess what we love, and he loved many things in music, although he developed a highly selective and very subjective taste of his own.

Here we are faced with a paradox. Stravinsky was essentially self-taught. He was twenty when he began to consult Rimsky-Korsakov about composition, and, although as time went on he filled in the gaps in his musical education, he did this *ad hoc* rather than systematically, acquainting himself with unfamiliar departments and spheres of music as the spirit moved him. In the case of *Pulcinella*, for instance, he familiarised himself with areas of eighteenth-century music that were new to him. ('*Pulcinella* was my discovery of the past, the epiphany through which the whole of my late work became possible.')[9] From this source sprang a new interest in the composers of the Baroque, and in the first place J. S. Bach, as seen in the *Octet* and the *Piano Concerto* written in 1923–4. In a precisely similar way – can it have been by accident? – Stravinsky 'discovered' Weber, whose virtuoso keyboard music prompted the *Capriccio* of 1929. On several occasions at different stages of his career he felt the need to study Beethoven seriously, and from his attacks on rigid traditional attitudes towards Beethoven's music there developed a jealously demanding attitude to that music, as we see in the *Piano Sonata* of 1922–4 and the *Symphony in C* (1940). The same happened later with Gluck (*Orpheus*, 1947), Gesualdo (*Monumentum*, 1959) and Schoenberg, whose music he had ignored for four decades after the appearance of *Pierrot lunaire*, only to embark on an enthusiastic study of it in 1952.

Even in old age Stravinsky never lost that amazing gift which forms, they say, an integral part of genius, the gift of wonder when confronted with the beauty of creation. Right to the end of his long life he preserved undimmed his ability to delight in musical beauty regardless of when, where, or by whom it was created – whether it was Mozart (whose *Così fan tutte* served as a model for *The Rake's*

Progress), or Guillaume de Machaut, Tallis or Weber. All these provided important stimuli to Stravinsky's imagination, to his active and fervent love of music. 'In order to create there must be a dynamic force', he wrote, 'and what force is more potent than love?'[10]

It was the continuous changes in these stimuli, in which it is by no means always possible to discover any regularity, that gave rise to Stravinsky's mercurial changes of style. He complained that his audiences having once accustomed themselves to the language of his early works were amazed when he embarked on any other – 'They cannot and will not follow me in the progress of my musical thought.'[11] He could answer them in Picasso's words, quoted by Dmitrieva:[12]

How is it possible to expect an outsider to experience a picture of mine as I experienced it? A picture has a long history. Who can tell how long I spent first on its conception, then on visualising it in my imagination and on painting it? The day after it is completed I myself am very uncertain of these things. How can an outsider penetrate my dreams, my feelings, my thoughts, that took so long maturing before they took on their final form?

Stravinsky spoke of his changing styles as 'manners'. They remained comparatively stable over definite periods, but during those periods there were variations, even changes in emphasis. Contrast, for instance, the emphasis on the sonority and articulation of wind instruments in the works written between 1920 and 1923 with the preference for long string melodies after 1928. The alternation of 'manners' of this kind was unpredictable and was particularly sharply defined round about the years 1920 and 1940: 'My manner comes from my personal relationships with the musical material. I discover my "laws" through that material. Even in Russia I worked, composed in that way. My "manners" are the birth-marks of my art.' The essential nature of these 'manners' and the meaning of their changing remained unclear to Stravinsky himself right to the end of his life. One thing is clear, however – the most important thing for him, within the terms in which a given work was conceived, was unity of style, or *tenue*, which was a favourite word of his. This is something which he insisted upon in the table which he drew up contrasting his own personal and individual characteristics with those of Schoenberg, a document full of ironic humour and very self-critical.[13] Nevertheless he admitted, 'although I have been interested all my life in musical "manners" I still cannot say exactly how to define them'.

It is time now to return to our analogy with Pushkin, for his works provide a more definite answer to the question posed but not answered by Stravinsky. Vinogradov observes that 'Pushkin counted a highly developed art of literary stylisation, parody and caricature, revealing the flexibility and high cultural quality of the language, as one of the hallmarks of a mature literature',[14] and Pushkin himself developed the ability of a virtuoso aesthete 'in penetrating as a creative artist the heart and essence of alien style'. It was precisely this virtuosity that constituted for Stravinsky Pushkin's irresistible attraction, as he worked – in Vinogradov's phrase – 'on the blending and combining of foreign styles', reinterpreting old models and adapting them to that cosmopolitan style which he, like Pushkin, tried to establish in his own original works.

A whole century, however, divided Stravinsky from Pushkin, and the whole artistic process consists of a succession of 'periods' each negating yet entailing the one that precedes it. The very tasks confronting the artist had now changed, and the virtuosity that served Pushkin as a means of expressing a high ideal became at times for Stravinsky an end in itself, thus casting a shadow over his work. There were unquestionably differences in their initial positions and thus in the direction of their interests as artists. Pushkin was vindicating what he called the 'European universality' of the Russian language and therefore sharpened his skill in alien styles, so that Russia should possess a mature literature.

During the first stage of Stravinsky's complex development – during his first fifteen years as a composer, that is to say – he asserted the 'European universality' of Russian music and achieved an enormous amount in this direction. Bursov's words about Pushkin's Protean character could well be applied to those years. 'This Protean character was not simply a natural trait of his genius: it was rather his greatest national characteristic.' In the same connection we might recall the well-known lines of Alexander Blok's: 'They are all clear to us – the Gallic wit and the gloomy German genius.'

Between 1920 and 1940 Stravinsky was concerned with obtaining a deeper comprehension of this clear vision of other nations and other epochs: it was then that his stylistic 'manners' began to accumulate, not now in order to expand the foundations of Russian 'European-ness' but from a desire to enlarge his consciousness of the full spiritual trajectory of European culture as a whole. And here we may find a second analogy, not with Pushkin but with Picasso, another 'Protean', another 'man of a thousand masks'. In 1920 Stravinsky and Picasso were accepted as brothers in arms,[15] united by their interest in the neo-classical movement, which we shall later investigate.

4

> ▶▶▶

Three stages

Stravinsky's first mature works date from 1908, his last works from 1968; and during those sixty years of indefatigable creative activity he tested for himself the true quality of a number of different artistic 'systems'. He began by mastering the Russian classical tradition of Tchaikovsky, Mussorgsky and Rimsky-Korsakov, which he enriched by the Impressionism of Debussy. He elaborated his own version of the diatonic system in many different directions and then, in his old age, introduced new features into that system by adopting his own version of serial technique. He, as it were, refracted through a single prism the many spectra of contemporary music, and at the same time – to change the metaphor – he absorbed the scents of earlier musical cultures, both recent and remote. No other contemporary composer can even faintly match this extraordinary universality of Stravinsky's; and yet whatever 'manner' he favoured, whatever model he selected, he remained unmistakably himself. His individuality is recognisable in the cut of his themes, the whole *facture* of his music, the character of his rhythmic organisation, his handling of the orchestra and in every stroke of his pen, every turn of phrase however small. His music gave expression to all the leading ideas of the twentieth century – our cruel, turbulent and magnificent age.

It was Stravinsky's aim to live, as he put it, *con tempo*, 'with the times'. He was keenly aware of the beating of the contemporary pulse, and it was for this reason that he excited the minds of successive generations of musicians. Yet at the same time he wanted to rise above the burning questions of the day and to stand aside from the bitter social struggles of the age, though as a great artist he could not of course fail to react to the events which gave that age its character. This reaction was seldom direct, as in *The Soldier's Tale* and *Symphony in Three Movements* which relate, respectively, to the events of the First and Second World Wars. More often it was oblique, as in *The Rite of Spring*, with its presentiments of fundamental changes in human history. His imagination was fired by the cultural achievements of the day and by movements of thought rather than by the social and political struggles behind them, though we must allow his due to the eminent artist who continued from one

23

Stravinsky in Russia, 1905

decade to another to polish and refine his skill, like a jeweller – and all .
in the name of Music with a capital M. It was in this assiduous
devotion that Stravinsky manifested his enormous creative energy
and the conviction that dominated him. We have already spoken of
the duality in Stravinsky's relationship to everyday reality, and this
duality accounts for the inequalities in his musical output, in which
the genuinely significant is sometimes overshadowed by formal
preoccupations and aesthetic virtuosity.

The quality of his music also varies according to the period in which it was written. His first three ballets launched Stravinsky on his artistic career like a three-stage rocket. Then, in the years immediately after the first war and during the twenties, came the dazzling zigzag of bold, totally unexpected *volte-faces*. From the middle thirties onwards his career became more tranquil, a kind of *diminuendo* which lasted until the fifties, when the volcanic forces in him gathered strength again and there was a new eruption. In the early stages of his career the violent character of his music made the impression of a tightly compressed spring suddenly released, each twist forming a spiral that seemed to contradict the one that preceded it. Although steep rises were often accompanied by corresponding descents, the logical nature of this complex 'unfolding' of Stravinsky's musical personality became clear when, as it were, the last twist was finally straightened out.

Each of the three periods into which his artistic career naturally falls is marked by a combination of disparate elements and the mutual interaction of different stimuli. In each, however, a single general characteristic marking this particular phase of his development imposes unity on the rich variety of figurative and stylistic *trouvailles*. The first, 'Russian' period lasted exactly fifteen years, from 1908 to 1923; the second, 'neo-classical' period lasted thirty years, from 1923 to 1953; and the 'late' period another fifteen, from 1953 to 1968. Those who will may see some symbolical meaning in this series of $15+30+15$, as though fate chose to give Stravinsky's evolution as an artist the same strict architectural perfection that he valued above all else in the arts. Not that the composer himself, of course, had any thought of number symbolism of this kind: he simply believed himself called, as he put it, to carry out certain definite artistic tasks. As he completed each of these, he turned in another direction, not arbitrarily (and still less following the fashion of the day), but fulfilling the interior process of his developing personality – a law established 'by himself for himself', in Pushkin's words.

Throughout his development as an artist Stravinsky unswervingly obeyed the provisions of this law; and this explains the fact that the details of his private life left virtually no mark on his music. In this he was an exception to the general rule of his era – in the separation of the artist's will from that mass of experiences which determines the emotional variability of everyday life. The singleness of purpose that marks his music was not disturbed even by the breaks in his existence caused by geographical changes of scene, from Russia to Switzerland during his Russian period and from France to the USA during the neo-classical. This is not, of course, to deny that the disasters of the two world wars played a part in precipitating and accentuating the changes between his stylistic periods.

Stravinsky experienced two moments of crisis in his artistic career. The first, around 1920, was less marked than the second and was soon surmounted. But the second, which began around 1935, was protracted, and we may presume that Stravinsky himself was increasingly aware of it the longer it lasted. The final pages of his autobiography strike a polemic note. 'The general public no longer gives [my music] the enthusiastic reception of earlier days . . . Their attitude certainly cannot make me deviate from my path.' [1] If he was proud to make this assertion in 1935, sixteen years later – after finishing *The Rake's Progress* – he acknowledged, 'This is the end of a trend.' [2]

The origin and the surmounting of any creative crisis present a complex psychological problem, for here the artist's personal fate is inextricably bound up with that of society, the law of his artistic being with the laws of social consciousness. We need only recall how painful Beethoven found the experience of such a crisis in 1817 (and Rimsky-Korsakov in the nineties, for that matter). Did Stravinsky experience comparable difficulties, and did he suffer acutely during the long period of his second crisis? We simply do not know; but it seems probable that any sense of catastrophic crisis was modified by the fact that the line of demarcation between the different stages of his evolution as a composer was not so clear as it may seem at first sight.

We have already observed that each successive period in Stravinsky's development appeared to his contemporaries as a negation of the preceding period. Now, in historical perspective, we can see that at the very heart of each period a new regulating principle was gradually forming. Let me give two examples. Four or five years before he wrote *Mavra* and completed *Les Noces*, early work on *Pulcinella* shows the aesthetic programme of neo-classicism is clearly formulated, although neo-classical features had appeared in earlier works. Similarly in the *Mass*, which Stravinsky began in 1944, we find an anticipation of the strictness and austerity of the composer's 'late' manner, although there were still seven years to go before he wrote the last of his large-scale neo-classical works, *The Rake's Progress*. Consequently, the chronological divisions between the three periods are comparatively conventional: there is an overlap between each period and the next, and for some clearly distinguishable length of time two periods synchronise in a kind of coexistence.

In establishing these periods of Stravinsky's creative activity another important factor must be taken into account. Any such division of an artist's career is based primarily on the physiological and psychological characteristics of youth, maturity and old age; and by maturity is meant the culminating stage of the artist's development, the peak of his creative career. This was certainly the sense in which it was first used, by Anton Schindler, of Beethoven. Stravinsky's case, however, is different, because each of the three periods is characterised by a different, specific content.

Stravinsky became a professional composer comparatively late, in 1905, after finishing his university studies. He was twenty-three years old. He had, it is true, a few harmony lessons during his last years at school, first with Akimenko and later with Kalafaty, with whom he also studied strict counterpoint.[3] Two years earlier he had begun to consult Rimsky-Korsakov, and from 1905 onwards these 'consultations' took place regularly, twice a week, though they came in fact increasingly to resemble consultations rather than systematic lessons. This period of youthful ripening was so short, and Stravinsky's rise so meteoric that, in contradistinction to most other composers', his first period of creative activity, which began with *Firebird*, appears as a period of maturity. In fact the quality of the works written during this 'Russian' stage suggests not only a period of mature technical mastery but rather – if we take into account the wide dissemination and the popularity of these works – an actual culmination, a high peak of the composer's career. And indeed they resembled a mountain-spring from which, in each succeeding period, the composer continued actively to draw the most vital of his creative impulses.

During the neo-classical period which followed, the composer's thinking was more remarkable for its breadth than its profundity. By this I do not mean in any way to depreciate the aesthetic value of the works composed during these thirty years, but only to indicate their different character, revealed in Stravinsky's assimilation of a number of different 'manners' and models. It was during this neo-classical period that Stravinsky reached his 'second maturity', at the age of about forty. And here we may see an analogy with Verdi, in whose career there were also two high points, the first represented by *Rigoletto*, *Il Trovatore* and *La Traviata* and the second by *Aida* and *Otello*.

There are, of course, many very real differences between the two cases. The second culminating phase in Verdi's career was the result of much research and of a new economy of expression, and these characterised a later, third stage in Stravinsky's evolution.

Beethoven's 'late' style is most marked in his piano sonatas and string quartets, and the corresponding phase in Brahms's development is also best seen in his chamber music. Beethoven was then in his fifties, Brahms about sixty, but Stravinsky's third period began in his seventies; and this was the more astonishing if we take into account the character of the changes brought about in his music by his individual use of serial technique. Verdi and Stravinsky were fundamentally different in character, indeed as individuals they had almost nothing in common; yet Stravinsky's final phase, like Verdi's, was based on the extensiveness of his artistic solutions and a maximum concentration of expression. This he achieved – in a way, once again, totally unlike Verdi's – at the cost of constricting thematic interest and correspondingly emphasising the fine, detailed work characteristic of chamber music in general and sometimes reminiscent of the late works of Beethoven and Brahms.

Characteristic of all three stages in Stravinsky's artistic development are the crossing and re-crossing of many different stylistic lines and images. These represent the Protean 'dominant' in his character as a composer, though this variety of 'manners' only manifests different aspects of Stravinsky's greatness. There are changes of emphasis, with one characteristic predominating and another taking a subordinate place; but in every work the dominant tendency of the period always makes the strongest impression on the listener. Intensity – extension – concentration: these are the chief hallmarks of the three periods in Stravinsky's career, and each demands careful investigation.

5

▸▸

The Russian element

The first public performance of Stravinsky's music was on 27 December 1907 at one of the Evenings of Contemporary Music given in the modest hall of the Petersburg Music School.[1] 'Nicholas Richter played my early piano sonata and this was the first music of mine to be performed in public. It was, I suppose, an inept imitation of late Beethoven. I myself performed there too, as accompanist to a singer, a certain Miss Petrenko, in my Gorodetsky songs.' These were *Spring* (*The Cloister*) and the *Song of the Dew* – 'mystic songs of the ancient Russian flagellants',[2] both recently completed. Other first performances followed soon afterwards. On 22 January 1908 the Court Orchestra under Hugo Warlich gave a private performance of the *Symphony in E flat major* written in 1906. The music is not markedly original and the idiom recalls that of Glazunov, whose reaction to it was negative, rather than Rimsky-Korsakov, who expressed reserves about the work. The young Myaskovsky's judgment, published in 1912,[3] was favourable. 'This work is brisk and springlike in mood . . . forthright, fresh, and clearly stated.' A warmer welcome awaited the performance of the three-movement suite *Faun and Shepherdess*, based on a Pushkin text and first performed on 22 January 1908, the *Scherzo fantastique* given two days later, and more especially *Fireworks* (9 January 1910). In the summer of 1908 these works constituted the whole of Stravinsky's output, not a large output for a composer of twenty-six, though we should take into account that the piano sonata – his first major composition – dates from 1904. From these works alone it is difficult to judge how the composer's musical personality was shaping and where his intellectual and emotional interests really lay. No less difficult is it to determine the stylistic sources of these early works.

His five years of close acquaintance with Rimsky-Korsakov had a great effect on Stravinsky. He gained experience of the technical side of a composer's work simply by observing his teacher, from whom he learned to love it. Rimsky-Korsakov developed the young man's strength of will, his resistance and his sense of discipline, and sharpened his awareness of the artist's responsibility to his art, the creator's responsibility to his own creation. It is even possible that the idea of order in art, which Stravinsky was later to preach with such insistence, was first inculcated in him by Rimsky-Korsakov's rationalistic turn of mind and, more generally, by his way of life, which was precise to the point of pedantry in everything – composition, teaching and general habits. Contact with Rimsky-Korsakov may well also have stimulated the young Stravinsky's natural love of knowledge and his inquisitiveness about life in general. Was it not, indeed, from Rimsky-Korsakov that Stravinsky even caught his characteristic passion for reincarnating a number of different 'manners'? He had, after all, the example of Rimsky-Korsakov's own 'late' style – the Panslavonic characteristics of *Pan Voevoda* and before that the primitive Slavonic *Mlada*; the evocation of Byzantine Christianity in *Servilia*, the epic quality of ancient Russian legend in *Kitezh*, the fairytale ambiguity of *Kashchei* and the satire of *The Golden Cockerel*. Finally, who was more likely than this teacher to arouse Stravinsky's interest in the whole ritual side of Russian peasant life and the archaic forms of Russian vocal music?

During these five years Rimsky-Korsakov exercised an un-questioned moral authority over Stravinsky, who felt for him a filial devotion that he seems never to have felt for his own father, who died in 1902. Many years after his teacher's death he remembered this 'as one of the saddest days in my life . . . and I shall remember Rimsky in his coffin as long as I remember anything. He looked so beautiful to me that I could not help weeping . . . Few people were as near to me as Rimsky-Korsakov, especially after my father's death, when he became a kind of adoptive father to me.'[3a]

If we take all this into account, it seems even stranger that Rimsky-Korsakov's music left no noticeable mark on Stravinsky's own. How is this to be explained? I doubt whether Freudians would succeed in discovering an 'anti-paternal', Oedipus complex in this relationship. Stravinsky himself cannot have been aware of any such antagonism or why should he have submitted all his works to Rimsky-Korsakov right up to *Fireworks*, the score of which arrived after Rimsky's death?[4] Here we again find ourselves faced with the problem of how Stravinsky's artistic personality was in fact formed. He did not, of course, escape the seductive refinements of the Queen of Shemakha's music or the delicate charms of *Snowmaiden*; and he certainly took very much to heart his teacher's insistence that music is not transposed for the orchestra but written for the individual instruments concerned.[5] It was with this precept in mind that he developed to perfection his own 'inner ear' and power of invention. No doubt he learned much more than this from Rimsky-Korsakov; but the fact remains that, apart from isolated points of method, Rimsky-Korsakov's music played only a small part in the formation of Stravinsky's style.

The role played by Mussorgsky was incomparably more signific-ant, though there again Stravinsky's ability to select revealed itself in a characteristic manner: what he took from Mussorgsky was not the same as what Debussy took – it was neither his melody, based on Russian speech, nor his harmony, liberated from pre-established rules. Though these did indeed influence him, it was only secondarily. What was important to Stravinsky was that Mussorgsky, unlike Rimsky-Korsakov, gave him a glimpse of the ancient Russian way of life before the reforms of Peter the Great, and, more particularly, its association with church ritual. Instances of such things are to be found in the bell-sonorities associated with funerals and the deathbed clothing in a monastic habit (*schima*), and with the ceremonies of 'glorification' (*slavlenie*) – in particular an echo of the scene of Boris's coronation in the funeral march in Act 3 of *The Nightingale*. As we shall see later, this 'bell sonority' formed an essential ingredient in Stravinsky's music, an organic element of his style. The same is true of the chant of the Orthodox Church, which Mussorgsky used on many occasions and Stravinsky sometimes echoed in his choral writing. Another instance is provided by the ritual songs of the Raskolniki, or Old Believers, with their archaic chants (cf. the *Song of the Dew* (1907) described by the composer as 'mystic song of the ancient Russian flagellants', and the *Sektantskaya* of 1919). It is also worth bearing in mind that in 1913 Stravinsky supplied the final chorus of the Old Believers for Mussorgsky's *Khovanshchina*. Speaking generally, we may say that it was Mussorgsky's archaic vocal style that attracted Stravinsky, and this was not without its influence on his 'children's' music, such as the *Stories for Children* and *Cat's Cradle Songs*.

Tchaikovsky's music exercised an even stronger and more lasting influence on Stravinsky, however paradoxical this may seem at first sight. Tchaikovsky and Rimsky-Korsakov were, after all, opposed to each other, and there were times when it was definitely tactless even to mention Tchaikovsky's name in the Rimsky-Korsakov circle. Do we, perhaps, have evidence here of some hidden antagonism between pupil and teacher? Once again I reject this insinuation, which might cast a shadow over the genuineness of Stravinsky's relationship with Rimsky. It seems to me far more probable that in his early days Stravinsky's artistic personality was shaped unconsciously: he was simply attracted by anything that helped him to develop his own individuality. Mussorgsky was one pole of attraction, Tchaikovsky another; and thus we can trace from the very outset of Stravinsky's artistic career a feature that was essentially characteristic of him – the pull of spiritual polarities.

We have already said that what attracted Stravinsky in Tchaikovsky was the search for 'Russian Europeanness', a field widely explored by Boris Asafiev ('Igor Glebov') in a book which appeared in 1929, before Stravinsky's *Chroniques de ma vie*, in which the composer acknowledged his deep love of Tchaikovsky.[6] In 1929 the juxtaposition of these two Russian composers so completely different in character seemed an unwarrantable caprice; but in fact Asafiev displayed his perceptiveness precisely by his ability to realise Stravinsky's affinity with Tchaikovsky purely from the spirit of his music, and not from any remark of Stravinsky's. According to Asafiev, what Stravinsky and Tchaikovsky had in common was, first, the 'festival' sonority of their music, and then the ability to adapt, and indeed to adopt as their own, the forms of musical speech characteristic of Russian folk-song and popular urban music. A further common trait is to be found in the two composers' 'taste for Italian melody, for French clarity and for dance-elements borrowed both from Russian folk-music and from Western Europe'.

It is hardly necessary to give instances of Stravinsky's admiration for Tchaikovsky, to which there are numerous allusions in the *Chronicle*. I should, however, like to give some typical quotations from an open letter which he wrote to Diaghilev on 10 October 1921. This was published in *The Times* of 18 October.

It gives me great happiness to know that you are producing that masterpiece *Sleeping Beauty* by our great and beloved Tchaikovsky. It makes me doubly happy. In the first place, it is a personal joy, for this work appears to me as the most authentic expression of that period in our Russian life which we call the 'Petersburg Period' . . . It is further a great satisfaction to me as a musician to see produced a work of so direct a character at a time when so many people, who are neither simple, nor naive, nor spontaneous, seek in their art simplicity, 'poverty' and spontaneity . . . Tchaikovsky in his very nature possessed these three gifts to the fullest extent . . . Tchaikovsky possessed the power of *melody*, centre of gravity in every symphony, opera or ballet composed by him. It is absolutely indifferent to me that the quality of his melody was sometimes unequal. The fact is that he was a creator of *melody*, which is an extremely rare and precious gift. Among us, Glinka, too, possessed it; and not to the same degree, those others . . . Tchaikovsky's music . . . is quite as Russian as Pushkin's verse or Glinka's song.

Incidentally, there were two occasions – one in 1921 and the other in 1941 – when Stravinsky rearranged and reorchestrated a number of pieces from *Sleeping Beauty*; and he often conducted performances of Tchaikovsky's Second and Third Symphonies and the *Serenade for Strings*. There is no doubt of Tchaikovsky's influence on Stravinsky, which is not confined to *The Fairy's Kiss*, or to *Mavra*, in which Stravinsky used a stylisation of Glinka's and Tchaikovsky's song idioms. There were further marks of Tchaikovsky's influence in methods of orchestration, in inventive touches in the treatment of the wood-winds and in his technique of melodic variation (a feature common to his early works, including *Firebird* and the neo-classical works) – as well as many other features which demand individual analysis. A comparative stylistic analysis of Tchaikovsky's *Italian Capriccio* and *Pulcinella*, in particular, would yield very interesting results.

The essential fact, however, remains the assertion that it is possible to give Russian music a general, European character. Stravinsky considered Glinka the first to explore that possibility, and it was Glinka whom he called 'the "musical hero" of my childhood . . . he was always *sans reproche* and this is the way I still think of him . . . all music in Russia stems from him'.[7] And after Glinka, Tchaikovsky who, he believed, brought Russian music even closer to the West. Debussy revealed to Stravinsky new perspectives in this rapprochement, and it is hard to overestimate Debussy's role in the emancipation of the young composer's musical individuality. Exactly how the two first became acquainted is not as yet clear. There is a vague reference in the *Chronicle* to his friend Pokrovsky introducing him to the music of contemporary French composers 'whose names I had hardly heard' – Franck, d'Indy, Chabrier, Fauré, Dukas and Debussy: 'I noticed a certain resemblance between the music of these composers and that of Tchaikovsky, a resemblance that became much more evident to me when I could examine and compare their works in the light of experience.'[8]

This was at the end of the nineties, that is to say long before Stravinsky began to study with Rimsky-Korsakov, so that even at that time he was trying to escape from the academicism of the Petersburg school, nicknamed the 'Belaievites' after their publisher, Mitrofan Belaiev. It was Tchaikovsky, the representative of 'Russian Europeanness' who provided him with the means of escape; there is still no mention of Debussy. It was only later, probably after 1906,[9] that Stravinsky became more thoroughly acquainted with his music, at the time when he was beginning to move in 'World of Art' circles and among the artists connected with the 'Evenings of Contemporary Music'. One of these, A. P. Nurok, was a great connoisseur of French art and also an excellent pianist, like V. F. Nouvel, another leader of the group and an old friend of Diaghilev, with whom he later collaborated in managing the affairs of the Ballets Russes. In any case, Yastrebtsev's notes of December 1907 contain a gloomy observation by Rimsky-Korsakov about 'the decadent-impressionist influence under which Stravinsky had fallen', and in another, dating from the preceding month, he says that 'Igor Fedorovich has become unnecessarily violently addicted to modernism.'[10] It is not clear to what works Rimsky-Korsakov is here referring. This 'influence' was still not very marked until *Fireworks*, and Rimsky-Korsakov died before the score of *Fireworks* reached him. Even so he showed great insight, for his pupil did indeed shortly afterwards become a 'Debussyite' for a short time, as can be seen from Act 1 of *The Nightingale* of 1908 (especially the orchestral introduction), parts of *Firebird*, the two Verlaine settings (1910), the cantata *Zvezdoliki* (The King of the Stars, 1911–12) and even the introduction to Part 2 of *The Rite of Spring*.

A nine-year friendship between Stravinsky and Debussy began after the first Paris performance of *Firebird* in 1910. Debussy at first regarded Stravinsky as a composer whose style was close to his own, but he was perplexed by the sudden acceleration in Stravinsky's development; and his attitude to *The Rite of Spring* was mixed, half approving and half doubtful, for here his young friend had broken with Impressionism and outstripped him.

It is impossible to say how important Debussy's influence was in Stravinsky's search for new harmonic laws liberated from the functional 'pulls' of the traditional diatonic system, for a melody springing from the intersection of 'arabesques' and also for the enrichment of his sound-palette. 'Musicians of my generation are indebted to Debussy, and I myself more than anyone else', he said, but three or four years after passing 'through' Debussy he no longer belonged to his 'followers' or remained, as did Ravel, in his shadow. Stravinsky took from Debussy that which enabled him to realise himself better as a Russian composer. This may seem paradoxical, but is not so in fact. Debussy, apart from helping him to abandon academic processes and patterns, also insisted on Stravinsky strengthening his ties with his national tradition. At the height of the 1914–18 war Debussy wrote to him: 'Be with all your strength a great Russian artist. It is so wonderful to be of one's own country, to be attached to one's soil like the humblest of peasants.'[11]

They also shared a common interest in Mussorgsky, whom Debussy rated very highly, going on one occasion so far as to say 'The whole of my *Pelléas* is in *Boris*', and we can imagine that they must have had many admiring conversations about Mussorgsky. 'The first time I visited him [Debussy] in his house, after *Firebird*, we talked about Mussorgsky's songs and agreed that they contained the best music of the whole Russian school.'[12]

Similar conversations may well have occurred in connection with the new edition of *Khovanshchina* in which Stravinsky collaborated with Ravel in 1913. There is further evidence of Stravinsky's warm admiration for Mussorgsky in a letter written on 15 November 1932, in which we learn among other things that Stravinsky could never forgive the conductor Napravnik for his underestimation of 'the real musical revelations' in *Boris Godunov*.

To sum up, then, we can say that Stravinsky's encounter with Debussy's music was an important lesson to him and that he was able, so to say, to extract from that music the hidden 'Mussorgskian' element that served him as motto in his search for a means to emphasise the 'Russianness' of his own music, something that at this stage of his career was of primary importance. Hitherto we have been discussing the influences under which Stravinsky's early style was formed, but it was Russian folk-song that came to him as a revelation; and he penetrated its essence the more deeply the more powerfully he felt the fascination of Debussy. This was in fact the original source of his innovations. Where and how did Stravinsky encounter this folk-song – as a child in Petersburg, at his wife's house at Ustilug where he lived after his marriage in 1906, or at the fairs in the neighbouring town of Yarmolintsy? He never spent long at Ustilug, and after 1910 he frequently travelled to Paris for the production of his ballets, very seldom to Petersburg; and he left Russia in July 1914 a few days before the outbreak of war. How, then, did he achieve such a profound and penetrating understanding of Russian folk-song? Like much else in Stravinsky's personality, this remains a puzzle.[13] One thing is certain, and that is that he did not normally use published collections of this music, which he mistrusted.[14] What he trusted was his own ear, and the selective faculty of that ear was altogether exceptional. Another surprising fact is that, although not a professional folk-lorist like Bartók, Stravinsky was able to observe the structural laws of Russian folk-song, which the classic composers of the nineteenth century had never fathomed. It was precisely these structures that aroused his interest, namely the characteristic harmonic and rhythmic construction of the melodies rather than the individual prototypes of the songs whose melodies – with the exception of some instances in *Firebird* and most noticeably in *Petrushka* – he did not use.[15] He showed a rarely informed knowledge in extracting from the Russian folk-song tradition what he needed for his own individual style.

Intermittently from 1912 onwards, with flying visits to Kiev, Stravinsky worked steadily on the texts of songs and fairy-tales, browsing in the Kireevsky and Afanasiev collections. By 1914 he had finished these studies, which had greatly helped his understanding of Russian speech and its connections with folk-song, and thus completed the stage of accumulating actual aural experience of folk-melody; and with this he also achieved the peak of his first period as a mature artist.

Having elucidated the question of the composer's stylistic sources, we must now, however, return to the point at which he embarked on his development as an artist, and to the year 1908. *Fireworks* forms the boundary-mark, as Stravinsky himself probably thought, since he included it in the programmes of his guest-concerts in the USSR in 1962.

On learning of Rimsky-Korsakov's death he composed *Chant Funèbre*, the score of which, to his great grief,

disappeared during the revolution . . . I can no longer remember the music, but I can remember the idea at the root of its conception, which was that all the solo instruments of the orchestra filed past the tomb of the master in succession, each laying down its own melody as its wreath, against a deep background of *tremolo* murmurings simulating the vibrations of bass voices singing in chorus.[16]

Stravinsky attached great importance to this piece, the first in an imposing list of works written in memory of friends; and echoes of the idea outlined above can be heard in the final chorale of the *Symphonies of Wind Instruments* dedicated to the memory of Debussy, in the *Ode* (*Elegiac Song in Three Movements*), in the trombone chorale of the Cantata *In Memoriam Dylan Thomas* and in the sonorities of the male-voice chorus with drums in the *Introitus* in memory of T. S. Eliot.

In fact Stravinsky's use of the poems of Sergei Gorodetsky for the texts of his 1907 songs determined, as it were, his further interest in Russian antiquity. The boldness and freshness of the young Gorodetsky's stylisation immediately attracted the attention of the Russian symbolist poets and later of Blok. There was a clear connection between them and *The Rite of Spring*, and it was another archaiser, Nicholas Roerich, whose *Pictures of Pagan Russia* (1910) suggested the scenario of the work. The path leading from the Gorodetsky poems to *The Rite* was not, however, a direct one.

In the summer of the year in which he wrote the *Chant Funèbre*, Stravinsky began work on his opera *The Nightingale*, for which S. S. Mitusov provided the libretto. What was it that attracted him in Hans Christian Andersen's story? Here we can see once again the influence of Rimsky-Korsakov, as we discover from the *Chronicle*:[17] 'This work was greatly encouraged by my master, and to this day I remember with pleasure his approval of the preliminary sketches.' In fact Rimsky-Korsakov's spirit is traceable in the Apollonian, Pushkin-like stylisation of ancient mythology in *Faun and Shepherdess*, in the fantastic character of the orchestral *Scherzo* as well as in Andersen's tale, where the life-giving spirit of art as it were exorcises death, and in *Firebird* – a personal variant of the older composer's *Kashchei* – in which beauty is again victorious over imprisonment, oppression and death. But musically speaking this mirror-image of the young Stravinsky was not so much a reflection as a refraction of his master's musical personality, and moreover an entirely original one. Thus in the *Scherzo fantastique* there are echoes not only of Rimsky-Korsakov (and the 'Flight of the Bumble Bee') but of Mendelssohn and Tchaikovsky, while in *The Nightingale* we are reminded of Debussy, and here and there of Mussorgsky and Dargomyzhsky.

As far as subjects are concerned, Stravinsky's indebtedness to his master can be seen in *Petrushka*, where the Shrovetide scenes closely recall the fair scene in *Sadko* and the wedding procession in *Kitezh*, despite many dissimilarities. The ritual scenes in *The Rite of Spring* too – especially the Auguries of Spring, Dances of the Young Girls, and Mock Abduction in Part 1 – go back in origin to many scenes in Rimsky-Korsakov's operas based on the rituals of the pagan Russian calendar. Naturally the stimuli which Stravinsky received from such scenes were transposed by him to different planes of style and imagery, and there is a clear contradiction between the aesthetics of master and pupil. If this was in fact the mainstream of Stravinsky's spiritual evolution between 1908 and 1913, there were a number of deviations. In his first theatrical works, *The Nightingale* and *Firebird*, he turned to the fairy-tale world which he treated, like Rimsky-Korsakov, humanistically, combining lyricism with fantasy. His interest in Chinese exoticism revealed a concern with stylistic refinements reminiscent of the 'World of Art' group, while the music initially recalled that of Debussy; and this mixture of 'Chinese' and 'French' showed a weakening of the Russian element which may account for the slowness with which work on *The Nightingale* proceeded. The first act was finished in the summer of 1909, before *Firebird*, while the second and third acts were not a stylistic unity. In the second act there are Japanese elements, while in the third the entr'acte, the chorus of spectres and the funeral march show a strengthening of the Russian element. In Asafiev's words 'the three acts of *The Nightingale* represent three stages of artistic development, and the third shows the most insight, being at the same time the most unusual and the most Russian of the three'.[18] Thus, *The Nightingale* may serve as documentary evidence of how the Russian character of Stravinsky's music became accentuated in 1914, an important point for the understanding of his evolution and one to which we shall return later in more detail. In the preceding years the important deviations were in two different directions – towards French music in the two Verlaine settings of 1910 and towards the exotic in the *Three Japanese Lyrics*.

Stravinsky also paid his tribute to modern poetry in his settings of Balmont: two songs later (1954) arranged for chamber ensemble, and the cantata *Zvezdoliki* (The King of the Stars) for male-voice chorus and orchestra, written in 1911 and finally orchestrated the following year. From the performance point of view the cantata is most impractical, since the music is complex and demands a huge orchestra, though there are no more than fifty-two bars, lasting only about seven minutes. This is probably the only instance of such impracticality in the whole output of a composer who was an expert at observing the proportions between musical inventiveness and practical performability. The cantata was dedicated to Debussy who, after playing it over with the composer at the piano, observed ironically 'this is probably Plato's harmony of the eternal spheres . . . and, except on Sirius or Aldebaran, I do not foresee performances of this cantata for planets. As for our more modest earth, a performance would be lost in the abyss.'[19] These ironic remarks about music 'for planets' refer in fact to Balmont's text. The first performance of the work was given by the Brussels radio in 1939, twenty-seven years after it was first' orchestrated.

Though the cantata was completed before work on *The Rite of Spring* was begun, it is interesting to compare fundamental differences between the two works. *The Rite* is essentially explosive in character, marked by great rhythmic variety: stamping rhythms, like those of the Coachmen's Dance in *Petrushka* only even more ponderous and ruthlessly persistent, alternate with wild, elemental, orgiastic rhythms. In the cantata, on the other hand, the sonorous complexes beginning with the motto of the opening chorus are not repeated but alternate with a slow regular pulse, the vocal melody has a swaying motion with much chromatic alteration, and despite the huge mass of sound the overall impression is an airy, tremulous pianissimo, the mystical symbol of limitless, star-strewn space. There are parallels with the handling of the chorus in the last act of *The Nightingale* and to some extent – in conception rather than in the means employed – with the enigmatic episode of Petrushka's death and the introduction to Part 2 of *The Rite*. Even so *Zvezdoliki* stands alone among Stravinsky's works. The whole element of 'airiness', which had played a part in *Scherzo fantastique*, in *Fireworks* and in some scenes of *Firebird*, disappears from the composer's music from now on.

Against the background of these multifarious influences, the unity of purpose behind the three ballets stands out all the more clearly; but the three stages of advance represented respectively by *Firebird*, *Petrushka* and *The Rite of Spring* were by no means simple. In *Firebird*, as Asafiev aptly observes, the composer was electrified by a sudden awareness of the vast possibilities of orchestral colour. Compared with the symphony written at most two or three years earlier, the ballet represents a huge leap into the unknown. It is true that the overwhelming richness of Stravinsky's imagination produces an almost monotonous effect of magnificence, which he was to modify in the later versions (1919 and 1945). The lyrical quality of the princesses' round-dances has an extraordinary delicacy, the lullaby is fascinating as pure sound; and while the fairy-like music of the Firebird has a glittering quality, the composer discovered wonderfully astringent colours with which to depict the dark, evil character of Kashchei's kingdom, and the *Danse infernale* has a 'Scythian' energy, only matched by the powerful sonorities of the triumphant finale. Even so, Stravinsky's attitude to folk-music was still not fully defined, and he was still weaving patterns on a background of folk-music rather than making that music his own and building on it. This is the reason why *Firebird*, for all the delicate pungency of its musical language, still stands at a crossroads in the composer's development.

In the spring of 1910, while he was finishing the score, he had the idea of a symphony with a finale which was to become the Sacrificial Dance of *The Rite of Spring*; and it was thus that the whole 'Scythian' element began to ripen at the very heart of *Firebird*. He himself has recounted how this came about:

One day, when I was finishing the last pages of *L'Oiseau de Feu* in St Petersburg, I had a fleeting vision which came to me as a complete surprise. I saw in imagination a solemn pagan rite: sage elders, seated in a circle, watched a young girl dance herself to death. They were sacrificing her to propitiate the god of spring.[20]

The ink was not yet dry on the score of his first ballet when he embarked on the new one, enlisting Roerich's assistance in devising the scenario.

A great deal has been written about the 'Scythian' movement (*Skifstvo*) in the Russian arts, as an expression of those wild elemental forces which were stirring in the years immediately before the revolution. This enriching of the composer's field of imagery demanded his penetration of the still unexplored material of folk-song. It was as though scales fell from his eyes and he suddenly saw the truth and, rejecting the traditions that still hampered him in *Firebird*, discovered deep, hitherto unexplored strata of the Russian past. The publication of the autograph sketches of *The Rite of Spring* has revealed the intensity and the thoroughness with which he worked this new territory, but at the same time he continued his explorations in a number of other directions. He was in fact entering the period when his creative powers were at their height. Thus it was that no sooner had he started work on *The Nightingale* than he wrote *Zvezdoliki* and *Petrushka*, which held up his work on *The Rite*, though not for long. *Petrushka* was in fact written between August 1910 and 26 May 1911, while the piano score of *The Rite* was finished on 4 November 1912 and the orchestration on 8 March 1913. These facts speak for themselves.

Stravinsky has told us how he first thought of Petrushka, the fair-booth buffoon whose nervous sensibility is wounded by the cruelty of life. He first conceived a musical image: 'I had in my mind a distinct picture of a puppet, suddenly endowed with life, exasperating the patience of the orchestra with diabolical cascades of arpeggi. The orchestra in turn retaliates with menacing trumpet-blasts.'[21]

The stage interpretation of this music was worked out with the help of A. N. Benois. Petrushka is the same mercilessly persecuted Pierrot as the figure in Blok's *Balaganshchik* (The Showman) and in Schoenberg's *Pierrot lunaire*, written at exactly the same time. But instead of Blok's and Schoenberg's abstract symbolism, Stravinsky surrounded his central figure with the carnival riot of the Shrovetide celebrations.

This wildness, or turbulence, is radically different from the wildness of *The Rite*. Here a real holiday festival is being celebrated, there an austere primitive ceremony. Imagery and musical origins are equally diverse, pre-historical Slavonic song in *The Rite*, in *Petrushka* popular urban songs or folk-song adopted and adapted by city-dwellers: the stylisation of antiquity on the one hand and the stylisation of the present on the other, a stylisation in the spirit of the past. These two musical poles – the archaic and the contemporary – form as it were in embryo the double, Janus-like character of Stravinsky's next productions, though they must not of course be regarded as antithetical. He was seeking for what is contemporary in the remote past and discovering in the contemporary an unbroken line going back to that remote past. Even so, *Petrushka* and *The Rite of Spring* are antipodal works, and from them there soon proceed different lines, or 'veins' of artistic creation, whose frequent crossing we shall try to trace.

If there is indeed an important borderline separating *The Rite* from *Petrushka*, the difference between *Petrushka* and *Firebird* is perhaps even more striking: it is as though the composer had rushed from a greenhouse into the wide open spaces and greedily absorbed the various sonorous impressions of everyday musical life. As I have already said, there is no folk-song archaising in *Petrushka*: native

Russian melody is treated like a popular print ('Vdol' po Peterskoi', 'Akh vy, seni' etc.) and we hear bourgeois songs (barrel-organ), echoes of the harmonica, calls from the gallery (based on the cries of street-vendors like those the composer used in *Renard*) and 'real life' dances (the Ballerina's waltz, with which it is worth comparing the *Easy Piano Pieces* of 1915). The Moor's music is a kind of grotesquely stylised Orient, and the Moor himself might indeed be considered as a native of the Queen of Shemakha's country. In short, the music of *Petrushka* is a concentrate formed of all the scraps of melody and the many-coloured impressions that Stravinsky received from the intense life of the Petersburg streets and squares of his youth.

In total contrast to this mercurially changing everyday existence stands the unchanging world of rite and ceremony. *The Rite of Spring* marked a shift of interest to the world of Russian pre-history, and with it an important turning-point not only in Stravinsky's style but also in the evolution of the ideas and images behind his music. It was an abrupt turning-point, and the reverberation was so great that for many years we can hear echoes of *The Rite* in other works of the composer's.[22]

Even before he had finished the score of *The Rite* Stravinsky had begun to collect the folk-texts for its vocal analogue, *Les Noces*. If in *The Rite* Stravinsky brought to life the old heathen ceremonies connected with the great sacrifice to Nature, in *Les Noces* heathen beliefs are intermingled with Christian and it is the eternal mystery of human procreation that is ritually hallowed. 'Russian choreographic scenes with singing and music' is the author's explanation of the title *Svadebka* (little, i.e. peasant, wedding). The work has no connection with ethnography: Stravinsky's object was to present in ritual terms an impersonal act. The bride in *Les Noces* resembles the Chosen Victim in *The Rite* in having no face, no individuality. Stravinsky was not concerned with the subjective, personal experience of either girl, or with giving a psychological picture of her attitude to what goes on around her. All that interested him was the essence, the meaning and the purpose of the ceremony as affirmed and established in the consciousness of succeeding generations and as bearing the universal imprint of a primitive, popular understanding of the world, an archetypal event in a national, Russian form. The same will be true of his handling of other subjects, such as the myths of Apollo and Orpheus, the tragedy of Oedipus, the Biblical stories and Russian themes, where he exposes the essential, the supra-personal and the age-old, but always as something alive and intransient and always embodied in the language of contemporary art, something totally different from any kind of archaeological documentation.

These ideas took shape during 1914 when the general musical plan of *Les Noces* was developed. In 1915 notices appeared in the press to the effect that Stravinsky had completed the work. The titles of the four movements were given, and reference was made to the highly individual scoring for some forty players. The first performance was announced for the year 1916, but Stravinsky could not immediately decide on the correct balance between voices and instruments and found the first version, which he completed in 1917, unsatisfactory.[23] Another six years were to pass before he finally decided to contrast the vocal part with six groups of percussion instruments and four pianos, which were also treated as percussion. This was a solution of genius, both simple and bold. According to the composer the instrumental ensemble is 'at the same time perfectly homogeneous, perfectly impersonal and perfectly mechanical',[24] and this emphasises all the more clearly the human, breathing character of the voices. Thus it came about that the composition of *Les Noces* was spread over almost a whole decade, something unique in Stravinsky's career as a composer. The final version dates from 1923.

The year 1914, when Stravinsky started work on *Les Noces*, is a landmark in his evolution as a composer, although of course the brilliant revelations of *The Rite of Spring* continued to illumine the works of the years that immediately followed. The composer himself recognised the novelty of his music in a letter to the son of his old teacher, Andrei Rimsky-Korsakov: 'Good Lord, what happiness I feel when I hear this music . . . It is as though *Firebird* were twenty years behind me rather than two!' Even so *The Rite* marks the end of a period rather than the beginning. In this connection it is interesting to note the composer's own words when he was eighty years of age. '*Firebird* was for me a fruitful beginning and in a sense determined the music that I wrote for the next four years.'[25] Those years included *The Rite of Spring*.

With the exception of individual works with no Russian associations, such as *Pulcinella* and *Ragtime*, the works of the next decade were planned during the short interval between finishing *The Rite* and beginning work on *Les Noces*. Stravinsky later recalled that in the summer of 1914 he had collected such a mass of material that a considerable number of sketches remained unused. There was more than enough textual material not only for *Les Noces* but for *Renard* and *The Soldier's Tale* as well as *Pribautki*, *The Cat's Cradle Songs*, *Four Russian Songs* etc. The full extent of the musical sketches dating from this time will only be known when Stravinsky's papers are made available to the public. One thing, however, remains quite clear: that it was in contact with Russian folk-song that Stravinsky perfected his style. All his vocal music up to *Les Noces* had been settings of contemporary poets; and it was only in 1914 that he completely assimilated not only the harmonic and the melodic–rhythmic characteristics of Russian folk-music but also its structural laws. Thus it is that *Les Noces* provides a key to the understanding of Stravinsky's 'manner' as a composer.

He elaborated a highly developed motivic technique. The structural material of the work consists of scraps of melody, and the direction of the movement is determined by the coupling, the rotation (to borrow a term used by serial composers), the pitch-, timbre- and metre-transformations of these motifs. An essential feature is the variable function of the word-stress, which Stravinsky learned by studying the phonetics of Russian folk-song, the actual play of syllabic accentuation in the songs. Shiftings and displacings of accents formed one of Stravinsky's favourite methods, and he used to speak of them laughingly as 'melodic–rhythmic stammering', insisting that this was an essential and specific stylistic feature of *Les Noces*. Asafiev has pointed to a typical example of such displacements – 'an oblique shift of verticals, their conversion into an inclined line, a kind of "oblique rain" of powerful constituents – a method producing powerful rhythmic contradictions and interruptions'.[26] This manner is most noticeable in the works written between 1914 and 1917. Motifs are short, their nucleus narrow in pitch-span and their connection with archaic folk-song phrases immediately noticeable; and it was this archaic form of diatonic modality that enabled Stravinsky to free himself from the trammels of the major–minor tradition. He was to describe himself in *Chronicle* as anti-tonal; and it was on this new folk-song basis that he elaborated his own original principles of tonal organisation.

An immediate result of these researches can be seen in a new concentration of expression, and it is significant that it was during these years that he abandoned large-scale composition and turned to miniature. An analogous taste for a minutely detailed style of composition, rather than broad fresco, was noticeable in his early works and again in a number of his neo-classical pieces; and it was to appear again in the works of his last phase. It may be observed in the *Three Japanese Lyrics*, which last only some four minutes in all, and in the timings of many subsequent compositions – *Three Pieces for String Quartet* (1914, 7 minutes), *Pribautki* (1914, 5 minutes), *Cat's*

Cradle Songs (1915–16, 5 minutes), *Three Stories for Children* (1915–17, 2 minutes), *Saucer Songs* (1914–16, 3 minutes), *Four Russian Songs* (1918–19, $4\frac{1}{2}$ minutes).

This newly discovered world demanded a new formulation of the problems of sonority and this led to the temporary abandonment of the large orchestra. Its place was taken by small instrumental ensembles, whose composition varied with the individual character of each work. The first example of this tendency is to be found in the *Three Japanese Lyrics*, written in 1912 after Stravinsky had made the acquaintance of Schoenberg's *Pierrot lunaire*, in which the virtuoso exploitation of the expressive qualities of each of the eight instruments made a great impression on him. Returning to Switzerland he persuaded Ravel, with whom he lived for some time, to write a work for voice and instrumental ensemble treated in a manner analogous to that of *Pierrot lunaire*. This was the origin of Ravel's *Trois Poèmes de Stéphane Mallarmé* and Stravinsky's *Japanese Lyrics* for voice and 2 flutes, 2 clarinets, piano and string quartet. There is an enigmatic quality about these miniature pieces, conceived in the spirit of the Japanese *hokku*, with their echoes of *The Rite*, of Debussy and even what appears in No. 3 to be Webern, whose music was at that time absolutely unknown to Stravinsky. These laconic pieces proved to be the starting-point for a series of other works of a similar kind, the most important of which were the *Three Pieces for String Quartet* written in the summer of 1914, immediately after the completion of *The Nightingale*. When these were first performed they were entitled *Grotesques* and the three pieces appeared as *Dance*, *Eccentric* and *Canticle*. The titles were later removed, but restored in the orchestral version begun in 1917 and finished in 1928. With the addition of a fourth piece, *Madrid*, they were eventually to form the *Four Studies for Orchestra*.[27] Each piece is highly charged and every smallest detail is significant. The musical ideas which they contain were later developed by the composer in other works. Thus there are threads connecting the first piece with the violin solo in *The Soldier's Tale*, the second piece with the fugue in Part 2 of *Symphony of Psalms*, and the chorale lay-out of the third anticipates the sonorities of the final chorale in *Symphonies of Wind Instruments*. Stravinsky's handling of the string quartet here was further developed in the *Concertino* of 1920, which also contains echoes of *The Soldier's Tale* and of jazz rhythms.[28]

Other works written at this time also contain anticipations of later pieces. The war had just begun and Stravinsky experienced what he himself called 'a nostalgia for home and for Russia'. He was seized with a wave of patriotism, wanted to volunteer for service at the front and hailed his 'dear liberated Russia'. In spite of material difficulties in Switzerland (or perhaps because of them) he was full of ideas, worked with great intensity, and after starting one work immediately switched over to another, laying aside the preliminary sketches of *Renard*, for example, to work on the *Saucer Songs*. Much that he planned and discovered during these years was, as it were, welded together in 1918, when he finished the first version of *Les Noces* and the 'buffoonery' of *Renard* ('The story of the fox, the cock, the cat and the ram') and began *The Soldier's Tale* – to be read, played and danced – which was finished after the end of the war in 1918.

This was a new turning-point within the 'Russian' period, marked by *Pulcinella*, which dates from 1919–20. Many of those who discuss the change in Stravinsky's style at this time ignore the fact that this change was not fortuitous, no mere caprice of the composer's, but was conditioned by the social and political changes of the day. The war, with its long tale of massacre and destruction, was over and Stravinsky felt a need to renew and brighten his palette. The music of *Pulcinella* is cheerful and sunny, the *Octet* is lively and brisk, and the comic opera *Mavra* is lit with smiles.

It must not of course be supposed that these changes of style and conception were sudden, as seemed at first to be the case. In actual fact they were slowly prepared so that, for instance, after 1914 Russian and 'universal' elements were combined in a paradoxical unity. The first of these lines, or 'veins', runs from the archaic, ceremonial world of *The Rite* and reaches its fullest development in *Les Noces*, while the second vein, with its contemporary and everyday concerns, starts from *Petrushka* and is modified and dispersed in different works and on different subjects treated by the composer as types. In speaking of 'veins' I have simply wished to emphasise the demarcation between these contrasting lines of force, one of which inclines towards primitive Russian themes while the other, though not excluding Russian subjects (as in the line stretching from *Petrushka* to *Mavra*), is more characteristically an attempt to give lasting form to that which survives not in ritual, but in daily life, including contemporary urban life. In short, the poles of these two 'lines' of force are on the one hand the permanent truth enshrined in the music of primitive ceremonial and on the other the truth that is achieving permanence in the popular music of modern urban culture.

We have already spoken of the archaic element, which Stravinsky realised in countless different combinations of images and themes, in characteristic scenes and phrases. Wedding ceremonies and buffoons' play, songs of celebration, mockery and joking, laments, counting-games, religious chanting, street-cries, yodelling, instrumental strumming, bell-tolling – Russian popular life provided ample means of expression and subjects for development, composition and musical formulation.

Children's music occupies a special place. Stravinsky had not concerned himself with this before and was not to do so again; and, although the fact that he now had children of his own was plainly an incentive, it does not seem enough to explain the considerable number of such works written about this time. These include *Memories of my Childhood* (three songs, 1913), *Cat's Cradle Songs* (1915–16), *Three Stories for Children* (1915–17); and *Pribautki* and *Renard* really belong to this group. In the *Cradle Song*, to his own words, Stravinsky used a bass ostinato, to be found also in *Tilimbom* from the *Three Stories* and in the opening numbers of *The Soldier's Tale*. The collection of easy piano pieces called *Les Cinq Doigts* (1920–1) belongs rather to the group of everyday song-pieces, as we shall see later.

In my opinion Stravinsky's interest in children was part of his interest in the archetypal, the original – the archetypal nature of children psychologically speaking – and this is confirmed by the similarity between these children's pieces and his primitive, ceremonial works. Nothing could be further from the conscious 'poetry' of Schumann's or Tchaikovsky's 'children's albums' than these children's pieces of Stravinsky's. They are more like those of Mussorgsky, who also exploited the imagery and phraseology of children's counting-games, their conspiracies and incantations, though not so thoroughly as Stravinsky was to do. He also touched on another sphere of interest in his music for children, that of domestic music-making, as in the three piano pieces with an easy part for the left hand – *Marche, Valse, Polka* (1914–15). These were followed in 1916–17 by five pieces with an easy part for the right hand – *Andante, Española, Balalaika, Neapolitana, Galop*. To the same group belongs the *Valse pour les enfants*, written in 1917 and published in *Le Figaro* in 1922. There are echoes of this world in the suggestions of the barrel-organ and in the ballerina's valse in *Petrushka*. Here it appears in more markedly grotesque and urban forms, emphasised by the character of the dances. But Stravinsky's originality in this matter deserves a short digression.

Mozart wrote dances for practical use, for dancing in fact. Their music organised, and at the same time reproduced, the rhythm of the dancers' movements, and in this respect it may be said to have possessed 'verisimilitude' – to have been, if you like, a kind of daguerreotype of a social prototype, a snapshot. But since this snapshot was taken by a genuine artist, Mozart's *German Dances* may be compared to an art-photograph. In his cassations, divertimenti and serenades the rhythmic movements are stylised: these pieces were not intended for dancing. Hence there appears a certain element of conventionality, a deviation from pure verisimilitude; and this element of conventionality is even more marked in the minuet movements of the Viennese classical composers. During the last third of the eighteenth century this once popular dance went out of fashion, and only its 'portrait' remained in music. In Beethoven's works the idea of the minuet is still further changed. Verisimilitude, i.e. a functional intention and a resemblance to the prototype in social use, is completely lost and the degree of conventionality becomes correspondingly greater, until in the Third Symphony the minuet is replaced by a scherzo.

Schubert, who belonged to a later generation, often improvised *Ländler* for his friends to dance to, but when he wrote down his improvisations he introduced a conventional element. The new Romantic age brought with it a new attitude to dance-music, which was now given a poetic content. Weber's *Invitation to the Dance* and Glinka's *Valse Fantasia* are two of the earliest examples of this poeticising of the waltz. Johann Strauss made his waltzes into lyric poems, without in any way neglecting their practical social purpose, and constructed his *Stimmungsbilder* (mood-pictures) on dance rhythms. In fact poetic 'portraits' of dances are frequent in nineteenth-century music. Obvious examples are Chopin's mazurkas (which he called *obrazki*, or pictures) and the waltzes of Berlioz, Tchaikovsky and later Ravel. Stravinsky too, it would seem, 'depicted' drawing-room dances, but not in the manner of a daguerreotype nor with the intention of 'poeticising' them. On the contrary, his intention was to tear away the antiquated poetic covering, and he reveals the picture only to ridicule it, to present it as it were in a distorting mirror. The essence of the waltz, galop and polka, the thrumming of the balalaika and the whole Spanish box of tricks are all presented by means of the grotesque or, as Pushkin would say, in the manner of 'conventional non-verisimilitude'. In other words, the convention is preserved: the characteristics of waltz, galop or march are reduced to type-models, deliberately exaggerated and given an ironical note, so that the social prototype is revealed by means of caricature. The consciously emphasised banality, the prosaic nature of the material, combined with a 'non-verisimilar' violation of the customary logic of musical development, were all part of Stravinsky's hostile attitude to the romantic 'poeticising' of life. This effect is produced by shifting rhythmic accents, by providing melodies with accompaniments which contradict them harmonically ('oblique rain', as Asafiev aptly called it) – by the use of unexpected, 'unsuitable' timbres and registers. Stravinsky's resourcefulness in deforming his material in this way proved quite exceptional, and his methods largely furnished the arsenal on which twentieth-century composers have drawn in order to express the grotesque.

At the same time similar methods mark the first signs of neo-classicism, which is founded on the stylisation of something – in this case the musical past – rather than its 'poeticising'. The deformation of the past involves a qualitative change of attitude: the past is simply seen through the prism of the present. *Mavra* furnishes an interesting example of this. The subject is taken from Pushkin and the musical type-models which provide the 'material' are the songs of Glinka, Dargomyzhsky and Tchaikovsky; but the material is so deformed that the opera represents a deviation from the composer's magisterial, 'primitive' vein and an approach to the style of his neo-classical period.

These two stylistic veins, or 'lines', cross each other in a unique manner in *The Soldier's Tale*. The music is a mosaic of old Russian folk-song, snatches of real-life tunes grotesquely transformed, echoes of jazz and chorale style. All this is expressed with great concision and concentration, and with the most economical forces, no more than seven instrumentalists. Stravinsky showed his very individual sleight of hand in concentrating in this work all that he had learned up to this time as well as the seeds that had been germinating in his most recent works. The chief characteristic of *The Soldier's Tale* is the universality of its conception. The subject is Russian, but although Stravinsky presents it in his Russian manner, he is already stepping outside the limits of the purely national. The subject itself has been 'de-nationalised': it is timeless and universal, but also topical. What gives the work its modern character is not so much the story-teller's narration as the pronounced urban traits in the music. These are particularly emphasised by Stravinsky's interest in jazz, which is confirmed by other works produced at the same time as *The Soldier's Tale – Ragtime*, *Piano-Rag-Music* and in part the *Three Pieces for Solo Clarinet*, the first of which is closely related to the Tango in *The Soldier's Tale*. Jazz attracted Stravinsky by its rhythmic subtleties, echoes of which can be heard in the solo cadenza of the first movement and in the finale of the *Piano Concerto* and in the unexpected 'break' in the middle of the finale of the *Piano Sonata*.

With *Pulcinella* a still further element enters Stravinsky's music, Italian melody. Was this a betrayal of himself, a going back on his former aesthetic principles? It was certainly a kind of side-stepping; but we should bear in mind that Stravinsky was following a long-standing national tradition, and that both Glinka and Tchaikovsky had paid their tribute to Italian melody. The 'Russo-Italian' element, as Asafiev calls it, is an essential characteristic of their music, and it is possible that Stravinsky was consciously following their example: he certainly admired them and considered them as pioneers on the path which he himself hoped to tread, though he was soon to disentangle himself from the roots that nourished the music of his Russian period.

It was not only melody that attracted him in Italian music: the instrumental writing of the pre-classical period also had a charm for him. The germ of this can be seen in *Pulcinella*, where the instruments of the orchestra became, as it were, active personalities in the comedy.

There is a direct line connecting *Pulcinella* with the *Symphonies of Wind Instruments* and the *Octet*, which were the last works for instrumental ensemble that can be counted as belonging to his Russian period. The beginnings of this same line are to be found in *The Soldier's Tale*; and it is worth recalling that both the *Symphonies* and the *Octet* employ only winds, which also play a leading part in *Mavra* and the *Piano Concerto*. Of the idea of the *Symphonies* he wrote 'This is an austere ritual which is unfolded in terms of short litanies between different groups of homogeneous instruments.'[29] There is a kind of family air about the perpetual return to the chordal sonorities which are summed up in the final chorale. The opening solo for flute, with two flutes accompanying, is Russian in character; the second section is pastoral, and the third a fast dance-movement, while the fourth is formed by the chorale already alluded to, written earlier in the form of a Funeral Chorale for piano solo and published as a supplement to the Debussy number of the *Revue Musicale*. The *Symphonies* last exactly twelve minutes, but the contrasting episodes of liturgical dialogue and the terse, concentrated style combine to make a powerful and unified impression. The Russian element is very clear, both in the echoes of *The Rite of Spring* and No. 4 of the *Four Russian Songs* (*Sektanskaya*) and in the bell-like sonorities.

The character of the *Octet* is quite different. This work lies on the borderline between two periods in Stravinsky's artistic career and already foreshadows his neo-classical works. The first movement is conceived as a solemn *intrada*, the second is a theme with variations in which the inclusion of similar intermezzi among the five variations suggests a rondo element. There is a clear connection with *Pulcinella* in the lively finale and a direct line links the *Octet* with the works of the next few years – the *Piano Concerto* and *Oedipus Rex*. There is even an anticipation of Jocasta's aria in one of the variations of the second movement, and of Kreon's aria in the third.[30] We have now reached the actual frontier dividing the first from the second period of Stravinsky's career as a composer, and it is time to form some general conclusions.

This period of intensive and varied artistic investigation had its effect on all Stravinsky's later work. All we need is to define it more clearly, not only by distinctive formal and stylistic features, but before all else by something in itself hard to define – namely the character of the artist's thinking. Speaking at an official reception in Moscow in 1962, Stravinsky said 'A man has only one birthplace, one fatherland . . . and his place of birth is an important factor in his life' – an interesting comment from a man who left Russia in 1914 and twice thereafter changed his nationality. In an interview published in *Komsomolskaya Pravda* on 27 September that same year he said, 'All my life I have spoken Russian, the whole essence of my personality is Russian. This may not be immediately clear in my music, but it is something deep down in its secret nature.' Even before this, in 1957, Craft had observed that Stravinsky always thought in Russian and, despite his mastery of French, German and English, he translated mentally from Russian when he spoke these languages.[31]

Hitherto this Russian something hidden in the 'secret nature' of Stravinsky's music has only been traced in the music of his first period, and in such works as *The Fairy's Kiss* and *Scherzo à la russe*. In analysing his later evolution scholars have generally stressed its international, universal character and what separated the composer from his Russian past. He himself never of course denied his Russianness or broke his ties with Russian culture, the genuine quality of which is vouched for by the warmth with which he speaks in *Memories and Commentaries* of his youth and his love of Petersburg and Pushkin, and finally by the nostalgia for Russia that he felt in his old age, particularly after his visit in 1962.

Russian echoes are clearly audible in many works of Stravinsky's neo-classical and later periods. Let me give a few instances. There are plain traces of this nostalgia in the *Symphony in C*, especially in the thematic resemblance between the first movement and Tchaikovsky's

First Symphony. Then the theme of the variations which form the second movement of the *Sonata for Two Pianos* and the *poco più mosso* episode in the finale both have a Russian cut. There are similar echoes, this time of *The Rite of Spring*, in the *Symphony in Three Movements*. Some of his works show the influence, as he himself said, of 'early memories of church music in Poltava and Kiev'.[32] These are to be seen not only in the *Mass* but in the 'Byzantine' cut of *Oedipus Rex* (where Mussorgsky's influence is also noticeable in the choruses), in the solo aria in Part 2 of *Canticum Sacrum* and also in *Symphony of Psalms*. Here the composer himself stated that his point of departure was the music of the Orthodox rather than the Western Catholic rite, and the 'Laudate Dominum' was originally composed to the words of the 'Gospodi pomiluy'.[33] How Russian, too, the chanting sounds in *Requiem Canticles*, in spite of the Latin text! Indeed, this Russian element can break through even in works deliberately stylised in a different national manner, like *Persephone*, which contains a reminiscence of the Russian Easter Liturgy; or *Pulcinella*, where the tenor's D-minor aria in Scene 4 is followed by what is in fact a Russian dance, and the soprano's aria in Scene 5 is closer to Tchaikovsky than to Pergolesi.

Another interesting reflection on Stravinsky's character is provided by the fact that after taking American citizenship he embarked in 1945–6 on the laborious task of revising the works of his Russian period, producing in some cases – such as the *Symphonies of Wind Instruments* – entirely new versions. He was once again on a borderline, this time between the neo-classical and the final period, and he was finding it difficult in his old age to acclimatise himself to the American way of living, which always remained fundamentally alien to him. It was then that he immersed himself, as it were, in the life-giving waters of his Russian works, searching and finding in them new creative impulses. Later, too, when he had adopted serial methods and might seem entirely to have abandoned his 'Russian' manner, he kept returning to the works that he had written between 1910 and 1920 and making free adaptations of them. The composing of new versions of this kind apparently gave him satisfaction, as though he were in love with these diatonic pieces, to which he gave a new polish and a new sonorous character; and in fact the terseness of expression that characterised the earlier works did correspond to Stravinsky's manner of composition in his old age. It seems likely, however, that it was not only this stylistic similarity that attracted him to the past, but that deep psychological factors were also engaged, as is suggested by Stravinsky's own admission that he was 'depressed by the disappearance of our old existence, our old domestic habits and way of life'.[34]

Just how strongly he felt this pull of the past is suggested by the fact that in 1965 – the year in which he finally ceased to compose – he wrote an orchestral canon on a Russian folk-song in which he used the theme of the *Firebird* finale.

It remains to make a careful study of the imagery and semantics in which Russian influence continued, in modified forms, to play a part in Stravinsky's last works. Asafiev used often to pick out two organic features of Stravinsky's style – his use of bell-sonorities and his percussive effects. The first examples of these are to be found in the early song *Spring* (*The Cloister*) and *Firebird* – the alarming tocsin that sounds as Kashchei's kingdom wakes to life. We find similar features in *The Rite* at the 'Procession of the Wise Elder' (bell sonorities in the high brass) and the 'Ritual of the Ancients' (deep antiphonal notes of muted trumpets and trombones). Asafiev called attention to the frequent use of *pizzicato* with a percussive or 'tolling' effect in *Pribautki*. *Les Noces* is the first instance of sound used neither descriptively nor for additional theatrical effect, he wrote, but as a fundamental principle of construction, an element that is organically present in the material and rich in possibilities for the composer. No other composer, not even Mussorgsky, achieved this.[35]

Obvious examples are *Tilimbom* from *Stories for Children*, *Sektantskaya* from *Four Russian Songs* – where the bell sonorities are further emphasised in the 1954 version – and 'Hymn' from the piano *Serenade*. Characteristic too are some of the episodes from the first movement and the end of the fourth variation in the *Concerto for Two Pianos*, Ricercar II for the Second Tenor in the *Cantata on Old English Texts* (the accented notes for the two oboes and violoncello) and finally, most impressive of all, the funeral sonorities of the *Requiem Canticles*.

What Asafiev calls 'the heavy tolling, or swinging, of complex groups of sonorities' is a characteristic feature of Stravinsky's music at all periods, and this is connected in the first instance with bell-sounds. The rhythmic power of such swinging movements is enormous, as in the Coachmen's Dance from *Petrushka*: Asafiev describes it as 'the breaking free of a contained energy trying to expand space', and he compares the dramatic function of such figures to the function of thrust in architecture.[36] This 'thrust' is so common in Stravinsky's music that it is hardly necessary to quote examples.

Generally speaking, we should perhaps associate the stability of Stravinsky's rhythmic figures with the phonetic quality of Russian speech, and this would reveal many Russian features in his last works. Particularly important in this connection are what the composer himself described as the 'melodic–rhythmic stutterings' produced by irregularities of accentuation; it was not for nothing that he discovered this mannerism when working on the articulation of the vocal lines in *Les Noces*.

It is not easy to isolate what is Russian in Stravinsky's treatment of non-Russian texts, whether these are French, Italian, Latin, English or Hebrew. The Russian element often protruded itself in these of course and, as we have seen, Stravinsky's individual amalgamation of Byzantine and Orthodox gives passages of chanting in his works a special significance. His handling of chorale-style is neither Gregorian nor Protestant in character, as is clear from the last of the *Three Pieces for String Quartet*, which became No. 3 of the *Four Studies for Orchestra* and might just as well have been entitled Hymn, according to the composer. 'Laudate' in the *Symphony of Psalms* has this static, hymn-like character which is Russian in derivation, as Stravinsky himself observed. This static quality is also to be found in the final chorale of the *Symphonies of Wind Instruments*, in the Hymn from the piano *Serenade*, the prelude to the *Cantata* of 1952 and the 'apotheosis' at the end of *Apollo Musagetes*. Vertical sound-complexes form the final sonorities in the coda of the *Octet* (cf. *Ebony Concerto*) and the *Symphony in C*, and indeed of the last of the *Requiem Canticles*, in which the preceding development is, as it were, synthesised and concentrated. Responsorial forms, similar to antiphonal practice common in church music, are common in Stravinsky's music and are to be found in *Les Noces* and the *Mass*. Contrasting chorales of trombones and strings answer each other in the cantata *In Memoriam Dylan Thomas* and in the *Introitus* in memory of T. S. Eliot. No further examples are needed, I think, to show that solemn Russian chant forms part of the bone and fibre of Stravinsky's music. He himself remarked of 'Laudate Dominum' in *Symphony of Psalms* that 'an apotheosis of this sort had become a pattern in my music since the "Epithalamium" at the end of *Les Noces*.'[37]

Such were the discoveries, the revelations and achievements of this first period of Stravinsky's career as a composer, which must be counted as the main period, not only on account of the aesthetic qualities of the works that it produced, but because of the significance that it had for the whole artistic evolution of the composer.

6

The theatre

When Pierre Boulez was interviewed by *Der Spiegel* in the autumn of 1967 he expressed a paradoxical wish. 'Just think what a collaboration between Stravinsky and Brecht in the twenties might have produced!' But the idea itself is an illusion, because even in his earliest works Brecht asserted the political role of the theatre, while Stravinsky was more interested in presenting the impersonal action of fate, something totally divorced from politics. Brecht's chief concern was with the didactic role of the theatre as a social and educative force, and he called his collaborations, first with Hindemith and Weill and later with Hanns Eisler, *Lehrstücke* – 'educational works'. What aroused Stravinsky's interest was pure 'play', the whole ritual side of drama, strict style within a given theatrical form. 'I was always attracted by new conventions and it was these that determined to a large degree my interest in the theatre.'

Yet, although the ideas of Stravinsky and Brecht were no doubt fundamentally different and their fields of activity never coincided, they were agreed on certain questions concerning the heightening of theatrical effect, and Boulez's paradox was not totally without foundation, however unrealisable it may have been in practice.

For Brecht the contrast lay between conventional theatre – the 'dramatic' theatre of illustration – and the 'epic' theatre of experience or transformation, based on a direct correspondence with living reality. Between 1910 and 1920, before Brecht that is to say, this same contrast, less clearly formulated, was proclaimed and put into practice first by Meyerhold and then by Eisenstein in his early works, by Gordon Craig, Jacques Copeau and a number of other men of the theatre.

In Brecht's view the theatre, appealing to the audience's desire for a likelife authenticity, demands an 'effect of presence'. It is based on the idea of an imaginary fourth wall, as it were separating the public from the stage and giving the illusion that the events on the stage were happening in reality. The opposite of this 'effect of presence' is the 'effect of alienation' – the distancing of the object presented – a distance dividing the audience from the stage, those taking part in the action from those watching it, actors from spectators. 'The theatre of illustration illustrates', as Brecht says. In the theatre of experience effect is calculated on the sharing of an experience, in the theatre of illustration it is calculated on observation and evaluation. The first demands the unification or amalgamation of all heterogeneous theatrical elements, while the second demands their separation; and the more extreme that separation is, the greater the 'effect of alienation'.

The inorganic nature of this unification or amalgamation became clear to Brecht in musico-theatrical works in which nineteenth-century romantic traditions still persist and are still carefully preserved today, in spite of their inner contradictions. According to Brecht, such contradictions should not be glossed over by means of an apparent synthesis: they should be brought to light and accentuated. 'The conventionality of opera', he wrote, 'lies in the fact that although it employs rational elements and introduces features of physical authenticity and reality, all these are suddenly cancelled by the music. The dying man is real, but when the dying man begins to sing, we are suddenly in a purely conventional world.' [1] He pointed out that the old dispute on the prior claims of gesture, music and stage presentation of character can easily be decided by a radical separation or disassociation of these elements.

Stravinsky was in fact the first composer to embark on this radical disassociation of the elements present in musico-dramatic works, and long before 1930, when Brecht wrote his *Observations on the Opera Rise and Fall of the Town of Mahagonny*. The young Stravinsky's views on the nature of the theatre were formed under the immediate influence of the 'World of Art' group. He was first initiated in the theatre by Diaghilev and Benois, with whom he collaborated on *Petrushka*; and it was Benois who first had the idea of separating the constituents of opera. We must presume that Stravinsky was acquainted with Meyerhold's early publications, in which he championed the principles of the conventional theatre with its rejection of stage accessories and the subordinating of the actor to verbal rhythm and plastic movement. Stravinsky naturally shared in the prevailing cult of the past which was proclaimed by members of the 'World of Art' group and, partly under their influence, by such producers as Evreinov, Tairov and, most importantly, Meyerhold. Their aim was to achieve a kind of transformed restoration of early theatrical traditions, the unsophisticated immediacy of the conventions of Shakespeare's day, of the *commedia dell'arte*, mediaeval mystery-plays, the popular show-booth, the fairground peepshow, the acrobats of the circus and the Japanese marionette-theatre, in which actors manipulate the marionettes in full view of the audience.

Just at the time when Stravinsky's career in the theatre began, a large number of people concerned with the theatre were working for a renewal of the 'play' element in stage production as opposed to the prevailing 'true-to-life' illusionism. Meyerhold adopted the pen-name of Doctor Dapertutto for the journal that he started publishing in 1914, devoting the first number to the discussion of a scenario based on Gozzi, and referring plainly to a number of methods similar to that of 'alienation'. Five years later, in 1919, Prokofiev completed his opera *Love for Three Oranges* which was based on Meyerhold's scenario. By this time, however, Stravinsky was already working on *Pulcinella*, which was in fact his seventh work for the theatre, and *Les Noces* was virtually complete except for the orchestration, which was not completed until some years later.

When Stravinsky started work on his first theatrical work, *The Nightingale*, he had no idea of a radical reform of the opera. Indeed, it seems unlikely that he had any plans of this kind even when he gave up work on the opera and turned his attention to *Firebird* in the autumn of 1909. It was a year after that that he conceived *Petrushka*, where we encounter the influence of these new ideas about the theatre. Here we can see reflected on the one hand an interest in the fairground peepshow, which is even clearer in *Renard* (and then in Satie's *Parade* and Milhaud's *Le Boeuf sur le toit* in which circus acrobats appear) and on the other a concern with the grotesques of the marionette theatre. The next stage in the discovery of a new form of convention, associated on this occasion with ritual and ceremonial action, was marked by *The Rite of Spring*.

What was novel in these works was more actively expressed in their music than in their theatrical form. It is quite possible that the details of that form were still unclear in Stravinsky's imagination. It was probably the theatrical experiments sponsored by Diaghilev that served to clear Stravinsky's mind on the subject. Two experiments of this kind were given at Benois's suggestion in the spring of 1914. The first was the production of *The Golden Cockerel* in the form of an opera–ballet, with the singers placed round the stage in everyday clothes, the action performed by dancers and mimes and the functions of singers and actors thus disassociated; and the second, given twelve days later in a similar manner, was the first performance of *The Nightingale* at the Maryinsky Theatre. Here too the principle of disassociating music and stage action was observed: the action was carried out by silent players at the front of the stage, the singers had music-stands with their parts on them, and the chorus stood motionless on the right and left of the stage.[2] So that if *Petrushka* may be said to have contained the embryo of *Renard*, Meyerhold's *Nightingale* may be said to have contained the principles of *Oedipus Rex*, where not only the chorus is motionless but the soloists also, who are dressed according to the author's instructions 'in special costumes and masks. Only their arms and heads move and they should give the impression of living statues.' Stravinsky was later to be more precise: 'The actors should stand on pedestals and wear cothurni [buskins], each person at a different height, behind the chorus . . . No one "acts", and the only individual who moves at all is the narrator, and he merely in order to show his detachment from the other stage figures.'[3]

A narrator, or speaker, had been introduced before this, in *The Soldier's Tale*. In *The Soldier's Tale* stage methods are 'reflected' or seen obliquely. On the stage are the *tableaux vivants* of the action, which is danced; the instrumental ensemble; and the Narrator representing the characters. Later, in *Persephone*, reader, singers, mimes and chorus are combined in this same 'disassociated illustration'; and at the of his life, in 1961–2, he called *The Flood* 'a musical performance for readers, soloists, chorus, orchestra and dancers'.

As far as the disassociation of the functions of singers and actors is concerned, *Renard* provides the clearest example; and it is worth observing that it was written before Meyerhold's production of *The Nightingale*, but soon after the Paris première. *Renard* is performed by clowns, ballet-dancers or acrobats preferably on bare trestles, with the orchestra placed behind. If it is to be given on the stage in a theatre, it should be played in front of the curtain, in which case the orchestra should be in its usual place. The singers should be in the orchestra.

A year before *Renard*, in 1914, Stravinsky started work on *Les Noces*. Evidently he already had a clear vision of a new kind of convention involving new laws to produce a counterpoint between stage and music. In each of the works that followed, Stravinsky discovered new aspects of this relationship, laying bare stage methods, 'illustrating illustration'. In one work he placed his singers in the orchestra, leaving the stage to mimes; in another everything – whether 'acted, read or danced' – was used for illustration; and in a third he insisted on the contrast between live action and statuesque immobility. In *Les Noces* all those taking part were brought on to the stage, not only the members of the chorus and the dancers but the four pianists and the percussion players.

The composer was absolutely satisfied by the Paris première in 1923, when Nijinskaya was responsible for the ballet and Goncharova for the sets. 'The curtain was not used and the dancers did not leave the stage even during the lamentation of the two mothers . . . But though the bride and groom are always present, the guests are able to talk about them as if they were not there – a stylisation not unlike Kabuki theatre.'[4]

Thus in *Les Noces* there is a triple counterpoint between music and action – chorus, dancers and players are disassociated, but at the same time united in a higher artistic unity. The principle by which the singers are not identical with the stage characters had already been used in *Renard* and was to reappear in *Pulcinella*, where masks from the *commedia dell'arte* take the place of Russian tumblers. But in *Les Noces* this 'counterpointing' is further complicated by the contrasting of singers and players. This was in fact the perfect realisation of Brecht's wish to separate the different elements of a musical spectacle.

The grotesque, which plays a considerable part in Stravinsky's works for the theatre, represents another feature of 'alienation'. (According to Gorky, Lenin observed that 'wherever a satirical or sceptical attitude to conventional beliefs is expressed, there is a wish to turn these beliefs upside down, to demonstrate the illogicality of existing conventions'.) Stravinsky was not of course the first or the only artist to use this method of interpreting the world. Alfred Jarry's *Ubu Roi* played an important part in popularising the grotesque with French writers in the early years of the century, among whom Guillaume Apollinaire is an outstanding figure with his play *Les Mamelles de Tirésias*. The grotesque also plays a large part in the work of Picasso, who stood very near to Stravinsky in his early days, and of course in the music of Erik Satie. This is not the place for a full examination of what led to this marked interest in the grotesque among the writers and artists at the beginning of the century. To trace this to its original source might well involve going back to the carnival parodies and distortions of the Renaissance. A few facts, however, should be borne in mind.

In the early years of the century there was a renewal of interest in the clowning and impromptu 'gagging' of the Italian *commedia dell'arte*, and it was not by chance that Stravinsky wrote *Pulcinella* or that Picasso provided the décor. The strong 'nonsense' tradition in English poetry was another important element – Edward Lear, for instance, whose *The Owl and the Pussycat* was chosen by Stravinsky as the text of his last composition (1966), Lewis Carroll and T. S. Eliot, who in 1939 produced *Old Possum's Book of Practical Cats*. All over Europe, too, there sprang up during these years cabaret or 'pocket' theatres characterised by eccentric acting styles and the caricaturing of everyday life and accepted opinions; and this taste for the eccentric was also to be found in the fashion for the circus, for acrobatics and clowns.[5] Stravinsky saw one of the most famous of these clowns – 'Little Tich' – in London in 1914 and was in his own words 'fascinated'. A contemporary historian of the circus has described Little Tich as 'like one of Goya's *Caprichos*'.[6]

It is hardly necessary to give examples of this vein in Stravinsky's music where, from *Petrushka* onwards, the grotesque is perpetually making an appearance, sometimes openly and at other times masked. And although, as has been said, he was not the only composer to tap this vein, he was certainly the most consistent, making use of it in his concert pieces and his theatrical works. This came naturally to an artist who never lost his curiosity in every manifestation of human existence (a curiosity that he shared with Pushkin) and was prompted by brilliant, almost uncanny powers of observation and a naturally ironical turn of mind.

Another contributing factor was Stravinsky's ability to give artistic form to the play-element which formed an integral part of his nature. Every game is based on the acceptance of a set of rules which govern it, but in the grotesque contradictory images and ideas are combined – the phenomena of real life are turned upside down, producing as it were a double set of rules, and this greatly complicates the game: the normal rules are observed and at the same time 'eccentrically' flouted. We referred to this earlier when discussing Stravinsky's use of distorting-mirror images, which we see most clearly in *Mavra*. But this same 'double game' appears in the Royal March in *The Soldier's Tale*, in the wheezy duet for double-bass and trombone glissando in *Pulcinella*. We see it again in the tragi-comic entries of the Joker in *Jeu de cartes* and in the *Circus Polka* – 'composed for a young elephant' – where Schubert's *Marche militaire* makes an unexpected appearance at the end; and again in the ragings of Baba the Turk in *The Rake's Progress*.

These passages often have a double significance. The grotesque may be both 'eccentric' and tragic, the humour both good-natured and malicious, the irony both sly and cutting and the most inoffensive joke can sometimes turn into sarcasm. All these different shades of meaning are richly represented in Stravinsky's theatre music, but their presentation is almost always marked primarily by the free play-element in its theatrical guise, and in an atmosphere of festival activity.

Stravinsky insists on this festival note in its most literal and immediate sense. He likes to begin a work with a definite *intrada* – with fanfares as in *Agon*, or with the preliminary parade which forms a familiar feature in the circus, the hippodrome and the bull-ring. Thus *Renard* opens with a processional march which accompanies the entry of the actors, and later their final exit; and in the same way *The Soldier's Tale* and all three scenes of *Jeu de cartes* open with a march. This deliberate theatricality also contains something of the play-element, which is present even in the Apotheosis at the end of *Apollo Musagetes* or *The Fairy's Kiss*, in the *Duo Concertante*, in *Scènes de ballet*, and in *Orpheus*.

We are, of course, far from having exhausted the list of Stravinsky's various solutions of the problem of theatrical form. He was most deeply concerned with this problem between 1910 and 1925, more particularly in the case of works belonging to the *genre mixte*. These pieces, which do not fit into the traditional framework of either ballet or opera, include *Renard*, *The Soldier's Tale*, *Les Noces* ('choreographic cantata'), *Oedipus Rex* ('opera–oratorio') and a number of others. It was these 'unclassifiable' works that exercised the greatest influence on the contemporary theatre.

Stravinsky's later works fall more easily into traditional categories. The alienation-effect is still present in them, but it is more deeply concealed and does not destroy the accepted stage form concerned. *The Rake's Progress*, for instance, is constructed on unexpected *volte-faces* and interruptions in the musical as well as in the dramatic development. These are manifest within individual scenes (e.g. the finale in the madhouse) as well as in the contrast between one scene and another. There is an important element of alienation in the actual methods of Stravinsky's stylisation, and particularly in his use of the harpsichord to accompany the recitatives.

Stravinsky was the author of five symphonies, not counting his first juvenile effort and remembering that the *Symphonies of Wind Instruments*, and the *Symphony of Psalms* are symphonies in name rather than in the traditional sense. He wrote four concertante works with orchestra – the piano and violin concertos, *Capriccio* and *Movements* – and two with chamber ensemble, *Dumbarton Oaks* and the 'Bâle' *Concerto in D*. In addition to this he composed twenty works for the theatre in the course of fifty-five years. These figures speak for themselves.

For years he was deeply interested in problems of the theatre, but to a different degree at different times. Theatre music dominates the fifteen years of his Russian period, during which he wrote nine theatrical works, if we include *Pulcinella*, which belongs stylistically to his next, neo-classical period, which lasted twice as long as the Russian and included nine theatrical pieces. It was not until the crisis of the mid-1930's that his interest in the theatre waned. After *Jeu de cartes* (1936) there were only two stage works, though *The Rake's Progress* is a full-length opera in three acts. Between 1939 and 1945 the world's attention was concentrated on the war, and Stravinsky's theatrical interests were therefore circumscribed. In his last period the composer's interest in the theatre further diminished, and there are only two theatre pieces from those years.

Having considered Stravinsky's innovations in the *genre mixte*, we must now turn our attention to his handling of the traditional forms, and in the first place ballet. It is an acknowledged fact that Stravinsky had a special love of choreography. In the ironical table which he drew up to demonstrate the differences between Schoenberg and himself[7] he quotes Schoenberg's dictum that 'ballet is not a musical form' and opposite this, in the Stravinsky column, he notes 'chief production is of ballets'. In *Chronicle* Stravinsky stated[8] his 'profound admiration for classical ballet, which, in its very essence, by the beauty of its *ordonnance* and the aristocratic austerity of its forms, so closely corresponds with my conception of art. For here, in classical dancing, I see the triumph of studied conception over vagueness, of the rule over the arbitrary, of order over hazard.' But is this true only of classical dancing, or was Stravinsky not perhaps narrowing the question down and ignoring another, deeper connection between all his music – not only that written for the ballet – and dance in general, the very nature of dancing as such?

For an answer to this question we must turn to Huizinga: 'It is not that dancing has something of play about it, rather that it is an integral part of play: the relationship is one of direct participation, almost of essential identity. Dancing is a particular and particularly perfect form of playing.'[9] Here we have the explanation of the primacy of the dance element in Stravinsky's music, of his passion for theatre-ballet, in which dancing constitutes the essence and meaning of 'play-activity', and the rules and discipline of the 'game' are strictly ordered.

It seems probable that Stravinsky did not immediately recognise his vocation, and that it was his meeting with Diaghilev that hastened that recognition. Through Diaghilev he met the great choreographers, all of whom were Russian born, an important fact in the circumstances. With Mikhail Fokine he shared the success of his first two ballets, though their ways then parted and relations between them were broken off. Of Vatslav Nijinsky's gifts as a choreographer Stravinsky expressed himself ambiguously, first with great enthusiasm and later (apropos of the same work, *The Rite of Spring*) with considerable scepticism; but he was wholly satisfied with the choreography of Bronislava Nijinsky (Vatslav's sister) for *Les Noces*. Other choreographers who worked with Stravinsky were Léonide Massine, Boris Romanov, Sergei Lifar, Adolf Bolm and finally George Balanchine (Georgii Balanchivadze), whom he first met in 1925. This was in connection with the new choreography for the symphonic poem *Song of the Nightingale*, which had had its première with Massine's choreography in 1920. The two men worked together on the Paris production of *Apollo Musagetes* in 1928, after which they collaborated closely for some forty years, their last joint production being *The Flood* in 1962. Western critics spoke of Balanchine as 'the twentieth-century Petipa' and it was he who revived the 'classical' ballets so much admired by Stravinsky. Balanchine's neo-classical choreography entirely corresponded to the composer's neo-classical ideals. Stravinsky produced eight full-length ballets (*Firebird, Petrushka, The Rite of Spring, Apollo Musagetes, The Fairy's Kiss, Jeu de cartes, Orpheus* and *Agon*); *Danses Concertantes, Scènes de ballet* and *Song of the Nightingale*; and three ballet pieces with singing, *Renard, Pulcinella* and *Les Noces*, making a total of fourteen works in all. This impressive figure does not include symphonic works of Stravinsky's used, in accordance with the practice of the day, for ballets by Isadora Duncan, Gorsky and Fokine. According to the list compiled in New York on the occasion of the composer's eightieth birthday,[10] some forty of his works, not counting the fourteen listed above, had been used for dancing, and the number has certainly grown since that time, confirming the significance that Stravinsky's musical innovations have had in the development of twentieth-century choreography.

It is true that not all choreographers have been willing to admit this. Lifar, for instance, who had a great success in the title role at the Paris première of *Apollo Musagetes*, was later (1939) to speak of the composer as 'a tyrant, a despot, the evil genius not only of the Diaghilev ballet but of ballet in general'. 'Stravinsky's music is not meant for dancing, rather the reverse – it kills dancing, destroying rather than enriching it. This music is so beautiful in itself that it does not need dancing.'[11]

Judgments of this kind are not numerous, of course, and they are expressed by choreographers who have no sympathy with the explosive rhythmic energy of Stravinsky's music, its characteristically aggressive and jerky movements, its sudden changes of accent, gait and dynamics – in fact the whole formal and expressive vocabulary with which Stravinsky enriched the language of contemporary choreography. This new vocabulary does indeed require choreographers to change their whole way of thinking and to abandon the old idea of 'merely duplicating the line and beat of the music', as Stravinsky accused Nijinsky of doing in his choreography for *The Rite*.[12]

In Stravinsky's opinion, 'choreography must realise its own form, one independent of the musical form though measured to the musical unit'. A counterpoint between the two must in fact be established. Choreography must not seek 'merely to duplicate the line and beat of the music', in the manner of Jaques Dalcroze; it must be a plastic transcription of the rhythmic figures, a transmutation of them into dance terms.

There is a close and interesting analogy between these ideas of Stravinsky's and Eisenstein's remarks about the role of music in the cinema, made in connection with Prokofiev's score for the film *Ivan the Terrible*: 'The combining of accents in the screen-image and the music does not consist in the crude metrical synchronising of the two, but in their complex interweaving, in which synchronisation is rare and exceptional – something determined strictly by the montage and the pacing of the dramatic development.' If we transfer this to choreography, I think that Stravinsky's opinion would coincide exactly with Eisenstein's.

Whether the fault lay with the conservative tastes of theatre-goers or with the insufficient inventiveness of his producers, Stravinsky's ballets enjoyed less success as theatre than might have been expected, and his music won greater acknowledgment in the concert-hall than in the theatre. *The Rite of Spring* is an obvious example.

None of these stage works fills a whole programme: even the largest lasts less than an hour and there are some that take less than half an hour to perform. This laconic character of Stravinsky's music represents a rejection, in principle, of the structure of the nineteenth-century three-act Romantic ballet. His terse, concentrated forms of expression are absolutely incompatible with the luxury and impressiveness of traditional spectacular ballets and their wealth of episodic intermezzos. It is not a case of miniature forms but of condensing the drama inherent in the music itself.

The aesthetics of the 'World of Art' group played a part in this concentration of expression during Stravinsky's early years, and it was effected by the condensation of the actual colours used. The *Firebird* music owes its brilliance and colour less to the inner meaning of the story than to the fantastic interweaving of Russian and oriental traits in its handling; and here Stravinsky, for all his subsequent assurances to the contrary, was completely captured by Fokine's imagination. In fact, had Stravinsky continued to compose in this vein, he and Fokine would probably not have parted company. But Stravinsky had other ideas, and he really found himself when Roerich proposed to him the scenario of *The Great Sacrifice*, as *The Rite of Spring* was called at first, though in the event this title was attached only to the second part of the work. Stravinsky had been acquainted with Roerich since 1904, but their decisive meeting was not until 1910, immediately after the completion of *Firebird*. In the autumn of that year Roerich said in a newspaper article:

The new ballet presents a number of scenes from the celebration of a 'holy night' among the primitive Slavs . . . The action begins during a summer night and finishes before actual sunrise, as the sun's first rays appear. The choreography consists of ritual dances, and the work will be the first attempt to reproduce life among a primitive people without using any definite dramatic story.

Two years later, in the autumn of 1912, when the sketches of the music were complete, Stravinsky called the work 'a mystery' and again insisted 'It has virtually no subject. It is simply a pattern of dances or a dance-drama.'[13]

Thus we have a ritual, an 'action in play': and with different modifications this was to be the fundamental character of all Stravinsky's subsequent ballets. Yet parallel to *The Rite* we find *Petrushka*, a ballet with a witty 'subject' and much picturesque action (the principles of which were defended by Fokine) enriched with new features. Asafiev has pointed out that the 'World of Art' group 'opened up a new path – instead of archaeological and ethnographical *vues d'ensemble* – a path to the beautiful, "sunny" forms of popular applied art, with its love for brightness and clarity'. This 'sunny', festival quality is solidly affirmed in Stravinsky's ballets – and not only in his ballets – both in the highly patterned structure of *Firebird* and in the decorative, gaudy touches of the fair scenes in *Petrushka*. But in *Petrushka* there are also elements of tragedy. The desperate, frenzied loneliness of Petrushka finds an echo on another stylistic level in the doomed, sacrificial loneliness of the Chosen Victim in *The Rite*; in the loneliness of the Emperor in *The Nightingale*, pinned down by death; in the tragic plight of Oedipus; and in the tragic loneliness of Rakewell in the madhouse at the end of *The Rake's Progress*. In the kaleidoscopic opening and closing scenes of *Petrushka* (the entry of the masks, for instance) the play-element forms an important part, as does the grotesque element used by Stravinsky for the purpose of theatrical alienation. New tendencies appear even more clearly in *Renard* and *The Soldier's Tale* and are reflected in a markedly original way in *Mavra*.

In *Petrushka*, however, there are still strong traces of Impressionist colour, although this was historically the first Russian ballet based on realistic scenes, *Firebird* containing many features that recalled Rimsky-Korsakov and Lyadov in their stylisation. (*Petrushka* still remains really the only one of its kind, if we are considering works with a permanent place in the repertory and not occasional ephemeral pieces.)

In the years immediately after *Petrushka* Stravinsky's music still preserved its strong Russian character, but no longer its picturesque note, and this accounts for the break with Fokine, who was the great master of the picturesque among choreographers. From now on, in contradistinction to *Petrushka*, the ballets that interested Stravinsky had only minimal subject-matter or none whatever.

In the first of these two classes belong the ballets in which the outline-pattern of the story is borrowed either from ritual (*Les Noces*), from mythology (*Apollo* and *Orpheus*), or from 'the rules of the game' – fairy-story (*Renard*), commedia dell'arte (*Pulcinella*), or card-playing (*Jeu de cartes*, which Stravinsky called 'a ballet in three deals'). In these it is not the story that is most important but the play-element in the story. *Scènes de ballet* (1944) has hardly more than a choreographic skeleton, and this was the prototype of the idea of Stravinsky's last ballet, *Agon* (1953–7), whose title might be translated as 'contest', 'rivalry' or indeed just 'game'.

There is no simple answer to the question of the musical form of Stravinsky's ballets. Tchaikovsky and Glazunov had given their ballet-music a symphonic character, preserving the connection with the structure of the Romantic ballet and using variations, adagio (*pas de deux*), pantomime (*pas d'action*) and so forth, but giving them more musical substance and musical development. In actual fact both Adam and Delibes had, within the limits of their capacity, attempted to do the same; but it was only Tchaikovsky, and after him Glazunov, who succeeded in liberating ballet music from its narrow functionalism. Their contemporary Petipa insisted on 'symphonic dancing' in his choreography.

In fact both composers and choreographers in the twentieth

century have enjoyed previously unimagined possibilities in the symphonic combination of music and dance; and under the pressure of these new ideas the whole structure of the old ballet-spectacle simply collapsed. The new principles of musical drama established themselves in two contrasting ways. The first of these involved a still further step towards giving ballet music a symphonic character and totally abandoning the old formal scheme. This was the path followed by Ravel in his *Daphnis et Chloé*, which he entitled a symphony in three movements, and in *La Valse*, which he called a 'choreographic poem'. Honegger, Hindemith and Bartók also wrote 'symphonies' or 'poems' for ballet. The second of these two approaches is represented in works based on the alternation and contrasting of a succession of dance episodes. There are plainly different ways of organising this variety from a musical point of view, but the importance lies in the principle of replacing the continuous musical development characteristic of poem and symphony by a suite-like succession of isolated 'numbers', each number having a different visual and stylistic *niveau*. Here again we should remember Meyerhold, who constructed his theatrical pieces as 'suites' of contrasting episodes. His pupil Eisenstein spoke of this stage method as 'a montage of attractions', and Stravinsky was a convinced supporter of this kind of 'composition', which Prokofiev also employed in his ballets. Prokofiev was concerned with the communication of what was individual and unique in his dramatic characters and with penetrating their inner world by means of gesture, manner and way of behaving. What interested Stravinsky, on the other hand, was the character of movement as such – that is to say as the universal, suprapersonal expression of life-processes and their deliberate, ordered alternation. It was not without significance that he added to the title of his last symphony the words 'in three movements', for each movement as it were vies with the others in summarising a particular variety and tempo of actual 'movement'. He also, of course, gave the title *Movements* to his last work for piano and orchestra.

There is a hugely varied repertory of movement-types in his ballet scores. They are inspired by the visual impressions of a keenly observant artist, and the potential visual element which they contain demands transposition into choreographic terms. I shall return to this again, but for the moment I wish to speak about Stravinsky's operas, of which there are only four – *The Nightingale* which Stravinsky called an opera in three acts, though in fact these are no more than scenes, the whole piece only lasting some 45 minutes; the one-act *Mavra*: the two-act *Oedipus Rex*; and his only genuinely three-act opera, *The Rake's Progress.*

All these works, with the exception of *The Nightingale*, are 'number-operas' in protest against the structure of the music drama, a term used by Stravinsky to represent all that he rejected in nineteenth-century opera, in particular Wagner's. He was in fact to make a clear distinction between 'opera in verse' and 'opera in prose'. 'Quite apart from their artificiality sub-divisions of this kind are essential to me in the process of devising form.'

What did Stravinsky really mean by this contrasting of verse and prose? We discussed earlier his conception of the part played by versification in his music. He contrasts the ordered rhythm and carefully devised regularity of verse with the irregularity of prose, the balance of verse with the continuous flow of prose'. The essential differences between the two demand the application of different principles in their dramatic handling. Rudnitsky has very justly observed that in the 'theatre of experience' the action tries to approximate to the uninterrupted flow of real life, and for this reason the details of the internal articulation of the drama are concealed, individual scenes forming whole 'blocks' or acts. In the conventional theatre, on the other hand, the action is divided into separate sections – episodes or 'numbers'. Rudnitsky goes on to explain this: 'The inner correspondence between the laws of the conventional theatre and the laws of poetry is determined by the fact that poetry is a condensed form of speech, in fact the most intense and closely woven form that exists.' [14]

It was precisely this condensed form of expression, this tight format of separate but interrelated numbers that Stravinsky aimed at in his ballets and operas.

He was nauseated by *verismo*, which he saw as an extreme example of 'true-to-life' emotional naturalism, something as alien to him as the ideals of Wagnerian music-drama, the *Gesamtkunstwerk* with its uninterrupted dramatic flow, of which he speaks so scathingly in *Chronicle* and *Poetics of Music*. [15] In fact, at the root of his hostility to Wagner lay a more general hostility to the whole Romantic conception of the theatre. What he introduced was a convention of a different kind, and different in each of his four operas.

The Nightingale is essentially a pictorial, one might even say a picturesque, work. Stravinsky's method of drawing situations and emotional states recalls that of the Impressionists, and there is an analogy here with another work written at exactly the same time,

Bartók's *Duke Bluebeard's Castle*. The method in fact goes back to Debussy's *Pelléas et Mélisande*. There is an out-of-doors element in the opera, represented by the Fisherman's song with which the Prologue opens and all three scenes end. There is also a festival, fairy element in the entr'acte between the first and second scenes; and there are touches of the grotesque, as in so many of Stravinsky's works. One specific characteristic of the opera, however, was mentioned by none of the contemporary commentators and was only referred to later, indirectly, by the composer himself, when discussing the composers of the Nationalist school. 'Cui did help me to discover Dargomyzhsky . . . and for that I am grateful . . . His writings drew my attention to the remarkable quality of the recitatives [in *The Stone Guest*], and though I do not know what I would think of this music now, it has had an influence on my operatic thinking.'[16] This was at the time when Stravinsky was composing *The Nightingale*, and apart from the 'World of Art' stylisations of the Chinese scenes (which are in any case not very important), the essential feature of this opera is the fluid, precisely formulated recitative in which the melodic lines are modelled on those of *The Stone Guest*.[17] Once again the analogy with *Duke Bluebeard's Castle* immediately suggests itself, for there too the melodic line is also coloured by the vernacular.

The Russian element in *The Nightingale* in fact deserves further study. I will content myself with the observation that the latent connection between this work and *The Rite of Spring* became manifest in the orchestral poem *Song of the Nightingale*, where the basic episodes of the second and third scenes appear shuffled together. As far as the musical character of the recitative is concerned, traces of Russian speech-intonations appear in Stravinsky's next opera, *Mavra*, whereas in the works written between 1914 and 1917 (including *Les Noces*) he used archaic folk-tunes. But the level of conventionality is very different in *The Nightingale* and *Mavra*.

Mavra and *The Rake's Progress*, written thirty years later, perfectly exemplify the comedy of the grotesque. There are great differences between the two works both in style and treatment. The grotesque comedy of *The Rake's Progress* is achieved by the accumulation of 'attractions', by the alternating contrasts of montage 'stills', interspersed with small islands of frank lyricism and clear hints of tragedy, though this lyricism is not emotionally direct and the tragic note is not severely controlled. The actors in the comedy are not so much real people as shadows borrowed from Hogarth's prints. There is something of a compromise, something even contradictory in the combination of the conventional and the naturalistic, the grotesque and the emotionally genuine. This contradiction is inherent in the very idea of the piece. The model chosen by the composer is fundamentally Mozart's *opera buffa*, but it has been stylised rather than rethought, whereas new means of expression in fact demanded a new kind of convention. This criticism by no means destroys the musical worth of the opera.

This conventional mode did in fact exist in *Mavra*, where 'illustration is illustrated' in Brecht's sense. *Mavra* might, if you like, be called a Russian transcription of *Pulcinella*: in both cases it is not the actual events on the stage that stir the audience, but the way they are illustrated. Only the 'masks' are different in the two pieces – the stock characters of the *commedia dell'arte* in the one and the equally (for Pushkin) stock setting of the old Petersburg suburbs in the other. The character of the music differs correspondingly: sunny and carefree in *Pulcinella* and grotesque in *Mavra*.

It is hardly necessary to speak in any great detail about *Oedipus Rex*, in which the conventions of the opera-oratorio are emphasised by the statuesque nature of the stage-setting and only the Speaker is directed by the composer to move. This idea matured slowly in Stravinsky's mind, possibly under the influence of Meyerhold, who as early as 1908 had written:

We need a theatre of immobility, which would be nothing new or out of the way. A theatre of this kind has long existed and to it belong the great tragedies of antiquity – *Antigone*, *Electra*, *Oedipus Coloneus*, *Prometheus* and *Choephori*. These are the models for any theatre of immobility. In them there is only Fate and Man as he finds himself in the universe – the essence of tragedy.[18]

Stravinsky seemed to be almost echoing these words when he said that in *Oedipus* 'the geometry of tragedy, the inevitable intersecting of lines, is what concerned me'.[19]

Meyerhold's production of Gluck's *Orpheus and Eurydice* at the Maryinsky Theatre in 1911 embodied his ideas on the subject of opera which aroused considerable discussion at the time. Stravinsky also knew the Paris version of *The Golden Cockerel* where the singers were motionless. This was however no more than a stage-form involving some violence to Rimsky-Korsakov's work, which belonged to a quite different theatrical tradition. When the ideas behind it were applied to the full in *Oedipus Rex*, a new kind of theatrical spectacle came into existence, and one which in many different interpretations has exercised a great influence on twentieth-century opera.[20]

To sum up then, I will give a list of Stravinsky's theatrical works classified according to their subject-matter. Six groups emerge, often mutually interrelated so that one work may well appear in several groups.

1 Fairy Tales:
    (a) those based on Hans Christian Andersen – *The Nightingale*, *The Fairy's Kiss*
    (b) those based on Russian fairy-stories – *Firebird*, *Renard*, *The Soldier's Tale*

2 Mask-pieces:
    Renard, *Pulcinella*, *Jeu de cartes*

3 Mythological works – Greek and Biblical:
    Oedipus Rex, *Apollo Musagetes*, *Persephone*, *Orpheus*, *The Flood*

4 Ceremonial or ritual works:
    The Rite of Spring, *Les Noces*, and in part *Oedipus* and *Persephone*

5 Realistic subjects:
    Petrushka and *Mavra* (early nineteenth century), *The Rake's Progress* (eighteenth century) – though both *Petrushka* and *The Rake* include non-realistic elements – *The Solder's Tale* (Stravinsky's only handling of a contemporary subject)

6 Works without a subject:
    Danses concertantes, *Scènes de ballet*, *Agon*

It is characteristic of Stravinsky that apart from Sophocles, Andersen and Pushkin there are no literary prototypes for the remaining works (sixteen), whereas myth, ritual and folk-lore are fundamental elements. Stravinsky's works may also be classified according to national origin and language. Thus nine of his Russian pieces, including *The Nightingale*, were composed to Russian texts, and Tchaikovsky's melodies are used in *The Fairy's Kiss*. Subjects taken from antiquity are increasingly important during his neo-classical period – *Oedipus* (Latin text), *Persephone* (French), while the subject of *Pulcinella* is Italian and both *The Flood* and *The Rake's Progress* have English texts. Four works may be classed as neutral in this respect – the three listed above as 'without a subject' and *Jeu de cartes*. This list of Stravinsky's works for the theatre presents a highly varied spectacle, emphasising the universal nature of the composer's spiritual interests; but it will be observed that Russian subjects still predominate.

I should like to end this chapter by drawing the reader's attention to a paradox on which I have already touched fleetingly. Stravinsky, we have seen, claimed for music a purely transcendental content. In *Chronicle*[21] he maintained that 'music is, by its very nature, powerless to express anything at all', and later substituted for this 'disappointingly imperfect' observation another that is in turn equally unclear – 'music expresses itself'. Any composer who holds such opinions would, one imagines, write music only for the concert-hall, so-called 'pure' or 'absolute' music, not involving any of the compromises inseparable from the theatre. We have seen, however, that during his fifty-five years' activity as a composer, he wrote repeatedly and enthusiastically for the theatre, and his theatrical works are in fact larger and more numerous than those in symphonic forms, properly so called. At first this seems difficult to explain. But it is not as paradoxical as it appears, because Stravinsky never compromised with the so-called 'laws' of the theatre: he accepted them as unavoidable conventions of the 'game' and, if they coincided with his artistic purposes, he observed the established rules and adopted them. He enjoyed 'working in chains' as he called it, that is to say within a pre-established framework; and a limiting framework of this kind was provided working both in the theatre and to private commission: 'The trick, of course, is to choose one's commission, to compose what one wants to compose and to get it commissioned afterwards, and I myself have had the luck to do this in many instances.'[22]

The attraction of the theatre for Stravinsky lay in the fact that the 'play-element' is more powerfully expressed there than in the concert-hall. A theatrical work is 'played', while music in the concert-hall is 'performed': the theatre provides a communal spectacle, while the concert-hall implies a 'concentrated solitude', because, while the action on the stage is watched by the whole audience, music in the concert-hall is experienced individually, 'for oneself'. These contrasts could be multiplied, but the idea behind them I think is clear.

Fascinated as he was by this whole conception of festival and spectacle, Stravinsky protested with his whole being against what he called 'the unintelligent, blasphemous interpretation of art as religion and the theatre as a temple'.

Art is not a liturgy but a game, not a sermon but a spectacle with the conventional attributes of a spectacle – hence the attraction for Stravinsky of the theatre and, more generally, of theatricality of expression. And this brings us to a further problem: the fact that what is 'seen' and what is 'heard' are inextricably connected for Stravinsky. This particular characteristic of his artistic perception will be further dealt with in a later chapter. I should like to say here only that latent in all his music is a visual element, and this fact explains why choreographers have been so anxious to make use of works that

Stravinsky himself did not compose for the theatre. Naturally this visual element is more clearly formulated in works where Stravinsky himself originally planned a joint effect of music and stage-spectacle, and where the visual element is actually transmuted into plastic, theatrical forms.

It may be objected that Stravinsky also wrote works not for the theatre, but for the concert-hall, whether they are orchestral, vocal and instrumental, or chamber pieces. To this I can only answer that the one does not exclude the other. I am only concerned to explain Stravinsky's preference for the theatrical forms in music. He certainly did not neglect the concert-hall: in fact he took an active part in concert life both as composer and performer, partly as conductor and partly as pianist and propagandist of his own works. If he criticised many features of today's concert life, the same could be said of his attitude to much in the contemporary theatre.

Unfortunately he never had a theatre of his own, as Richard Strauss may be said to have had at Dresden, where most of his operas had their first performances and a solid musical and dramatic tradition of interpreting his works was developed. When Diaghilev's company, which had given Stravinsky's first ballets, was disbanded, the first performances of his works were given in different theatres all over the world. He was more fortunate with his choreographers than with his operatic producers, none of whom played a decisive part in his development as did some of his choreographers, or remained in contact with him over long periods.

One final question – how are we to interpret the musical form of these theatrical works of Stravinsky's? Is it immanent in the music itself, or is it something ' applied ', in fact a secondary consideration in cases where there is a conflict between the laws of music and the laws of the theatre? The mere putting of the question implies an uncertainty about the absolute value of Stravinsky's music, and the answer is to be found in the facts of the case – these theatrical scores of Stravinsky's continue to be played in the concert-hall even when they are not given in the theatre. Nor is this a matter of surprise, since we know that on many occasions the musical idea, or kernel, of these pieces preceded the actual construction of the 'chassis' formed by the story and its stage presentation. Take the case of *Petrushka*, for instance, perhaps the most effective of his ballets, and a graft from the stock of a *Konzertstück* for piano and orchestra. *The Rite of Spring* had a similar origin and *The Soldier's Tale* was originally conceived not as a piece for the theatre, but as an instrumental suite.[23] Nor should we forget the subject-less, 'abstract' ballets. It appears, therefore, that for Stravinsky the prime, determining factor in any work was always the musical idea, though the theatre might provide different forms of stimulus. Indeed, such extra-musical stimulus was frequent with Stravinsky, who found it in conversations and in books (though only rarely in literary characters), and most importantly in visual impressions. Among those that most excited his imagination were visual impressions of the theatre, a 'field of vision' which was greatly enlarged after 1910 when he travelled abroad. The taste for travel grew on him and became insatiable, bringing with it a new wealth of impressions and a well-nigh universal range of interests. His assertion of neo-classical principles may be regarded as both a cause and an effect of this, and we must now go on to consider how he realised these ideas in practice and what in fact neo-classicism meant to him.

7

Neo-classicism

There is a well-known phrase in a letter from Pushkin to Prince Vyazemsky – 'I have observed that everyone here has a vague understanding of Romanticism' – and Vyazemsky in turn wrote to Zhukovsky, 'Romanticism is like the "brownie": a lot of people believe in it and there is a general conviction that it exists, but no one can say where it is to be observed, how to define it or how actually to put one's hands on it.' Exactly the same can be said of neo-classicism, a word that has been widely used by a large number of people who, however, have only a 'vague understanding' of it and attach to it a meaning that is either too wide – in which case almost all Western European music of the twentieth century may be called neo-classical – or too restricted, in which case Stravinsky alone bears the load of guilt for the sins of neo-classicism.[1] And in fact it is not easy to 'put one's hands' on it.

I do not agree with those who look for the sources of twentieth-century neo-classicism in the nineteenth century. It may be difficult to find another word for the classicising tendencies that we find in the music of, say, Brahms or Saint-Saëns, Taneev or Reger; but the fact remains that the neo-classicism that appeared in many branches of Western European art during the years immediately after the First World War was something quite different in character, a new

Stravinsky in Biarritz, 1923

phenomenon in fact. It is an interesting fact, indeed, that twentieth-century neo-classical musicians reacted negatively to the music of the 'classicising' composers mentioned above, and certainly recognised no connecting link with them. The truth is that these two generations were divided by the catastrophe of the war and the social unrest and disturbances in post-war Europe. There was a deep division among Western artists who had lived through these catastrophic events and wished to understand their real significance for the culture of the future. Some of them saw the dawn of a new era in human history announced by the October Revolution in Russia, and these began to play an active part in life, some earlier and some later. Others, realising sadly that their faith in the realisation of the humanistic ideals of the nineteenth century was weakened, tried to stand *au dessus de la mêlée*, though in many cases their belief in those ideals was badly undermined. There were many differences and often real contradictions in their artistic attitudes, rooted in the plurality of ideas and styles associated with the crisis of the bourgeois consciousness that marked the first years of the century. In every case there was a marked opposition, whether latent or overt, to the whole legacy of the nineteenth century, and the most consistent and most principled form taken by this opposition was neo-classicism.

Stravinsky clearly defined his attitude in *Chronicle*, and again later: 'It is in the nature of things . . . that epochs which immediately precede us are temporarily further away from us than others which are more remote in time, and it is this which determines the uninterrupted march of evolution in art quite as much as in other branches of human activity.'[2] He repeated this in other words when he said that 'it is one of the laws of nature that we often feel nearer to remote generations than to those which immediately precede us'.

In these categorical but abstract terms Stravinsky was merely affirming the fact that there is a break in the link connecting one generation of artists to the next; he was not revealing the essence of the artistic phenomenon, and we must now ask ourselves in what that consists.

The appearance of neo-classicism was part of a general cultural movement in search of some way of renewing European civilisation. The rejection of nineteenth-century humanism prompted the search for something like a point of support in an amalgamation of cultures, a correlation of past and present, an indissoluble linking of historical periods. It was in this form that the legacy of the past came to be envisaged. Once the genetic tie between the generations has been destroyed, however, the question arises as to what is to be selected from the rich storehouse of the past to serve as the new artistic model. And closely connected with this question is another – how is the question of 'tradition' to be decided once the limits of the 'artistic legacy' have been made so unimaginably wide? Is it to be regional, that is to say limited by national boundaries, or universal?

These questions can hardly have suggested themselves to either Stravinsky or Picasso when they embarked on their neo-classical works. Their choice was intuitive, and it only turned out later that they were both on the same path. When Stravinsky in 1915 wrote his pianoforte *Polka for Three Hands*, he can hardly have supposed that it would be – as he later called it – 'a sort of variety of neo-classicism', any more than Picasso's enthusiasm for a drawing in Ingres's manner in the same year can have seemed to the painter the possible start of his involvement with the neo-classical movement. Neither can have imagined that the attraction that they felt towards this 'method of modelling' would in the end influence their own creative imaginations – in Picasso's case almost at once, in Stravinsky's only after some two decades. The evolution of both men had already been marked by great impulsiveness, though the time-scale was different in each case. Picasso in 1901, at the age of twenty, was already an independent artist, whereas Stravinsky at nineteen was a university student for whom working with Rimsky-Korsakov was still only a dream. Picasso passed quickly through his 'Blue' (1901–4) and 'Pink' (1905–6) periods, and in 1907 initiated his Cubist period with *Les Demoiselles d'Avignon*, the picture that destroyed the traditional conception of painting. The corresponding explosion in music was the Paris première of *The Rite of Spring*, which Honegger later compared to the atom bomb. *The Rite* may be regarded as analogous to Cubism in painting, whereas *Firebird* and *Petrushka* were phenomena parallel to the violent colour-schemes of Les Fauves. It may be said, therefore, that on the eve of the 1914–18 war Stravinsky in a single gigantic spurt raised the level of his work to that of Picasso's. Not that their paths coincided for long, diverging in the middle of the twenties and more seriously as the thunder-clouds of the Second World War came nearer. Nothing could be more characteristic of their differences than the productions of the year 1937, when Picasso painted his *Guernica* and Stravinsky wrote his *Dumbarton Oaks* – the one a symbolical Expressionist vision of mounting cruelty and destruction, the other a classically transparent vision of confident hope.

We must return, however, to the first beginnings of neo-classicism, the true significance of which soon declared itself. There was a new restriction of material range and expression, and the accumulation of sheer volume was replaced by a clarity and finesse of design, already visible in *The Soldier's Tale* and still more noticeable in *Pulcinella*. In contrast to the nightmares of war appeared intelligence and orderliness, 'restraint'; and the rage of destruction was replaced by the joy of creation, sometimes touched with the ironic, mocking character of a game and destroying the last vestiges of the false pathos of Romanticism. During the twenties Stravinsky looked for support from a number of different models – mostly the Baroque as far as music was concerned (though he also 're-thought' Weber and Tchaikovsky) and for subject-matter the classical antique and occasionally the Bible, which was to occupy a more important role in his compositions of the fifties and sixties. Picasso also showed a preference for mythological themes, although even in the early days of his neo-classical period there appear sudden returns to his earlier explosive manner, a phenomenon more frequent in his case than in Stravinsky's.

About 1920 the work of both men reflected interests revealed in many other artistic fields and given individual expression by different artists. Thus Paul Valéry was preaching a return to classical simplicity, and so in his characteristically extravagant manner was Erik Satie, followed by his then henchman Jean Cocteau. At the same time Guillaume Apollinaire was calling for the renewal of poetic sonorities by the reintroduction of classical rhythms, while Ferruccio Busoni dreamed of resurrecting a 'young classicism'. There was a strange variety of demands among these representatives of the classical renewal. In general philosophical terms there was an assertion of clarity, organisation and a certain festival activity and energy to replace the emotional over-heating of the Expressionists, with their nightmare visions and unreal, mystical themes. In the realm of expression there was a repudiation of the subjective and a concern with objective content (sometimes involving an 'over-cooling' of the feelings), a cultivation of the supra-personal and hence an interest in mythology, ritual and the conventions of 'play'. Finally there was a huge expansion of existing ties, a new sense of participating in a world culture, a universal tradition, and hence a plurality of 'manners' and a freedom in the choice of artistic models. Here there is a parallel with Meyerhold, whose methods as a director were based on the age-old theatrical traditions of many different countries and epochs. He never felt constricted by any one style and his theatrical judgments were always made from this universal standpoint.

To sum up, then, the contradictions within the movement were violent: there was never a single neo-classical 'platform'. What has been said above is of course a formulation in retrospect and chiefly applicable to Stravinsky, because he remained a neo-classicist for a longer period and with greater consistency than any other leading artist of his day. Indeed he never repudiated the fundamental theories with which he was so closely linked, even when the Second World War demonstrated the illusory nature of neo-classical premises and, as he himself said, the neo-classical schoolmen had dogmatised themselves to a standstill. He remained faithful to these theories even in his last dodecaphonic period. Perhaps the clearest statement of some of these theories is to be found in T. S. Eliot's *Tradition and the Individual Talent* (1917), although whether Stravinsky was actually acquainted with this book I do not know: it was only considerably later that the two men knew each other personally. The important fact is that such ideas as these were, as we say, in the air and that they attracted Stravinsky. I will therefore give a free transcription of them here.

Eliot is discussing poetry and literature but what he says is equally applicable to the other arts. According to him the individualistic consciousness of the artist is a blind alley. The crisis is not to be overcome by capricious experimentation: real originality consists not in trying to be original, but in understanding cultural traditions. The fundamental task of the artist is not self-expression but the transmission of the supra-individual (impersonal) – that which most clearly manifests the immortality of the great poets of the past, the total aggregate of their artistic experience. The one great thing is the significance of tradition, and in order to understand this a sense of history is essential. This sense provides the feeling that the past has not disappeared without leaving a trace, but exists in the present. This historical sense enables a poet to write not only from the point of view of his own generation but as though the whole of European literature – beginning with Homer and including the literature of his own country – existed simultaneously and formed a single indissoluble whole. This same historical sense endows the poet with a feeling of both the eternal and the temporal, or transient. It impels him to realise both his place in history and his contemporariness. Thus he will be able to see with exactly the same eyes the best production of the present day and those of the last two or three centuries.

A comparison of these ideas of Eliot's with Stravinsky's often-repeated remarks about the role of tradition reveals a striking resemblance between the two men's conceptions of the artist's experience of the past as forming part of his experience of the present. In fact Stravinsky might well echo Eliot's words in *Four Quartets*. 'History is a pattern of timeless moments' ('Little Gidding'). 'Tradition', says Stravinsky, 'is inherited understanding. It is not only transmitted from fathers to children, it follows the life processes, being born, growing, reaching maturity, declining and sometimes being reborn.' And in *Poetics of Music*:[3]

A live dialectic demands that innovation and tradition develop together, in mutual aid. Tradition is entirely different from habit, even from an excellent habit, since habit is by definition an unconscious acquisition and tends to become mechanical, whereas tradition results from a conscious and considered acceptance. A real tradition is not the relic of a past that is irretrievably gone; it is a living force that animates and informs the present ... It appears as an heirloom, a heritage that one receives on condition of making it bear fruit ... A method is replaced: a tradition is carried forward in order to produce something new. Tradition thus assures the continuity of creation.

At the age of eighty Stravinsky could speak even more categorically: 'Did not Eliot and I set out to refit old ships? and refitting old ships is the real task of the artist. He can say again, in his way, only what has already been said.' If we accept this metaphor it is easier to understand Stravinsky's method of 'working from a model', and we must now enquire into the specific nature of this method, which had such an importance for all neo-classical artists. Questions of this kind irritated Stravinsky, who used to say that it was absurd to imagine him as a man rummaging in the past and declaring his adaptation of what he has stolen to be a new style. He was particularly annoyed by people who saw in *Pulcinella* no more than a clever imitation of the eighteenth century; and no doubt Prokofiev's witty joke about Stravinsky's instrumental works of the twenties – 'Bach with wrong notes' – must have enraged him. He broke off relations with Schoenberg and ceased to listen to his music after Schoenberg published his op.28 in 1925, in which he satirised the neo-classical tendencies of a certain 'Modernsky'. In fact the failure to understand the principle of neo-classicism – Adorno spoke of him as 'a music-restorer' – continued to plague him for a long time; and it has not really disappeared even now.

Painters were immune from this misunderstanding. They used models in any case, both living and 'pictorial'.

As Dmitrieva points out,

When Rembrandt sketched and, as it were, distorted Leonardo da Vinci's *Last Supper*, this was not so much a 'study' as a quarrel with the principles of the Renaissance, but the quarrel was a friendly one – as though across the centuries the one artist were saying to the other 'I understand what you want to say, but I should have expressed it differently – like this.'[4]

One can imagine a kind of secret link, a freemasonry among artists of all ages. And when Van Gogh painted from black-and-white reproductions of Rembrandt, Millet, Doré or Delacroix he was experiencing the delight of belonging to this great fraternity. The list of such free adaptations could easily be added to, and some of the most famous examples are Manet's *Déjeuner sur l'herbe* based on Giorgione, the sleeping Venuses of Giorgione and Titian (which might be compared with Manet's *Olympia*) and Velasquez's *Las Meninas*, which served Picasso as theme for a series of free variations.

The musicians of the Baroque certainly felt themselves to be members of this sort of freemasonry. Bach, and more particularly Handel, 'distorted' other composers' ideas, and indeed their own, without being considered guilty of plagiarism. Johann Mattheson even encouraged this method of composing, which he called 'the method of parody', on condition that the new work added something to the old. And, after all, even Mozart followed this fashion occasionally.

This 'method of parody' was very common among the poets, not least among them Pushkin. Vinogradov quotes Ostolopov's *Slovar' drevnei i novoi poezii* (Dictionary of old and new poetry) of 1821, in which five kinds of parody are precisely listed: that quoting whole lines or individual phrases, that with verses containing alterations or substitutions, and finally complex species of parody (the reproduction and renovation of another style and even the distortion or comic confusion of themes) – all this while preserving the structural characteristics of the original.[5]

In grotesque situations Stravinsky also liked to use the methods of distortion, confusion or, as we should say, deformation of familiar material, always 'preserving the structural characteristics of the original'. These are what I have called 'distorting-mirror' images. But in general, despite momentary similarities, Stravinsky's use of 'parody' is not the same as his method of 'working from a model', because this is not a question of reproducing or 'renovating' another style, of copying or 'stylising' it.

When a composer develops his musical language by making use of the methods and constructions of his immediate predecessors we do not call this stylisation, but simply the continuation of a tradition. We use the word stylisation only of an 'imitation' of a style that is historically remote, in which case the composer must suggest what we call the 'spirit', the atmosphere, the colour, even the social manners or the 'dance-culture' of the age in question. In cases of stylisation the composer, as it were, dresses up in the clothes and adapts the way of speaking of another age, as Tchaikovsky does in *Mozartiana* and Grieg in *Aus Holbergs Zeit*.

Stravinsky's case is different. He is not concerned with such things as 'spirit', atmosphere, colour or any such categories, and unlike Prokofiev he very rarely writes minuets or gavottes. His aim was not to simplify but to enrich his own musical idiom, introducing and distorting the methods and structures of other musical periods. Good examples of this are *Pribautki* (1914) and *Renard* (1915), in which he discovered for himself a new technique based on the play of speech-accents in Russian folk-song, and he perfected this technique in *Les Noces*. Jazz is another example. He first became acquainted with this in 1918, not from hearing performances but from sheet-music that Ansermet brought back from the USA. He was interested by the idea of jazz improvisation, and his 'portrait' of this can be seen in *Piano-Rag-Music* and *Three Pieces for Clarinet Solo*. In the same way he was attracted by what he called the 'concision and clarity' of Bach's *Two-Part Inventions* and it was with them in mind that he wrote the last movements of the *Octet* and the *Piano Sonata* (1922–4).

This reworking of the methods and constructions of other musical periods or other composers continued to interest Stravinsky for many years, as we can see from his adaptation of Weber at the end of the twenties and his 'rethinking' of Webern at the beginning of the fifties. The two cases are indeed analogous; for just as the contact with Weber did not make Stravinsky a Romantic – indeed his opposition to Romanticism remained unchanged – so his contact with Webern and his use of serial methods left unchanged his attitude to Expressionism, which he continued to regard as a manifestation of early-twentieth-century decadence. Another interesting fact about these works of Stravinsky is the variability of their quality, which showed marked fluctuations, crests of creative energy being succeeded by troughs. Nor is this surprising if we consider the unusual length of his creative activity.

Stravinsky was keenly aware of the continuity between present and past. His enormously wide interests had their origin, and later their support, in his passion to understand and to absorb the spiritual values of Western Europe. This passion was insatiable and showed no sign of diminishing with age. In this he was at one with Eliot and able to listen to Gesualdo in exactly the same way as he listened to Webern. In fact we might paraphrase Eliot's words quoted above and say that Stravinsky wished to compose not only from the point of view of his own times but also as though the whole of European music existed simultaneously and formed a single indivisible entity. Going beyond the framework of a single national school, he wanted to universalise the Pushkin tradition, to extend it over the whole cultural world.

This enlargement and complication of his creative mission inevitably involved certain losses. The law of development has its own immutable character: all progress is normally accompanied by such losses. Thus the enormous scientific and technical progress of the present day has compelled civilised humanity to abandon the patriarchal foundations of life, just as youth is replaced by maturity, experience and knowledge, while what constituted youth's charm is lost. In the case of Stravinsky's evolution as an artist this general law is, indeed, to some extent corrected. We have seen how his abandonment of Russian themes for those of a universal character involved the loss of that abundant 'Fauviste' power that so captured the imagination of his contemporaries. If it recurs, in isolated flashes, in his later works, it is held in check by a new strictness and austerity of manner. When Stravinsky was asked in his old age what he loved most in Russia, he replied 'The violent Russian spring that seemed to begin in an hour and was like the whole earth cracking.'[6] Later, however, he lost the feeling of this spring madness – whether because he left Russia or perhaps because he was nearing forty and the time for neo-classicism had come, it is impossible to say.

' Experience is the child of painful mistakes', as Pushkin said, and if Stravinsky's experience was indeed enormous, he did not of course avoid mistakes. The path on which he entered in the twenties was beset with them, and they were made more serious by the attraction that he felt towards technical virtuosity – 'art for art's sake'. Even so he was to write a number of significant works both then and in the years to come, because his spiritual horizon was growing wider all the time and the formal structure of his music was gaining in variety and capacity.

Valentin Kataev wrote of Picasso that 'his genius lay in the fact that he had a universal spirit – universal both in time and space'. These words, I believe, are with some qualifications applicable also to Stravinsky.

8

>-

World classics

Stravinsky's 'universal spirit' was reflected in his choice of subjects and styles belonging to different eras and different countries, which together formed a highly variegated picture during his neo-classical period, with its unexpected succession of artistic 'models'. It is difficult to decide what dictated these various choices. Stravinsky was subject to sudden enthusiasms, and his musical evolution was not guided by reason so much as by the many, often unconscious, changes of psychological impulse that marked his career. He himself declared that he was no rationalist.

Without attempting to discover any law governing his adoption of these different styles or manners, we may perhaps establish a certain cyclical character in their succession. These changes were certainly impulsive and explosive; but each of his sudden enthusiasms was rationally interpreted and consciously defended with complete conviction, and became a perfectly finished stylistic manner which, it always seemed, once firmly established was shortly replaced by another.

This was what occurred about 1920, at the beginning of Stravinsky's neo-classical period; but before considering this we must glance for a moment at the ground that he had already covered. We have already pointed to a definite cycle of 'manners' within the Russian period, which is marked by a greater stylistic unity than any other, later period. Each cycle appears to have lasted about four years. The first, from *Firebird* to *The Rite of Spring*, covered the years 1910–13. The second opened with the *Three Pieces for String Quartet* and ended with *The Soldier's Tale*, *Les Noces* occupying the most important place (1914–18); and the third opened with *Pulcinella* and ended with *Mavra* (1919–22). *The Soldier's Tale* theoretically marks a stepping outside the framework of Russian themes, but these were completely abandoned only in *Pulcinella*, although Russian and foreign elements may be said to have co-existed in Stravinsky's music up to 1923. How highly the music of *Pulcinella* is rated will depend on individual taste, and we are more concerned to determine the part this work played in the composer's subsequent development. Personally I regard this work as the great, perhaps the fateful temptation of

Stravinsky and his first wife, 1937

Stravinsky's career. It represents his first attempt to give his music a Latin character. Although in *Pulcinella* he captures something quite specifically Italian, in this particular context the distinction between Italian and French is unimportant, for after all it was always fundamental characteristics – in this case the 'Latinity' shared by both French and Italian – that Stravinsky chose for his own purposes. Many Russian artists have felt this same attraction, including Glinka, Gogol and, among painters, Alexander Ivanov. This was the temptation with which Stravinsky now found himself confronted.

This Latin strain in Stravinsky's music has been even less studied than the Russian, and it is not easy to establish their interconnection. We still need to examine the different changes in his personal life in the West and their possible relationship to the emergence of different priorities in his music. Certainly *Pulcinella* represents his first contact with Latin themes, and after this Stravinsky was to solve his problems in a number of different ways. These problems confronted him when he wrote works with Catholic texts, when he used Latin in preference to a contemporary language and more especially when he set out to recreate a specific tradition such as *le goût français*, as in *Apollo Musagetes* and *Persephone*.

The Latin spirit is essentially a cult of clarity, preciseness of expression, persuasive eloquence and strict stylistic *tenue*, and this to a certain extent reinforces the need for order in music. One particular manifestation of the Latin spirit is to be found in a taste for that 'play of intelligence' denoted by the French word *esprit*. As we have said above, the 'play element' is something characteristic of all Stravinsky's music. The Latin form of this element is often subtle, refined, and marked by an aristocratic elegance of manner. This 'play of intelligence' may indeed lead to elegant, superficial solutions in which the actual content of an idea is of secondary importance as, for instance, in *Jeu de cartes* and a number of other works commissioned during Stravinsky's early years in the United States.

In the same way Stravinsky found the very shapeliness of Italian melody – and we should not forget, perhaps, that *formosus* (i.e. shapely) is the Latin word for beautiful – a great temptation. He was plainly exercising self-restraint when he attempted to surmount the conventional, formula-like cut of Pergolesi's themes in his re-working of them – the brevity of their motivic coupling, in which the actual organisation of harmony and rhythm implies a motor impulse. Hitherto he had shown no interest in the so-called *protyazhnie* – literally 'long-drawn-out' – songs of Russian folk-music, with their extensive melodic structures. Now, however, he was charmed by the long, protracted melody of the Italians with its strong tonal contours, and he was to pick out Italian traits in Glinka and Tchaikovsky (clearly reflected in *Mavra* and *The Fairy's Kiss*). For his own polemical purposes he was even to champion Bellini, as a melodist, against Beethoven.[1]

Stravinsky was not by nature, and could never become, a melodist of the Bellini type: his intellectual nature was offended by all open, naked expression of feeling. But his music now became more sensual in contour and the actual 'climate' (as he called it) of many of his works became softer and more lyrical. Some of the lyrical nuances that he adopted seem to me, personally, alien to his personality, which they distort – nuances of melancholy and elegiac delicacy that are to be found in his neo-classical works and more particularly in *Persephone*. In the critical period at the beginning of the forties this sweetness could become almost saccharine, in the Broadway manner that Stravinsky himself disliked. There are examples of this in *Scènes de ballet* and other works of this period.

Neo-classicism, therefore, while widening Stravinsky's spiritual horizon, involved a number of real losses. But he would not have been the genius that he most certainly was had he not been able to overcome the temptations that he encountered in his development as a composer. They had appeared earlier, in *Zvezdoliki* for example; but it was now, at the height of a crisis in his personal life, when he was threatened with the loss of his country and his native tongue, that he was faced with the desperate need to make new artistic decisions. Nor was he alone in being uprooted from the life to which he was accustomed; the war was shaking the very foundations of a whole civilisation that had hitherto seemed stable. Was not this in fact the reason why the idea of order in art suggested itself to him so forcibly? He certainly became its most uncompromising prophet; and this would explain his attempts to moderate the wild outbursts of Dionysian forces in his music and his insistence, in the face of the facts, that he was himself an Apollonian artist, though he was later to admit that he was mistaken in this. Was it not perhaps the fear of such forces that made him persevere more single-mindedly than ever along the path that had presented itself to him in those significant years in Switzerland, when he stood alone? Was it not indeed this same fear that caused him, immediately after the war, to embark in yet another direction in his search for stability and support? Losing, like Antaeus, his vital powers when separated from his mother earth, he felt the need to establish even more firmly his connections with universal tradition as a fulcrum. There was no weakening in the attraction that he felt for the unexplored or in his passion for invention; but now, as he went forward, he more frequently turned his gaze backward, comparing the old with the new and parting more reluctantly than before with the past.

This is of course no more than an hypothesis and, as such, needs verification and further discussion. I hope to contribute to this by an analysis of the 'cycle' of manners that can be distinguished in his neo-classical period, and I therefore return to *Pulcinella*. Although it was a commission of Diaghilev's that sent Stravinsky to Pergolesi, it would be naive to suppose that a chance commission such as this could play a crucial part in the composer's development. Stravinsky was plainly prepared for such a step psychologically, and simply needed some external stimulus to follow what was already an unconscious impulse. His new acquaintance with eighteenth-century Italian music provided that stimulus.

Stravinsky accepted this music as an artistic fact, a cultural manifestation demanding an interpretation. He studied and adapted, modified and adopted for his own purposes everything that was new to him and that he found in any way interesting or surprising. It had been the same with Russian folk-music, with his 'portraits' of popular social music, including jazz; and it was through the music of everyday life that he came to Pergolesi.

We have already discussed the Italian element in Russian music and its presence in the drawing-room songs of Glinka and Tchaikovsky with which Stravinsky was so familiar. This formed a natural bridge to Italian music itself, which proved to contain new and undreamed of potentialities for the composer.

Adapting his chosen musical model, Stravinsky proceeded to isolate the types of structure that he encountered there, whether these were melodic, rhythmic, or matters of *facture* and compositional procedure. This in fact was what he did in the case of Pergolesi's music, retaining the method of the original while changing its character and making it brighter, softer and simpler. The atmosphere of *Pulcinella* is quite different from other works composed at about the same time, such as *The Soldier's Tale*, *Ragtime* or the *Three Pieces for Clarinet Solo*. The explanation of this may lie in the fact that in the case of *Pulcinella* he departed from his normal practice and built his composition by using, as it were *verbatim*, already existing music, and therefore 'stylising' that music itself. He was later to resort to an analogous method in both *The Fairy's Kiss* and *Norwegian Moods,* using Tchaikovsky's music in the first case and genuine models of folk melodies in the second. He soon abandoned this method, however, attracted by the possibilities of another, different source from which he hoped to revivify his music.

The result proved to be quite unexpected. The polymodality of his earlier works was abandoned; rhythms became simpler and terser, while the homophonic element was given a more significant part – in fact Stravinsky was returning to traditional tonality.

Contemporary reactions are not difficult to understand: *Pulcinella* was regarded as an act of treachery on the part of Stravinsky, a betrayal of his own aesthetic ideals, as indeed it was from the standpoint of *The Rite of Spring* and *Les Noces*. But Stravinsky's work has multiple 'layers' and each of these in turn, with its own style and imagery, occupies a dominant position in his music. When speaking of his Russian period we came upon two of such layers, conventionally distinguished as the archaic and the everyday, the former polyphonic or 'poly-modal' and the second homophonic, based on traditional tonality. *Pulcinella* belongs wholly to the line which stretches from *Petrushka* to *Mavra* and includes the three- and four-hand piano pieces which were later used as material for two orchestral suites. For this reason I very much doubt whether Stravinsky considered *Pulcinella* to be a crucial turning-point in his career, although the atmosphere of this 'Italian ballet with singing' is markedly different from that of the works written between 1918 and 1922, among which it occupies a unique position – rather like some harmless prank of genius, as Stravinsky's own words suggest: 'Picasso accepted the commission to design the décor of *Pulcinella* for the same reason that I agreed to arrange the music – for the fun of it.'[2]

The central event of those four years was the completion of *Les Noces*. The very Russian-feeling *Symphonies of Wind Instruments* was characterised by a fundamental seriousness, with contrasting alternations of fanfares and prayers and pastoral and tragic episodes recalling the 'Sacrificial Dance' in *The Rite of Spring*. It was in *Mavra* that Stravinsky finally bade farewell to Russian themes; and in fact this might be counted, in terms of music theatre, as a kind of Russian *opera buffa* corresponding to the Italian *Pulcinella*, despite the important stylistic changes that closer inspection of the two works reveals.

The important fact is that through the medium of Pergolesi Stravinsky assimilated the principles of toccata- and concerto-style and the variation-technique of Baroque instrumental music. The pre-classical sonata also aroused his interest, and the first glimmer of that interest is to be seen in the solo role of the first violin in *Concertino*. Another feature, and one that goes against the general tendency of *Pulcinella*, is an increased attention to the timbre and articulation of the wind and, with it, to 'hard' sonorities. The *Symphonies of Wind Instruments* is revealing in this connection and the winds assume a new importance in *Mavra* also, while in the final version of *Les Noces* (1923) the instrumental ensemble is dominated by hard, percussive sonorities. This quality of percussiveness is another characteristic feature of Stravinsky's instrumental thinking, although he had already made experiments in accentuation in his vocal music between 1914 and 1918. At first he was attracted by the cimbalom, which he used in *Renard* and *Ragtime*, while the pianoforte is used percussively in both *Piano-Rag-Music* and *Les Noces* and was in future to appear in many of Stravinsky's orchestral scores as a percussion instrument – often associated with the harp, producing a very individual effect in combination with the strings' *martellato* and *pizzicato*. Other contemporary composers followed his example in this, notably Bartók and Orff.

The pianoforte and the winds may be said to symbolise the

transition to a new stylistic manner in Stravinsky's music. With the exception of some very early works (such as the *Sonata* and *Four Studies*, both of which were written before 1908) and the *Konzertstück* transplanted into *Petrushka*, Stravinsky had not written for the pianoforte as a solo instrument before 1918, although he always used it when composing and it was one of his central interests. Now, however, he was to write a series of piano works – the *Concerto* (1923–4, second version 1950), the *Sonata* (1922–4), *Serenade* (1925), *Capriccio* with orchestra (1928–9), and in a different stylstic 'key' the three transcriptions from *Petrushka* (1921). As far as the winds are concerned, as early as 1913 Stravinsky, referring to the introduction to Part 1 of *The Rite of Spring*, observed that he had 'deliberately excluded the strings as too sensual and too reminiscent of the human voice, with their *crescendo* and *diminuendo*, and instead of them had moved into the foreground the wood-winds, which are drier, more precise and less rich in minute nuances'.[3] He also speaks in *Chronicle* of his growing interest in different combinations of winds during the twenties.

The *Octet* stands at the beginning not only of a new 'cycle' of manners but of the second, neo-classical period as a whole. Its significance was not grasped by many of his contemporaries. An exception was Aaron Copland, then studying with Nadia Boulanger in Paris, who wrote that this work 'establishes a new, universal ideal of music, based on classical forms and contrapuntal procedures, while the melodic material is borrowed from different epochs but unified by the individuality of the composer'. Cocteau solemnly hailed this change in Stravinsky's manner: 'In 1916 our *maître d'école* was Satie. In 1923 we heard Stravinsky and discovered that he spoke our language better than we did.'[4] In connection with the *Octet*, Stravinsky embarked on a programme of articles which formed a kind of artistic manifesto. He gave a large number of interviews; and since he never, either before or after this, published manifestos of this kind, particular importance attaches to the article published in January 1924.

In 'Some Ideas about my Octuor'[5] Stravinsky says that he chose wind instruments because they seemed 'more apt to render a certain rigidity of the form I had in mind', while 'the suppleness of the strings serves better the individual sensibility of the executant'. He goes on to say that 'the difference of the volume of these instruments renders more evident the musical architecture', and in fact the chief formal element of the *Octet* is to be found in the confrontation of the different timbres and registers and the different forms of 'attack' and style proper to each of the instruments. The basis of the work lies in the density and volume of the sonorities and the resourcefulness of their interplay, the other element being 'the movements in their reciprocal connection'. The third is counterpoint which lends itself perfectly to 'an architectural construction'. Finally dynamics:

I have excluded all nuances between the *forte* and the *piano* . . . Therefore the *forte* and the *piano* are in my work only the dynamic limit which determines the function of the volumes in play.

This exclusion of gradual *crescendo* or *diminuendo* implied a return to what Busoni called the *Terrassendynamik* – terraced dynamics – of the Baroque period.

Here, as always, Stravinsky's dislike of literary writing about music leads him to avoid touching on the formal essence of a work and to confine himself to matters of technique and style. Apart from the *Octet* the clearest examples of this style are to be found in the *Piano Concerto*, *Oedipus Rex* and, further enriched by a synthesis of what he had learned in the intervening years, *Symphony of Psalms*. This cycle of 'manners', partly reflected in the *Sonata* and the *Serenade* for piano, lasted exactly four years, from 1923 to 1927. A new cycle began with *Apollo Musagetes*.

The *Octet* is linked with *Pulcinella* by its Italianate traits, but, whereas the music of *Pulcinella* is predominantly homophonic in character, counterpoint plays an important part in the *Octet*. The shadow of Bach hovers in the background, evoked by Stravinsky's favourite use of equal note lengths with variable accentuation. The barline that serves to regulate the metre is both a support and an obstacle, and Stravinsky normally retains it even in the most complicated rhythmic combinations.[6] The discrepancy between rhythm and metre, often accentuated by the use of ostinato figures that do not coincide with the barlines, serves to enhance the energy with which the movement unfolds. The music 'spins forward like a well-oiled machine', as the composer said, and on one occasion in 1931 he spoke of his *Concerto* to the present writer as 'tractor-music'. He was later to admit to an excessive use of ostinato during this period, but he also remained characteristically faithful to two-part writing. In spite of its undeviating nature the development is fragmentary and consists of mutually dependent episodes, with each episode implicit in the one preceding it, thus forming a complex web, with many arch-like passages. Thematic material has no independent interest and is not always structurally fashioned: its role appears only in the combinations of motif and rhythm in which it becomes involved. This is the consequence of the motivic techniques so perfectly elaborated by the composer in the 'cycle' headed by *Les Noces* and dating from the years immediately after the First World War. Another characteristic of these works is the appearance of secondary motifs, that detach themselves during a development section and sometimes assume more organic significance than the theme itself. Bearing this in mind, we can more easily understand how sonata form in general was not particularly sympathetic to Stravinsky, who was inclined to treat it schematically. His development of the variation principle proved much more rewarding, but it was the *concertante* principle that played the most important part, and we shall pay special attention to this later. Stravinsky's return to tonality was gradual, and it was no longer as simple as it had been in *Pulcinella*, but was sometimes diatonic and sometimes complicated by chromaticism. These works naturally contain polytonal combinations and complex sonorities in which different harmonic functions are combined. What Stravinsky emphasised was the polarisation of these complex sonorities, in which the functional relationships of traditional tonality are, as it were, exploded from within. We might in fact compare the role of tonality in Stravinsky's music, acting at the same time as a controlling and supporting force, to the role of the barline.

We must next determine the significance of timbre and dynamics in his music. Stravinsky's music is composed of blocks of sonorities, either juxtaposed, alternating or accumulating. He applied to such 'blocks' the concept of volume or density, that is to say he felt them as a kind of material substance having weight that was distributed spatially. (He was later to say that he checked even the intervals in his series 'by touch'.) Whether these volumes were large or small, solid or transparent, heavy or light, they were dynamically correlated. Terrace-dynamics served to give prominence to individual lines by isolating and differentiating the sound-sources. If Beethoven formed his climaxes within the overall musical development, the Romantics' desire to communicate multiple impressions led them to introduce a large number of climaxes, as is shown most typically in Mahler's music. Stravinsky dispersed his climaxes, which appear like shifts in the relentless forward movement of the music. There are pauses between or even within his 'blocks', sometimes prolonged and at other times compressed. The pressure of muscular energy may well conflict openly with the metrical grid, destroying the even flow; so that we find interruptions in what is by its nature continuous, stability within what is unstable and static moments in what is essentially dynamic. Dislocations and interruptions of this kind destroy the inertia of gravitation, producing a kind of giddiness in the listener. Lévy-Strauss has spoken of this as 'a delicious sensation of falling', 'an apparent release from any firm support and a feeling of being hurled into empty space, though in fact this is due simply to the fact that the foothold we are instinctively seeking appears in an unexpected place'.

Some of these considerations apply to all Stravinsky's music, others are not applicable to his later works (his treatment of the melodic element, for instance), but the gist of what has been said above is true of the cycle of 'manners' that we have been analysing – ranging from the *Concerto* and *Oedipus Rex* to the *Symphony of Psalms*, though this lies outside our stated chronological limits.

Essential differences apart, the first and last movements of the *Concerto* are both marked by great rhythmical refinement and refreshed by jazz elements. *Oedipus* is more backward-looking, static and homophonic, certainly if we compare it with the double fugue in the second movement of the *Symphony*. These three works are linked by a unity of imagery and emotional mood, which suggest such phrases as 'inflexibility', 'punctiliousness', or 'unsentimental severity'. It is significant, for instance, that in the *Concerto* there are no strings except double-basses; that the chorus in *Oedipus Rex* contains no women's voices; and that in the *Symphony* there are no violins or violas, while the winds are augmented and two pianos are added to the percussion.

This elimination of the sensual colours of the higher strings and of women's voices would appear to be an individual trait, but a characteristic one – as characteristic as Stravinsky's use of the pure, unified sonority of the string sextet in *Apollo Musagetes*. Winds and percussion now take a second place and the chief role is played by the violin. We are in fact on the threshold of a new cycle of 'manners'.

This division of Stravinsky's works into 'cycles' must not of course be understood as a rigid scheme. As we have seen, one cycle grows imperceptibly out of another and we find cases, such as *Symphony of Psalms*, in which an earlier manner will reappear in the middle of another cycle. There may also be anticipations of the still-distant future, as in the case of the *Mass*, which was begun as early as 1944. Artistic creation is a living process that cannot be submitted to schematic pigeon-holing, and this is particularly true of any artist as impulsive by nature as Stravinsky.

Compared with the *Concerto* and *Oedipus*, both the *Sonata* and the *Serenade* are gentle in atmosphere. The middle movement of the *Sonata* recalls late Beethoven, with its free recitative passages, but at the same time Stravinsky shows an inclination to a form of melodic patterning that he was, in my opinion, to abuse in other of his neo-classical works.[7] The finale is akin to Bach's *Two-part Inventions*, with the same jazz-like rhythmic interruptions that we noted in the *Concerto*. The virile tone of the Hymn in the *Serenade* anticipates the opening chorus of *Oedipus*, just as we noticed anticipation of the *Octet* in the Russian period. The *Serenade*, which is a suite in four movements, has a chamber-music character, and the Romance is positively tender. It was in this way that the transition from one cycle of manners to another was prepared. The new cycle is again dominated by the line of influence initiated in *Pulcinella*, but enriched by the influences of Tchaikovsky (*The Fairy's Kiss*) and Weber (*Capriccio*). A new Romantic vein suddenly makes its appearance in Stravinsky's music, which becomes decorative, elegant, impetuous, with a note of something that has its origin in the traditional tactile character associated with the ballet – but with Delibes rather than Tchaikovsky. If this music still remains essentially 'Stravinskian' it is chiefly by its sonorous and rhythmic character.

Each stage in the composer's development is dominated by some antithesis – hard and soft, angular and fluid, abruptness and roundedness of contour, asperity and melodiousness. At the same time Stravinsky's thinking becomes increasingly instrumental. Having lost his native language, he turns less and less to vocal music and theatrical genres become increasingly rare. Prominence is given to the instrumental forms of sonata, concerto and symphony. As we shall see later, this correlation of genres and musical character will change again in Stravinsky's third period, when vocal music once more plays a leading part.

Apollo (1927–8) and *The Fairy's Kiss* (1928) are works that throw light on Stravinsky's compositions of the next decade, and echoes of features that occur in them appear even in the forties. I should not call them 'generalising', for after all there was the *Symphony of Psalms*, the *Violin Concerto* and even the *Mass* – but even so there was a strong temptation towards the purely decorative, the 'elegant', the 'lyrical'. This was the reverse side of that Apollonianism to which Stravinsky was dedicated during these years. At the same time he now felt the wish to write music that was 'appreciated at the first hearing'.[8]

But let us return to facts and listen to the composer's own words. In *Chronicle* he speaks of his delight in the 'cultivation of canto, of melody' that originated in Italy. And how characteristic of his perpetually enquiring nature it was, this enthusiasm for the strings to which he had refused a leading role in the music of his most recent cycle of 'manners'! Now he was hypnotised by the sonority of the violin, and this passion was further strengthened by a meeting with the young American violinist Samuel Dushkin. Following *Apollo*, both *The Fairy's Kiss* and *Capriccio* are marked by an increase in the importance of the strings, and in *Capriccio* we find, side by side with the solo piano part, solo passages for violins, violas, cellos and even double-basses. Violin works followed each other in profusion – the *Concerto* (1931), *Duo Concertante* (1931–2), a transcription from *Mavra* (Parasha's song) and a suite from *The Fairy's Kiss* (*Divertissement*).

It was not only the strings' *cantabile* that attracted Stravinsky, but their long 'breath'. Earlier he had worked with themes that resembled formulae, severely limited in sonorous capacity, motifs or phrases determined by the articulation of actual speech. In fact Stravinsky spoke of the music that he wrote at that time as 'phoneme-music', emphasising the importance of the 'cell' of intonation and rhythm contained in every word. Now he wanted to write purely instrumental music not governed by speech-articulation, but extended lines of melody. There are signs of this new approach in the *Octet* and in *Oedipus Rex* (e.g. the arias of Creon and Jocasta). Now he gave such melodies to the strings, with their long 'breath'. 'Apollo was my largest single step towards a long-line polyphonic style, and though it has a harmonic and melodic, above all an intervallic, character of its own, it nourished many later works as well.'[9] Much earlier he had written in *Chronicle*:

It seemed to me that it was not only timely but urgent to turn once more to the cultivation of this element from a purely musical point of view. That is why I was so much attracted by the idea of writing music in which everything should revolve about the melodic principle. And then the pleasure of immersing oneself in the multi-sonorous euphony of strings and making it penetrate even the furthest fibres of the polyphonic web![10]

He was finishing *Apollo* when, at the end of 1927, he was approached by Ida Rubinstein with a proposal that he should write a ballet based on Hans Christian Andersen's *Snow Queen* for the repertory of her newly founded company, a work to celebrate the thirty-fifth anniversary of Tchaikovsky's death. Stravinsky was on the threshold of his fiftieth year and, as he found himself communing with the muses of his boyhood favourites Tchaikovsky and Andersen, he looked back over his own past and remembered his *Scherzo fantastique* and the fairy scenes of *Firebird*. In reaction against the compact solidity, the weight and the sheer sonorous volume that had marked his latest cycle of 'manners' he now emphasised the fairy element with its ethereal lightness and elasticity.

The Fairy's Kiss is linked musically to both *Apollo* (especially by the long melodic lines) and to *Capriccio*, which was to follow it and also belongs to the world of high-flown Romanticism. The more austere music of *Apollo*, on the other hand, anticipates another, later ballet also based on Greek antiquity, *Orpheus*. The close connection between *The Fairy's Kiss* and *Capriccio* is immediately plain in the soloist's opening passages, which are borrowed from the coda of the *pas de deux* in the third scene of the ballet, the influence of which can be traced in other works of the same period – most noticeably in the *Violin Concerto* and only slightly less in the *Duo Concertante*, of which we must now say something.

This five-movement suite is remarkable for the number of different musical currents that can be traced in its pages. The first movement (Cantilena) is a lyrical piece based on two figures, the first of which is similar to the instrumental introduction in *Symphony of Psalms*. The second movement (Eclogue 1)[11] recalls the Royal March in *The Soldier's Tale*, while the third (Eclogue 2) recalls Aria 2 in the *Violin Concerto*. The fourth (Gigue) recalls the *pas de deux* in *Apollo*, while the fifth (Dithyrambe) is a kind of threnody, one of those funeral laments to which Stravinsky attached a special importance, beginning with the *Symphonies of Wind Instruments* in memory of Debussy. The eclectic character of the *Duo Concertante* is clear from this list of 'reminiscences', though what would otherwise be a blemish is made up for by what the composer himself would call its 'unity of *tenue*'. Occasional suggestions of the Baroque manner are characteristic, and it was this that prompted one commentator to say, with more wit than charity, that Bach might have written such a work if he had known and liked jazz.[12]

The *Violin Concerto* is on the same plane, but its general character is more energetic. Even so the decorative character of the music creates serious stylistic discrepancies. The whole lay-out of the work points to Baroque models, and more particularly the concerto principle deliberately emphasised by the composer. ('My chief interest was concentrated on the different combinations of violin and orchestra.') An example of this is the Bach-like duet between the soloist and the leader of the first violins (cf. figures $\boxed{87}$ and particularly $\boxed{94\text{--}5}$). There are occasions on which a Russian note creeps into the music, recalling the solo violin in *The Soldier's Tale* or the *Concertino* (figure $\boxed{14}$ in the first movement and $\boxed{123}$ in the finale). Moments such as these are organically integrated in the polyphonic texture, while reminiscences of *The Fairy's Kiss* are altogether different. The solo part in Aria 1, for instance, could come from any traditional ballet score, though Aria 2 with its Bachian features is altogether more solid. Various episodes in the finale have the same winged, ethereal character that is to be found in *Capriccio* and sound to my ears too 'balletic' – or too Tchaikovskian.

I began the account of this cycle of manners with *Apollo* and carried it up to the *Duo Concertante*, that is to say from 1927 to 1932. Does this represent the full extent of the cycle, with *The Fairy's Kiss* occupying the central role? No, the chronological limits of this cycle were extended, and this indicates a break or slowing down in Stravinsky's artistic evolution. His 'manners' now become less consistent and less distinct, vaguer and more eclectic, evidence of the approaching crisis in his development. It may well be that the composer was unaware of this and continued to compose in the same vein simply from inertia. The break had to come, a new 'cycle' had to appear and some individual work had to initiate it; but this work was not *Symphony of Psalms* and this makes it all the more astonishing to find that work flanked by *Capriccio* and the *Violin Concerto*, which are stylistically so remote from it.

Stravinsky was later to say[13] 'I did start to compose the Psalms in [Church] Slavonic, and only after coming a certain distance did I switch to Latin.' He also spoke of the section 'Laudate Dominum' as 'a prayer to the Russian image of the infant Christ with orb and sceptre'. Nevertheless *Symphony of Psalms* is an expression of the austere spirit of the Gothic, particularly the second part in which the composer made use of elements of musical symbolism, such as we shall find later in *Canticum Sacrum*. Without destroying the overall musical structure, powerful dynamic features make their appearance, like sudden squalls. One of these, the opening of the finale, was inspired, according to the composer, by the vision of Elijah's 'chariot of fire' whose rumbling, in Russian popular belief, was the cause of thunder.

Symphony of Psalms was commissioned by Serge Koussevitzky for the fiftieth anniversary of the Boston Symphony Orchestra, for which Hindemith wrote his *Concert Music for Strings*, Prokofiev his Fourth Symphony and Honegger his Third Symphony. The European and American first performances of the work in 1930 were almost simultaneous (13 December, Brussels, and 19 December, Boston) and the composer himself conducted the first Paris performance in February 1931. Stravinsky removed the titles given to the three parts at the Brussels performance (Prelude, Double Fugue, Symphonic

Allegro) and they could be characterised according to their nature and content as 'prayer for help', 'song of hope' and 'song of praise'.

If the music of this work still reminds us, however slightly, of the *Violin Concerto* and the *Duo Concertante*, it was strikingly different in character and atmosphere from the mélodrame *Persephone* on a text by André Gide (1933–4). The subject was again taken from Greek mythology; but it was handled in a different way from *Apollo* or *Orpheus*, both of which contain tragic nuances, whereas *Persephone* is dominated by an elegiac colouring and a tender grief. In no other work did Stravinsky make such excessive use of the minor mode: more than half of the seventeen numbers of *Persephone* are melancholy, minor-mode pieces. This may have been dictated by Gide's conception of Persephone descending voluntarily to the Nether Regions, not under compulsion as in the original myth, thus making the whole work a hymn of compassion. It is also possible that Stravinsky was consciously adapting his music to the demands of French taste: he was after all on the eve of standing – unsuccessfully as it turned out – for the Académie Française. He had once before set a French text – the Verlaine poems of 1910 – not very successfully, and this second attempt was to be his last.

The score of *Persephone* unquestionably contains a number of purely artistic *trouvailles*, such as Eumolpos's invocation and the choruses of nymphs and shades; but the use of spoken declamation against music – free, and not notated as in Schoenberg's *Sprechgesang*, cannot be counted successful. In addition to this the text is altogether too profuse, and elements of stylisation often creep into the music also. The opening chorus, for instance, contains unexpected reminiscences of the pastoral intermezzo in Tchaikovsky's *Queen of Spades*, as Yarustovsky pointed out.

After *Persephone* Stravinsky finished his *Concerto for Two Pianos*, the first movement of which had been written in 1931, i.e. at the same time as the *Violin Concerto*, while the other three date from 1934–5. Some musicologists consider the *Concerto* as the culminating point in Stravinsky's neo-classical period, and this may be true. If so, however, we must count *The Rake's Progress*, written as a kind of farewell to his neo-classical ideals, as a second peak.

The *Concerto* is one of the composer's strangest and most enigmatic works, restless and disturbed in character, over-saturated with chromaticisms, which is rare for Stravinsky, and extremely complex polyphonically. Ten years earlier, in the *Serenade*, Stravinsky had treated the piano as a chamber instrument, writing mostly in two parts which moved in parallel intervals. Now, on the other hand, he made use of many different technical devices – repeated notes that recall the cimbalom, many-tiered chords, *martellato*, wide-spreading passage-work as in *Capriccio*, complicated ornamental passages both there and in the second movement of the *Sonata* or the Romance in the *Serenade*. In Stravinsky's own terms the density of the resulting sonorities is excessive: blocks of sound are piled up and, despite the energetic, even aggressive nature of the music, especially in the second half of the cycle, these blocks have a static rather than a dynamic effect. In general the *Concerto* is more impressive for ingenuity of workmanship than for freshness of invention. Although the organisation of contrasts is masterly, in the actual invention there is some lack of primary inspiration, something essentially secondary. Nevertheless the *Concerto* is a significant work, and it offers an occasion for a number of observations.

The toccata-like movement in equal note-values was adapted by the composer from the Baroque and is admirable, but he tries to combine in one the Bach-experience and the Beethoven-experience – as in the first movement, where a sonata-like form (with rather ill-defined subsidiary sections) is 'symphonised', and the transition from the Baroque to the classical is noticeable. It was to be even more marked in the *Symphony in C*.

The colouring of the Nocturne, which forms the second movement, is characteristic of a number of the neo-classical works. The music as it were vibrates and sways, it is interrupted by intermittent accentuation. The ornamental *fioriture* and melismas give the whole movement an air of refinement and an atmosphere of uneasy calm, such as we also find in the second movements of the *Sonata*, *Capriccio* (*poco più mosso* section), in Aria 2 of the *Violin Concerto* and in the second movements of the *Dumbarton Oaks* concerto, the *Symphony in C* and the *Symphony in Three Movements*. Analogous movements can be found in Bartók's fourth and fifth quartets and in the *Music for Strings, Percussion and Celesta*. These bold, fresh expeditions into the irrational, with their clear, subjective colouring, are among Bartók's most original innovations, while in Stravinsky the lyricism is objectified and is more speculative in character.

The third movement of the *Concerto* consists of variations, and the variation form is, as it were, an organically natural form of development in Stravinsky's case. He first used classical variation-form in *Pulcinella*. After that he used it for the most part freely, employing fragments of a theme and individual features of timbre, harmony or rhythm and less frequently the passacaglia form with ostinato bass. In fact Stravinsky's variation technique, which is inseparable from his use of counterpoint, deserves a special study.[14] The idea of the variations in the *Concerto* is an interesting one, involving the gradual crystallisation of the theme, which ᵣorms the cantus firmus of the fugue in the finale. The last two movements are played without a break and are the most highly organised of the 'cycle'.

Stravinsky particularly admired the art with which Bach 'developed accumulations of intensity'. He himself succeeded in achieving the same artistic result in these movements, though the prelude before the fugue is perhaps rather limp. The *concertante* principle of the two pianos competing with each other is particularly notable in the variations, where the fourth has a typical Baroque splendour and in the last the fugal theme stands out with increasing clarity and is then heard in cancrizans form. The finale is short and its explosive power is not so much exhausted as interrupted.

In connection with the *Concerto* something should be said about the *concertante* principle in general and its place in contemporary music. Without exploring the possible sociological reasons for the increasing importance of virtuosity in twentieth-century music, we may safely say that it is connected with the general progress of technology. Today we find not only athletes but musicians – soloists, ensembles and orchestral players, even the gramophone industry – all anxious to establish 'records'. This concern with virtuosity is naturally reflected in orchestral music itself, and in the concerto. What concerns me, however, is to explain the revival of the Baroque musical forms which Stravinsky cultivated with such zeal and versatility, becoming the prophet and champion of new stylistic tendencies.

We must return now for a moment to Huizinga's study of the part played in all culture by the 'play-principle'. According to Huizinga, culture became increasingly serious after the eighteenth century, and the play-element began to occupy a subordinate position. We are of course speaking of the Age of Enlightenment and its culmination in the French Revolution, when the play-element began to be replaced, even suppressed, by the rational. The attempts to revive the play-element in the twentieth century may be explained by the wish to free the spiritual forces of the individual from the fetters of civilisation and to counter the cult of technology – which produces *homo faber*, the 'doer' or 'business'-man – by insisting on *homo ludens*, the 'play'-man. Hence the return to the theatrical forms of pre-industrial society that we discussed in chapter 6, and the revival of Baroque musical forms, i.e. free manifestations of the will in the form of joint, shared play as originally suggested by the word 'concert', the root meaning of which is precisely 'joint music-making'.

What Stravinsky revived in these works is the *Spielfreudigkeit* of the Baroque composers, no doubt including Bach – the delight in the actual process of 'playing'. It was this quality in Stravinsky's music that captured his contemporaries, who shared his experience of the fascinating resourcefulness of the imagination at 'play'. The quality of Stravinsky's imagination during the thirties and forties was variable, it is true, sometimes leaping up like a flame and at others dying down again, and on those occasions less convincing. The concern with imparting this 'free manifestation of the will' in ensemble-playing developed gradually in Stravinsky. Speaking of his development between *Firebird* and *The Rite of Spring*, I. Vershinina wrote that 'the purposeful manifestation and reinforcing of the dynamic and constructive functions of orchestral timbre eventually created what may be called a "counterpoint of timbres"'. Original as this was, it was only the first step towards mastering the *concertante* principle, as can be seen from the opening wind solos and the play of timbres between the different orchestral groups in the Introduction to Part 2 of *The Rite*. Speaking of his work in 1917, Stravinsky said that his instrumental ideas were then directed towards an individual solo style; and this style was in fact realised in *The Soldier's Tale*, in which a total of seven instruments covers the whole range of sonorities. Each instrument not only has its own timbre and register but is also distinguished by its own kind of articulation and attack, and these specific qualities are used to form different combinations – as, for instance, the clarinet's legato, the cornet-à-pistons' *staccato* and the violin's chords in the 'Little Concert'. The instruments 'concertise', i.e. they make their appearances as individual 'characters' in the common 'game'. And when Stravinsky said that in the *Violin Concerto* his chief interest was concentrated on the different combinations of violin and orchestra, he was in fact stating the principles of *concertante* music. In exactly the same way these principles are manifested in the *Symphony in Three Movements* by the contest between piano and harp, which has a definite formal significance. Finally, the method of using an obbligato instrument to strengthen an operatic role – like a kind of satellite – as Stravinsky does in *Oedipus Rex*, was clearly borrowed from the Baroque.

Both the *concertante* and the variation principles are inextricably bound up with counterpoint in Stravinsky's music. The personified instruments do not simply confront each other, displaying their characters and their virtuoso possibilities, as Rimsky-Korsakov does, for instance, in *Sheherazade* and *Capriccio espagnol*: they also appear in direct contrapuntal relationships. This is an inimitable feature of Stravinsky's music and one that has not yet been studied in detail.

The hallmarks of this *concertante* style are to be found in any one of his works, and in many they play a leading and decisive role. The overwhelming majority of these cases belong to the neo-classical period, and it is to Stravinsky that the honour of reviving Baroque forms in the twentieth century really belongs.

We are now at the heart of the neo-classical period, the rise of which may be dated from the *Octet* and the *Piano Concerto* to *Symphony of Psalms*. This was followed by a slowing down, marked by a number of breaks; and now, after the *Concerto for Two Pianos*, the downward movement is a zig-zag in which the descent is interrupted by individual inspired utterances. We may consider the cycle of earlier 'manners' concluded (a space of eight years divides the *Concerto* from *Apollo*), although their influence continued to be felt for another decade. From 1935 to 1945 Stravinsky went through a prolonged creative crisis during which he was unable to discover new themes or forms or new means of expression, either in the sultry, storm-laden atmosphere of the late thirties or in the catastrophic years of the war.

These were the years of Fascism in Italy, National Socialism in Germany and the Spanish Civil War, which turned out to be the prelude to the Second World War. When that storm broke, it did not spare Stravinsky but forced him to emigrate from France to the United States. Before that, however, both his wife and his daughter died of the consumption that also struck him down. Having lost two members of his family and been forced to change his whole accustomed way of life, he found himself at nearly sixty separated from his friends and acquaintances and compelled to build a new life, with his second wife, in a world whose cultural and social life were to remain alien to him for the rest of his life. A sense of perplexity and confusion can be felt in his actions and in his involuntary concessions to American taste.

In his music this sense of perplexity is most marked during the early forties. The beginnings of the crisis are to be found in *Jeu de cartes* (1936), which had its first performance at the New York Metropolitan in 1936; in the chamber concerto *Dumbarton Oaks* (1937–8), the last work that he finished in Paris; and in the *Symphony in C* (1938–40), the first two movements of which were written in France, the last two in the United States, where the work had its first performance. Each of these works has its own individuality and is typical of the composer's stylistic preferences.

Jeu de cartes is a three-scene ballet (Stravinsky calls it 'ballet in three deals'), in which the Joker is continually interfering and trying, like some imp of the perverse, to confuse the game, though he fails to do so. This was not a new idea for Stravinsky, if we think of the Conjurer in *Petrushka*, the Devil in *The Soldier's Tale* and, later, Shadow in *The Rake's Progress*, all different personifications of the devil-figure which controls people and their actions as though they were marionettes. In *Oedipus* this role is played by fate, the geometry of destiny. In these works the devil (or fate) is triumphant and this gives the drama a tragic note, made more emphatic in *Oedipus* and *The Rake's Progress* by the fact that in the dénouement the person of the hero is transfigured.

The dénouement of *Jeu de cartes* is in an altogether different key, light-hearted and unpretentious. In addition to this, the drama of the piece is so abstract that it can almost be counted among the 'subject-less' ballets. The music too is unpretentious. The composer himself thought that it was the 'most German' of all his works. He also pointed to the fact that the march-like Introduction to each 'deal' plays the part of the 'master of ceremonies' inviting the players to the card-table, and he recalled the voices of the croupiers that he had heard at German spas in his youth. This, he says, explains the Romantic colouring of the score; and in fact the general spirit of the work is indeed Romantic, just as its style is eclectic – indeed *Jeu de cartes* might be called a kind of 'concentrate' of the eclectic element in Stravinsky's music. There are echoes of Strauss (waltzes and *Die Fledermaus*), of Ravel (*La Valse*), of Beethoven (second movement of the Eighth Symphony) and of Rossini (overture to *The Barber of Seville*, which is at one point quoted verbatim, one of the few examples of collage in Stravinsky's works). Generally speaking the 'godfathers' of this pasticcio may be said to be Delibes and Tchaikovsky, so that we have here the final point in the line that stretches from *Pulcinella* to *The Fairy's Kiss*, though in fact the harmonic language here is simpler than that of *The Fairy's Kiss*, since we find not only the assertion of traditional tonality but even the triads on which that tonality is based.

The bright palette, simplified structure and eclectic style are all symptoms of the coming crisis which led Stravinsky to write works that were a kind of simplified version of what he had already written. Or is this judgment perhaps too severe? I do not deny the right of *Jeu de cartes* to existence, particularly an existence in the theatre. Nobody can find fault with a composer for feeling a need for distraction, and *Jeu de cartes* was written immediately after the restless, anxious *Concerto for Two Pianos*. Music such as this can provide a form of relaxation and real aesthetic enjoyment, and what is artistically valuable need not necessarily be profound. Mozart, for instance, wrote divertimenti and serenades as well as the last three symphonies and the G Minor Quintet. And in fact the parallel with Mozart is justified, despite the difference of epoch and individuality, by the fact that each composer had a natural inclination to 'art for art's sake', something that accounts for the 'Protean' character that they shared. It is not the work itself that is open to question so much as the tendency that it expresses; and, as in the case of *Pulcinella*, the tendency to produce 'simplified versions' was a great temptation to Stravinsky and one that at the beginning of the forties he was unable to resist.

The *Dumbarton Oaks* chamber concerto is on quite a different plane and represents the high point of Stravinsky's Baroque-based works. It takes its name from the estate of the American art patron R. V. Bliss, who commissioned the work when Stravinsky was in the United States to conduct the first performance of *Jeu de cartes*. He took Bach's *Brandenburg Concertos* as his model, finding in them a perfect example of the 'personification' of individual instruments in an ensemble work. The music breathes freely, especially in the first movement and the middle section of the second, the instruments competing freely with each other in complex contrapuntal combinations (the last movement is a fugato) while remaining strictly subordinate to the general rhythm and movement of each section. There is a superb urgency, almost like an *idée fixe*, in the return of the persistent motif in the second movement, perpetually reappearing in new instrumental combinations. Vlad has compared the high pressure and the inexorably mounting intensity of the finale to similar characteristics in Honegger's *Pacific 231*, though I cannot agree with him and Yarustovsky in finding a resemblance between the opening motif of the last movement and the fanfare with which Tchaikovsky's Fourth Symphony opens. The resemblance seems to me purely formal and the character of the two passages absolutely different.

Dumbarton Oaks is a complete unity, an unshadowed piece both wholly contemporary in spirit and specifically Stravinskian. It also represents the composer's farewell to the Baroque, to which he was only occasionally to return in the future. In the *Symphony in C* he returned to the Viennese classics. This new course, traceable in the *Concerto for Two Pianos*, was to last for ten years, until *The Rake's*

Progress in fact. Stravinsky tells us that he chose Haydn and Beethoven as models for his symphonic 'cycle' but it is impossible not to add Tchaikovsky's name, if only because the germ of the theme in the main part of the first movement of the *Symphony in C* is demonstrably almost identical with the analogous theme in Tchaikovsky's First Symphony. In fact the three-chord phrase on which the theme is based and the repetition of its many variants are what give Stravinsky's music its Russian colour. What I have in mind is something else, a 'balletic' note in his music that is hard to define but connects it very closely with *The Fairy's Kiss* or, more exactly, with the melodic matrix from which that ballet grew – Tchaikovsky, in fact. It is worth remembering that not long before completing the *Symphony* Stravinsky arranged some numbers from *The Sleeping Beauty* for the depleted orchestras of the war years, and he used the same reduced orchestra for the *Symphony*, forming as it were another link with Tchaikovsky.

As for Haydn, Stravinsky said that he loved this composer's work for 'the different lengths of its sentences and its asymmetrical rhythms',[15] which he found sympathetic and adopted in the construction and transformation of his own symphonic themes. In fact it was the symphonies of Haydn and Mozart that he had in mind when establishing the durational proportions of his works – thus the four movements of the *Symphony in C* last twenty-eight minutes and the *Symphony in Three Movements* lasts twenty-four. This is not a formal index: the processes of symphonic development, the time that music lasts, are determined by structural principles chosen by the composer, and it is worth comparing with Stravinsky the principles of the protracted unfolding of the 'events' in the symphonies of Mahler and Shostakovich.

And Beethoven? At this time Stravinsky spent much time at the piano looking through Beethoven's sonatas and searching for the key to their craftsmanship, and what I think must have most aroused his interest was Beethoven's technique of thematic development. He had gone beyond constructing his thematic material from existing formulae, and since *The Fairy's Kiss* he had been trying to soften the abrupt outlines of sound-complexes by giving more plasticity to transitional passages; and he had found himself obliged, at least in part, to give up graduated in favour of 'terrace' dynamics. This renunciation was not of course complete, and could never be so without Stravinsky renouncing his own personality; but his own specific, individual earlier manner revealed limitations. In his new manner he had to find other ways of spacing the strong points of his climaxes. The unfolding of the symphonic action demanded a genuine *Durchführung*, or through-development, rather than a fragmentary one.

If we ask ourselves why in fact Stravinsky felt the need to make this break, the answer may be that he was tired of standing alone and hankered for wider contacts, attracted by the acknowledged and generally accepted treatment of the different musical genres, and artistic problems in general. The crisis in his creative life led him temporarily – and, mercifully for him, no more than temporarily – to a kind of conformism. It is in this light, which may be a harsh one in speaking of a composer of such genius, that I view his works of the early forties.

As always, of course, it was the sheer boldness of his creative imagination that saved Stravinsky. There is a wide sweep and a powerful élan in the first movement of the *Symphony in C*, and the Italianate cantabile of the Larghetto concertante is balanced by the complex rhythmic structures of the Allegretto, which consists of two sections – the first based on a polymorphic alternation of dance-rhythms and the second taking the form of a fugue in which the subject appears first in cancrizans form. The Largo has an impressively dramatic character despite its static nature, and this serves as a transition to a finale dominated by dance-elements. In the coda these are solidified, as it were frozen, so as to form colonnades of vertically constructed chords.

Stravinsky expressed a preference for the even-numbered among Beethoven's symphonies and he greatly admired the Seventh. Echoes of Beethoven's symphonies, and particularly the Fourth, are therefore not difficult to find in the *Symphony in C*.

Here I should like to interrupt our chronological study. In the years 1940–5 Stravinsky was adapting himself to a new life, and his compositions follow no definite plan and manifest no unity of purpose. Works written for his own concerts include the two *Symphonies, Danses concertantes* (1941–2) and the *Sonata for Two Pianos* (1943–4) for performance by himself and his son, but more numerous were works written to commission. Private commissions included *Ode* (1943) commissioned by Serge Kussevitzky and the cantata *Babel* (1944) commissioned by the composer Nathan Shilkret, and in 1946 his first post-war European commission, *Concerto in D*, for Paul Sacher and the Bâle Chamber Orchestra. There were also commissions from film-producers, though the films were never made and the music was performed in the concert hall – *Norwegian Moods* (1942), a kind of sinfonietta in four move-ments, and *Scherzo à la russe* (1943–4). Unused film-music was also incorporated in the second movement of the *Symphony in Three Movements*. Broadway theatres commissioned music for 'shows' (*Scènes de ballet*, 1944) and he wrote *Ebony Concerto* for a jazz ensemble and *Circus Polka* for a circus. The variety is bewildering, and also the energy of a man already past sixty.

When he was a very old man, twenty years later, he spoke of these works reluctantly and with a slight note of disgust, observing that he could judge works that he had written fifty years earlier (during his Russian period, that is to say) with impartiality, but that he found it hard to estimate the works that he had written during the forties. Even so he made some sharp observations about *Danses concert-antes* and about *Orpheus*, which he criticised for it metrical monotony and its rhythmic 'greasiness'. He was particularly hard on *Scènes de ballet*, saying 'it is featherweight and sugared'; and he criticised the coda of the finale of *Symphony in Three Movements*, which is one of his best works, for 'the final . . . rather too commercial, D flat sixth chord – instead of the expected C'.[16]

Before going on to discuss the *Symphony in Three Movements* I should like to draw the reader's attention to a significant psycho-logical trait of the composer's character. When he ceased using Russian themes at the beginning of the twenties, Stravinsky did not forget the music of his native country. I have already had occasion to point out a number of Russian nuances that appear in the works written between 1920 and 1940, but now these become clearer and more definite, perhaps evidence of a nostalgia that increased with the sufferings of the Russian people during the war. We have already mentioned the 'Russisms' in the *Symphony in C*, and even the title of his *Scherzo à la russe* was borrowed from Tchaikovsky's op.1. This work was originally arranged for jazz ensemble and later for full orchestra. There are marked Russisms in the *Sonata for Two Pianos*, where the second part of the theme on which the variations are based has a noticeably Russian cut, and the *poco più mosso* episode in the finale recalls the kind of popular song that we find in *Mavra*. This same clear Russian colouring is to be found in a number of episodes in the *Symphony in Three Movements*, particularly in the develop-ment section of the first movement and in the finale, though here it is the Russia of *The Rite of Spring* that Stravinsky recalls.

He spent a long time over the *Symphony*, from 1942 to 1945, and it seems probable that it was the work expended on this piece that helped him to find a way out of the creative blind alley in which he found himself, to rediscover the strength and inflexibility of purpose that characterise his best dramatic works. In fact the *Symphony* occupies a situation in Stravinsky's development not unlike that of *The Soldier's Tale*, the early work serving as a focus for the stylistic researches of the years 1910–20 and the later synthesising much of what the composer had learned – the rhythmic refinements and the relentless energy of *The Rite*, the interior discipline and intensity of *Symphony of Psalms*, the exploiting of contrasting sonorities and volumes in the *Octet* and that worship of spontaneous melody that played such a large part in his works between *The Fairy's Kiss* and *Jeu de cartes*. These different stylistic impulses do not appear in a kind of eclectic medley: their individual characteristics are carefully selected and thematically unified.

It has been said that Stravinsky's model for the *Symphony in Three Movements* was Beethoven's Fifth, but the comparison is far-fetched. Dramatically the two symphonies are constructed quite differently, for whereas the centre of gravity lies in Beethoven's finale, to which all the 'events' in the earlier movements point forward, Stravinsky sets his centre of gravity in the first movement. There is perhaps a faint resemblance between the two works in the concentration of the drama, in the quickened pulse of the development, but even this is achieved by quite different means. A closer analogy is provided if we analyse the significance of the chief theme, which serves as a kind of motto in the first movement of both works. Even such a generalisation as this is true only in a limited sense, for if Stravinsky's main theme recalls that of any other symphony, it is not Beethoven's Fifth so much as Brahm's Third.

Beethoven's technique, however, which was certainly developed in his own way by Brahms, was not without its influence on Stravinsky. He once referred casually to the importance in his music of what he called – in English – a 'pull idea'. That is to say, the initial stimulus, the impulse from which a whole movement grows, whether that impulse is one of rhythmic attack, of timbre or of harmony. In the *Symphony in Three Movements* that impulse is provided by the intervallic structure of the 'motto', which is incessantly modified during the development in the first movement. This has a significance analogous to that of the three-chord phrase in the *Symphony in C*. Although such modifications partly reveal Stravinsky's acquaintance with Beethoven's technique of thematic development, they exemplify even more clearly Stravinsky's own individual method of development through variation. In addition to this he once again shows his virtuosity in organising the play of sonorous volumes and planes, something not at all characteristic of Beethoven.

For his new symphony Stravinsky adopted the three-movement form, and he seems to me to have been generally more successful in displaying the unity of an instrumental work in this rather than in the four-movement form. The idea of four movements is that the two middle movements should provide a kind of distraction from the vital pulsation of the first and the last, and it is for this reason that they concentrate respectively on the lyrical and the scherzo elements, whether this last is humorous, demonic, or fantastic. In the classical symphony the third movement was given a touch of everyday reality by the use of dance-forms, and this served as a transition from the purely symphonic to the genre-like character of the finale. There was a similar touch of the everyday in the *Symphony in C*, where old dances are stylised. In Stravinsky's music the pressure is in fact so strong that no scherzo element is really needed, and if we do find it, it will be in the delicate lyrical movements to which we have already referred.

It is characteristic that the three-movement scheme is regularly used for concertos, where the dynamics of the drama are clearly established. Although there are nineteenth-century exceptions to this rule, such as Brahms, they are rare. This dynamic quality is inseparable from Stravinsky's music and this, I believe, explains why his three-movement works, with their brightly coloured contrasts, are better integrated. (I am not speaking here of instrumental works written for the theatre, or those adapted for the concert-hall from his theatre-music, as the principle of their construction is quite different.)

The *Symphony in Three Movements* sums up and closes the list of the discoveries in the field of instrumental music that the composer had made during the neo-classical period. These include the concerto; and concerto characteristics, which were confined to the second movement of the *Symphony in C*, here express the essence of the music, which in its original version was in fact a concerto for piano and orchestra. *Ebony Concerto* and the *Concerto for Strings*, written not long after, are no more than footnotes to this symphony.

Thus it is possible to speak of 1945 as marking the beginning of a new upward movement in Stravinsky's development. Right into the fifties, however, this was a splintered development. *Orpheus* (1946–7) and *The Rake's Progress* (1948–51) showed a renewal of interest in neo-classical theatre, while the cantata *Babel* (1944) and the *Mass* (1944–8) have their roots in the Baroque and still earlier musical periods. These represent a renewed interest in church music which was to become increasingly important.

We have already spoken in chapter 6 about the theatre-pieces, but must here add some further points. Stravinsky's last work for the theatre before the outbreak of war was *Jeu de cartes* and now, ten years later, he returned to the ballet with quite different aims. *Orpheus* is based on the classical myth and the action is linked and directed by three orchestral interludes. There is one in the first scene and there are two in the second, the third forming the very short, purely static scene of Orpheus's Apotheosis. The work is divided, as is usual with Stravinsky, into separate numbers. There are twelve of these and they fall, choreographically, into the traditional solos (*air de danse*), duets (*pas de deux*) and *pas d'action*, in which the corps de ballet is employed. These separate numbers, however, are not arranged as Petipa would have arranged them, as a large suite. Stravinsky's music establishes a number of different intersecting arcs which ensure the work's balance and proportion. For example, the second scene revolves round the dances of the Furies and Bacchantes (nos. 5, 8 and 11): but within the scene the Interlude (no. 7) is framed by Orpheus's 'dance arias'. In these arias the harp has a *concertante* part that points to a connection with the second movement of the *Symphony in Three Movements*, and there is a similar connection between the Dionysiac Dance of the Furies (no. 8) and some episodes in the first movement of the *Symphony*. The fugue in the Apotheosis forms a link between the ballet and the other, opposite manner used by Stravinsky at this period. He was very proud of the fact that the fugue was conducted in the spirit of the old masters (cf. sections 143–9 in the score). There are three relatively independent strata. A slow melody is stated by the trumpet (with the violin, at the beginning and the end), like a cantus firmus; two horns provide a complex contrapuntal pattern, while the harp contributes a measured ostinato bass – thus bringing back Orpheus's solo, with which the ballet opens. This suggestion of the archaic gives the work an unexpected colour, because the ballet as a whole is melodic, and the fact that Orpheus's dances are called 'arias' is not without significance, since they are touched with an operatic expressiveness. It is clear that Stravinsky felt a need to write an opera at this time; and it was a museum visit in 1947 and a chance acquaintance with Hogarth's two series of prints that provided him with the impulse to write *The Rake's Progress. Così fan tutte* also, according to the composer, influenced him, though this perhaps need not be taken too seriously. If we are to look for artistic models, we shall find them not in Italian *opera buffa* but in the *opera semiseria*, and *The Rake's Progress* is nearer in character to *Don Giovanni* than to *Così fan tutte*.

The form of *The Rake's Progress* is close to that of its eighteenth-century Italian prototypes – what is sung is in verse and the parlando recitatives are in prose, with harpsichord accompaniment – and it is of course in disconnected 'numbers'. The music itself contains echoes not only of the eighteenth century but of a medley of different *bel canto* styles including Rossini, Verdi and perhaps even Puccini. There is a two-fold 'alienation-effect': the farcical moments destroy the dynamic situations, while the experiences of the characters are given a grotesque flavour by the musical parodies, though even so a natural, unforced manner prevails. The music unquestionably possesses that genuine comic *brio* which Pushkin, in speaking of Rossini, compared to the foaming bubbles of champagne. Equally beyond question is the tragic note in the two final scenes. The scene in the churchyard and the card game recall *The Soldier's Tale*, and the mythological figures in the madhouse scene recall *Orpheus*. This was not the first time that Stravinsky set an English text. The little seven-minute cantata *Babel*, for male-voice chorus and orchestra, is of interest not only in itself, but as a symptom. It was essentially an occasional work commissioned as part of a 'symposium' Biblical oratorio by the successful, though not very gifted, American composer Nathan Shilkret. Among the composers he approached, some of whom accepted the commission like Stravinsky, were Schoenberg, Milhaud, Toch and Tansman. The project as a whole, however, never materialised.

Stravinsky chose the story of the building and destruction of the Tower of Babel. The English Biblical text is read by a Narrator against orchestral accompaniment, as in *Persephone*. The first and last sections are purely instrumental, an opening Largo accompanying the account of the building of the tower (fugato) and a longer, concluding 'Con moto meno mosso', the account of its destruction. This is a kind of passacaglia in which, of course, counterpoint is more important than actual variation. The music is archaic in character, partly reminiscent of the second part of *Symphony of Psalms* but also anticipating the fugue in *Orpheus* mentioned above and, more particularly, the musical prosody of the *Mass*. The cantata, in fact, contains hints of the composer's further journey, from the Baroque to the Middle Ages.

A significant milestone on that journey was the *Mass* for mixed chorus and wind ensemble (2 oboes, cor anglais, 2 bassoons, 2 trumpets, 3 trombones), a setting of the Latin text consisting of Kyrie, Gloria, Credo, Sanctus and Agnus Dei. The specification of the ensemble was probably determined by the composer's wish to imitate the sonority of the organ, and the absence of strings and even flute marks a return to that taste for 'hard' sonorities which had marked the early twenties. Similar considerations explain his desire that boys' rather than women's voices should be used for the soprano and alto parts, as in *Symphony of Psalms*.

The *Mass* was composed over a period of five years, the first two sections in 1944 and the last three in the winter of 1947–8. What had he in mind in writing it? It is difficult to know whether he intended the work for liturgical performance. He had in fact written a number of small *a cappella* pieces for use in church – 'Our Father' (1926), 'I believe' (1932) and 'Mother of God, to thee' (1934), and in 1949 he made new versions of these with Latin texts (Pater Noster, Credo and Ave Maria); and he may have hoped that the *Mass* would be adopted for liturgical use, which has only rarely happened. This, however, is not important if we think of Verdi, Brahms and Dvořák, of Tchaikovsky's *Liturgy* and Rachmaninov's *Vespers*. We need not therefore enquire why Stravinsky, an Orthodox by conviction, set the *Mass* and much later a *Requiem*. Why, after all, did the Protestant Bach write Catholic Masses? and was Beethoven an orthodox Catholic believer when he wrote the *Missa Solemnis*? In questions of deep personal religious conviction it is a mistake to give any hasty, dogmatic answers. One fact stands beyond question – that religious consciousness was firmly rooted in Stravinsky, manifesting itself less strongly at some times and then asserting itself with a new strength, and predominating in his final creative phase, when it found expression in works based for the most part on biblical or gospel themes. Stravinsky's handling of these was not conventionally Orthodox: he was not an ecclesiastical composer. In old age he was increasingly attracted by the sublime and the supra-personal, and it was from subjects of this kind that he drew his inspiration. Yet a religious consciousness was always happily combined in Stravinsky's case with a robust feeling for life, and he was neither a hypocrite nor an ascetic. He took what life offered him with both hands, and indeed this was a necessary condition of that 'festival', life-accepting quality of which we have spoken at such length.

The polarity of Stravinsky's intellectual and emotional interests has already been emphasised in these pages, and the antithesis represented by this polarity is suggested by such words as 'austere/decorative', 'hard/soft', 'angular/flowing'. The composer's final period was to be dominated, as we shall see in a later chapter, by austerity of manner, although the decorative was still to play a part in his music, if in a rather different form. The present digression has been rendered inevitable by the need to understand the part played by the *Mass* in Stravinsky's general development as an artist and the stylistic changes involved.

Russian liturgical choral singing reproduces the chordal character of Orthodox canticles. In the *Mass*, on the other hand, as in the *Orpheus* fugue, Stravinsky employed the polyphonic principles of the old masters. Furthermore he also turned to Gregorian chant, to the florid mediaeval style of trope and sequence and the technique of faux-bourdon. The rich variety of these means of expression served to convey great interior intensity, a dynamic power within static forms.

The archaic character of the music stirred associations with early Russian diatonicism, perhaps without the composer being fully aware of the fact; and I. Blazhkov has even noted the influence of Georgian canticles in the Gloria and Sanctus of the *Mass*. Particularly characteristic in this music are the linking of small intervals and the 'chanting' tone, which was also to become a marked feature of Stravinsky's last works. Also remarkable is the frequent use of antiphonal forms, both between chorus and instrumental ensemble and between wood-winds and brass within the ensemble itself.

The central movement of the five forming the *Mass* is the Credo, for the most part strictly 'chanted', with static wood-wind chords accenting the breaks in the flow of the chant. In the Gloria and the Sanctus which frame the Credo there are a number of correspondences and parallelisms, as the composer called them, which underline this musical framing – thus the tenors' florid major seconds at the opening of the *Gloria* correspond to the florid oboe figure at the opening of the Sanctus, though the construction of the two movements is different, the Gloria forming a chain of interconnected episodes while the Sanctus is developed by a system of mounting intensities. The fugue at 'Pleni sunt coeli' is marked by displaced rhythmic accents in the cantus firmus very characteristic of Stravinsky, and leads through the strongly but evenly accented Benedictus to the ecstatic explosion of the 'Hosanna in excelsis', which recalls similar episodes in *Symphony of Psalms* and *Les Noces*. In the short Kyrie the vocal line is controlled by the steady movement of the wood-wind (two oboes and bassoon). In the Agnus Dei the three *a cappella* episodes are punctuated by instrumental ritornelli which recall the chorales of *The Soldier's Tale*.

Three years after he had completed the *Mass* Stravinsky started work on the *Cantata* on old English texts, which marks the borderline between the neo-classical and the last period, to which it properly belongs. We shall therefore not consider it here, although it contains clear links with the *Mass*.

Stravinsky at nearly seventy years of age was entering a new period of composition. He had conquered in himself that sense of constraint inseparable from the changed conditions of life in the United States, and his connection with Europe was re-established by the Bâle commission, the *Concerto in D*. Thus it was at Bâle, in 1947, that he had his first European première since the Paris première of the *Concerto for Two Pianos* (1935). In 1948 the *Mass* was performed in Italy; and from now onwards the majority of his major works were to be given their first performances in Europe.

I should like to add one point in conclusion. Between 1945 and 1950 Stravinsky revised the scores of a number of his earlier works – *Firebird* (1945), *Petrushka* (1946), *Symphonies of Wind Instruments* (1947), *Apollo Musagetes* (1947), *Oedipus Rex* (1948), *Symphony of Psalms* (1948), *Pulcinella* (1949), *Capriccio* (1949), *Persephone* (1949), etc. He did this for two reasons, the one financial and the other artistic. In the United States authors' fees were paid only for the performance of works written there and, by revising his earlier works, Stravinsky as it were 'authorised' them. Artistically he was concerned to make these works more practicable and easily performable. Unlike Hindemith, who made important changes of form and style when re-editing his earlier works (such as *Das Marienleben* and *Cardillac*), Stravinsky confined himself to details, some significant and others less so – what painters call *retouches*. Later he was to rework or transcribe a number of his compositions, but these belonged to his Russian rather than his neo-classical period. This reviewing of his own past output, at once critical and creative, served him as a point of support in his new artistic speculations.

9

>->

Movement

In 1927 Stravinsky received a commission for a ballet from the American Library of Congress, and the subject he chose was the myth of Apollo Musagetes – Apollo inspirer of the Muses. He reduced the number of the Muses from nine to three – Calliope, Polyhymnia and Terpsichore,

as being the most characteristic representatives of choreographic art. Calliope, receiving the stylus and tablets from Apollo, personifies poetry and its rhythm; Polyhymnia, finger on lips, representing mime. As Cassiodorus tells us: 'Those speaking fingers, that eloquent silence, those narratives in gesture, are said to have been invented by Polyhymnia, wishing to prove that man could express his will without recourse to words.' Finally, Terpsichore, combining in herself both the rhythm of poetry and the eloquence of gesture, reveals dancing to the world, and thus among the Muses takes the place of honour beside the Musagetes.[1]

This description is very characteristic of the composer, for it contains in a compressed form the most important impulses of his own creative life. Poetry and rhythm were what he wished his music to communicate because, as we have seen, with him the process of composition resembled versification ('at the present moment I am busy with serial versification'). Expressiveness, eloquence of gesture – this was the 'speaking gesture' whose outline is so clearly drawn in his works. Significant too is the repetition of the word 'rhythm', the organising element in Stravinsky's music.

Visual images are of the first importance in all these definitions, and this was not by chance. We have already quoted his remark about visual impressions having inspired him with musical ideas on countless occasions. He was in fact an astonishingly sharp observer, and it is significant that many of his earliest childhood memories were visual – the village where he used to spend the summer . . . 'a huge peasant sitting on the end of a log and dressed simply in a red shirt. His naked legs covered with red hair, no sign of white, though he was an old man'. That Stravinsky, being before all else a musician, should remember the sounds made by this blind old man is entirely understandable; but these visual details reveal a visual memory, the memory of an artist, and a long memory too.

114

There are a number of interesting things of this kind in the conversations with Robert Craft – freely drawn, precise caricatures of people whom he had seen decades earlier. Thus he remembered Vsevolozhsky, director of the Maryinsky, wearing a square monocle and odd triangular pince-nez, and Felia Litvinne who had an unusually small mouth for a singer. When Gide spoke, only his lips and mouth moved: his body and the rest of his face remained motionless. Debussy's daughter Chouchou had exactly the same teeth as her father, like fangs; and Franz Werfel had 'large, lucid, magnetic eyes . . . indeed the most beautiful I had ever seen'. After more than half a century he remembered exactly the yellow of Petersburg buildings, and the precise differences between oil and gas lighting. He could draw from memory an almost perfect plan of the apartment in which he spent his childhood. He remembered the whitish-golden colour of Rybinsk, like the sets of Rimsky-Korsakov's *Tsar Saltan*, the blue-and-gold churches and yellow government buildings at Yaroslavl, and the white gloves in which Napravnik conducted. He remembered the horses which drew Nicholas the Second's carriage and the black horses in the Paris première of *Firebird*. He remembered the sets of many productions, including the beeswax yellow and the black costumes of *Les Noces*, and could sketch those of *Pulcinella*, the curtain and the Devil's costume in *The Soldier's Tale* and many other things of the same kind.[1a]

Diaghilev introduced Stravinsky to a number of artists, chief among them Valentin Serov, whom Stravinsky greatly admired, Alexandre Benois, Golovin, Roerich, Bakst, Larionov, Goncharova. These were all great names and famous artists who played a part in producing the great spectacles organised by Diaghilev for his 'Ballets Russes'. Golovin was responsible for the sets and Bakst for the costumes of *Firebird*, Benois for *Petrushka*, Roerich for *The Rite of Spring*, Benois for *The Nightingale*, Larionov for *Renard*, Goncharova for *Les Noces*, Benois for *The Fairy's Kiss*.[2] Other artists with whom Stravinsky was on close and friendly terms for many years were Picasso, René Auberjonois, Giacometti and the Russian-born Marc Chagall, Eugene Berman, André Barsak, Leopold Survage, Nikolai Remizov and Pavel Chelitchev. Nor was it simply a matter of personal ties with artists: Stravinsky himself was an excellent draughtsman and his elder son, Theodore, is a professional artist and a pupil of Braque's.

It would be no exaggeration to say that Stravinsky's interest in painting was lifelong. He began to be attracted by painting in the nineties, when he was still a boy, possibly under the influence of his father, who was an artist as well as a remarkable singer. Benois, recalling his first meeting with the young Stravinsky, observed that 'Unlike the majority of musicians, who are completely indifferent to everything outside their own sphere, Stravinsky was deeply interested in painting, architecture and sculpture.' In his Los Angeles house, according to Robert Craft, two-thirds of the library of several thousand books were devoted to the visual arts. When he was on tour, Stravinsky would often make long journeys to see a favourite picture or building, and he continued to do this right into old age. It was a real passion of his and something that he was anxious to understand thoroughly, maintaining that 'of all our organs the sense of sight is most closely connected with the intellect'.

If we bear this in mind, we shall hardly find it surprising that visual impressions of movement, line and pattern so frequently 'suggested' musical ideas to Stravinsky. He has indeed himself given us a number of examples, including his account of the origins of *Petrushka* and *The Rite of Spring*, both visual images that occurred to him suddenly, pictures inspired by the dynamic movement of dancing. These surely provide undeniable evidence of the primacy of his visual imagination, whereas he never on any occasion speaks of literary images playing any part in his ideas or in the actual process of composition. He was in fact a declared enemy of all literary influence in music, and in this, as in many other ways, he was the exact opposite of Schoenberg, whose early *Verklärte Nacht* and *Pelleas und Melisande* are permeated with literary associations. Even the seventy odd pictures that Schoenberg left are thoroughly literary in character.

It is also significant that one of the few works in which the events of the war find some reflection – the *Symphony in Three Movements* – was inspired not so much by the scenes of Nazi brutality that he had witnessed while on a visit to Munich in 1932 as by much later visual impressions obtained from films. What is still more striking is the fact that a work of visual art should have prompted an opera, as Stravinsky tells us: 'Hogarth's "Rake's Progress" pictures, which I saw in 1947 on a chance visit to the Chicago Art Institute, immediately suggested a series of operatic scenes to me.'[3]

Once again we have a case of an instantaneous reaction to visual impressions. Later, even the intervals in a series presented themselves to him as something material, as though invested like tangible objects with a visible, palpable covering.

Is not this the reason for Stravinsky's long affection for the ballet, with its 'graphic' purity of movement, and especially for classical ballet? – for his interest in rhythmic accentuation, which translates the gestures of mime, becoming thereby a 'speaking geature'? Does it not explain what Asafiev calls the 'muscular-motor' energy of Stravinsky's music, which is founded on the resourceful accentual variation of a motif – the feature which he explored with such insistence in the years immediately after the First World War, and with such perfect mastery in *Les Noces*? It was this kinaesthetic interconnection between exterior and interior motion, between muscular action and feeling, that Stravinsky had in mind when he refused to trust people who listen to music with their eyes closed ('what they are actually doing is abandoning themselves to the rêveries induced by the lullaby and its sounds'). He was convinced that a performer's movements actually assist the listener's perception of the music. This is such an important article in his aesthetic creed that I must quote his own words:

I have always had a horror of listening to music with my eyes shut, with nothing for them to do. The sight of the gestures and movements of the various parts of the body producing the music is fundamentally necessary if it is to be grasped in all its fullness. All music created or composed demands some exteriorisation for the perception of the listener. In other words, it must have an intermediary, an executant . . . Why not follow with the eye such movements as those of the drummer, the violinist or the trombonist, which facilitate one's auditory perceptions?[4]

From this it is possible to construct a formula which contains a profound meaning for Stravinsky: music arises from bodily movement, from gesture. These motor sensations were an important creative stimulus in his case and this was a reason for his liking to compose at the piano. 'Fingers are not to be despised: they are great inspirers, and, in contact with a musical instrument, often give birth to subconscious ideas which might otherwise never come to life.' Our formula remains valid even if we invert it and say that Stravinsky's music is associated with gesture and evokes the idea of movement, because it is governed by the energy of a motor impulse. In fact this is a specific characteristic of Stravinsky's music.

At the same time he did not accept what is called 'painting in sound'. For him this was a belittling, a profanation of the possibilities immanent in music. It would be a poor thing if music were reduced to such a purpose – music should be loved for its own sake and should not seek to incorporate in sound 'the forms of Nature and the fantastic'. He was hostile to all forms of description or illustration in music, disapproving of the Russian Nationalist composers, for instance, because he thought them too inclined to picturesque illustration, and for the same reason rejecting Berlioz, Wagner and Richard Strauss. In short, he was a violent opponent of all so-called programme-music and could therefore hardly share Debussy's belief that piano preludes can communicate such notions as a *cathédrale engloutie* or a *fille aux cheveux de lin*.

How did these views of Stravinsky's manifest themselves in his music?

A static object cannot be described or painted in sounds: but when that object is set in motion, music can by analogy reproduce the character of that movement – its tempo (a measurement of pace), its rhythm (a mode of periodicity), its amplitude (a degree of intensity) and so forth. In this way a visual is transformed into a musical image. Hence it is not with the illustration of an object as such that Stravinsky is concerned in his music but with the nature (tempo, rhythm, dynamic amplitude) of that object's movement. It is therefore easy to understand why different forms of motoric energy – and particularly the clearest manifestations of these, namely the dance – occupy such a significant place in determining Stravinsky's musical forms. The origin of every ritual lay, as he believed, in the dance, which was also the origin of the symphony. All ritual, as we know, is based on the same principle as 'play', and this element is powerfully expressed in dancing. Thus in Stravinsky's music the visual-element and the play-element form an indivisible unity. In the same way we can understand how essential he felt it to be to catch exactly the character of musical movement, the definition of which corresponds most precisely to that of the French word *mouvement*. This he emphasised in the titles of two of his later works: *Symphony in Three Movements* (a sense lost in English) and *Movements for piano and orchestra*. That is why he never tires of insisting that the relation between a musical idea and its tempo are for him a primary problem of musical order, and that he cannot compose until he has found the right tempo for his ideas. 'Any musical composition must necessarily possess its unique tempo (pulsation) . . . A piece of mine can survive almost anything but wrong or uncertain tempo.'[5] It was this that he always demanded of conductors, with whom he found fault for failing to interpret correctly the character of the 'movement', not only in his own works but in those of Mozart and Beethoven. He even introduced a special term of his own, 'rhythmic diction', to denote the articulation or 'pronunciation' of rhythmic structures. Rhythm, he believed, was the chief problem in the performance of new music. No other twentieth-century composer can be compared with Stravinsky in the virtuoso elaboration of different types and species of movement; and it was the intensity of his visual impressions, his artistic sharp-sightedness, that helped him to capture the fine gradations of such movements in actual life and to transform them into musical shapes. Movement, however, does not unfold in an abstract continuum, but in time; and this brings us to another difficult problem.

The scientific study of art at the present time has introduced a new concept, that of 'artistic time'. This is distinct from both 'everyday' (or psychological) and from objective (or physical) time. It is used specifically of the tempo and phase-correlations in the development of all the processes involved in the artistic system or the artistic production concerned. Scholars of literature and of art both use the term, borrowed from painting; but its clearest application is to music, which is by its very nature a 'temporal' art.

We must first consider temporal processes in general. All temporal relationships are defined by the contrasts suggested by 'earlier–later', 'before–after'. The temporal intervals that separate 'before' from 'after' are organised by rhythm, and it is to rhythm that we owe our ideas of regularity and periodicity of movement, its structure in fact. Thus rhythm reflects a definite order in time and registers the alternating phases of that movement. This is not, however, simply an ordered uniformity – the essence of rhythm is dynamic, that is to say the increase or decrease of temporal intervals and also the measure of the speed at which the rhythmic processes occur; and it is this that establishes the tempo of a movement.

Each historical period, each historical style develops its own characteristic norms of rhythm and tempo in the 'artistic time' of its music. These norms produce definite structures within the process of duration, the arrangement of alternating phases, the measure of a movement's pace. Thus, for example, the structures of the solo concerto and the symphony, which took shape towards the middle of the eighteenth century, had pre-determined temporal limits – 12 to 15 minutes for a concerto and 20 minutes for a symphony, according to the theories of Mattheson and Quantz. The Romantics, belonging to a different period, represent a different historical style. With their characteristic polarisation of artistic ideals they both compressed the temporal limits of a work to miniature proportions, in order to establish the artistic 'moment', while at the same time hugely expanding these limits in order to obtain disproportionate formal contrasts, as in Mahler's symphonies, which resemble novels.

I have not been able to give more than a few historical examples of the treatment of 'artistic time' in music, and it is a subject that has not yet been fully explored scientifically, despite its importance. There are of course different approaches to the problem and these depend not only on the historical period but, in the case of major composers, on individual character. The essential nature of these processes relating to time remains the same, unchanged despite superficial variation; and this is an ontological premiss of both music and the visual arts. It was this that Rilke had in mind when he defined music metaphorically as 'time standing vertically to the heart's beat'. Thomas Mann asked the same question in *The Magic Mountain*: 'What is time? Something disembodied and omnipotent – a mystery, an indispensable condition of the world of appearances, a movement inextricably connected and blended with the existence of bodies in space and their motion.'[6] Mann often returned to these questions about the nature of music which, he says, can give to a certain space of time maximum saturation, fullness and extension. The 'artistic time' of music is 'an aperture in human, terrestrial time, into which music is poured in order to elevate and ennoble it indescribably'. Lévy-Strauss expresses himself even more precisely, calling music, like myth, 'an instrument for the abolition of time in the objective, physical sense, because music organises the listener's subjective, psychological time by means of tempo and dynamics, by the repetitions and parallelisms in its development'. These observations of Lévy-Strauss are important because they chime in some ways with Stravinsky's views. According to him both music and myth need time, but only in order to refute it. Beyond the plane of sounds and rhythms music acts on the waste-land of the listener's physiological time. This time is absolutely 'diachronic', i.e. it does not synchronise with psychological, subjective time, because it is irreversible. Music converts the space of time spent in listening to it into a synchronous self-enclosed unit. Listening to a musical composition arrests the flow of time by virtue of the interior organisation of that composition. Like a veil fluttering in the wind, it both covers and curtails that flow. It is only listening to music, and only at the time when we are actually engaged in listening, that we come close to something like 'immortality'.

Compare this with Stravinsky's theoretical generalisations in *Chronicle*:

Music is the only region in which man realises the present. The imperfection of his nature is such that he is doomed to experience in himself the flow of time, perceiving it in the categories of past and future and never being in a position to feel it as something real, and consequently a stable 'present'. The phenomenon of music was given us uniquely in order to introduce order into all that exists, including especially the relationship between man and time.

In his attempt to establish a resultant balance in this connection, Stravinsky distinguished two fundamentally different approaches to the time-flow. The first seeks uniform regulation, while the second is, as it were, an attempt to destroy the time-flow by the compression represented by climaxes, by incessant interruptions in character of movement, by alternating *accelerando* with *ritardando* and so forth. This second form of music, super-saturated with emotions and psychological factors, was alien to Stravinsky, who maintained that the first approach corresponds more truly to the purpose of music as such. In this a definite order in the development of the rhythm and tempo of movement is consistently maintained, and according to him this is the 'classical', the other the 'Romantic' approach. In the terminology of Pierre Souvchinsky,[7] with whose views on this matter Stravinsky identified himself, 'classical' music is 'chronometric' (i.e. the expression of *chronos* – time) and Romantic music is 'chronoametric' (i.e. the violation of order in time).

This is not in fact a new distinction, although its interpretation may be new. Nietzsche had contrasted two types of musical movement, *Zeit-und-Affekt-Rhythmik*, meaning respectively the ordered succession in time of rhythmic waves (*Zeitwechselswelle*) and the succession of rhythmic waves dictated by the emotions expressed in them (*Stärkewechselwelle*). The first of these he called 'Apollonian' and the second 'Dionysian'. Souvchinsky's classification, which Stravinsky accepted, was not uninfluenced by Bergson but was nevertheless individual in a number of ways. Souvchinsky's 'chronometric' music is more static and analytical, while his 'chronoametric' music is dynamic and based on a continually developing flow. Stravinsky naturally felt himself nearer to the first of the two types, and it is from this point of view that we should consider Souvchinsky's classification rather than from that of the objective critic.

Characteristically Stravinsky admitted that he found it painful to listen to music in which 'the events unfold at a tempo radically different from that of my own music', and he quoted the slow movement of Bruckner's Eighth Symphony as 'too slow for my temperament, while Schoenberg's *Erwartung* is too fast'. This really means that he felt the time-correlations and the measure of duration of the rhythmic processes as retarded (unnaturally slow) in Bruckner and accelerated (unnaturally fast) in Schoenberg. He got bored turning over the pages of Bruckner's score, while he could not turn the pages of Schoenberg's fast enough. In fact, listening to either of these two works, he was like an infantry-man who cannot keep in step with the rest of the column.

Stravinsky asserts a unity within a multiplicity of variants – instead of what he considered the Romantic principle of antithetical contrasts; this means logically replacing contrast by analogy, constructing with 'parallelisms' depending on identity and repetition. His ideal was what he called *calme dynamique*, and I should call 'unstable stability', as opposed to Schoenberg's ideal which might equally be described as 'stable instability'.

In *Conversations*[8] he attempted to explain by a diagram what he meant by this 'dynamic calm', and the diagram is instructive because it reveals how he imagined his own music visually, with his 'inner eye'. It is chiefly distinguished by parallel lines ('constructing with parallelisms') interrupted in places ('stammering') and with sudden upward strokes ('I am naturally explosive by temperament') and white circles marking strong points ('the intervals in my series incline to tonality . . . and this to a certain degree means that I compose tonally'). The bottom line of the diagram, running parallel to the top line, is an essential feature ('my musical thinking is always concentrated round the bass'). If we compare this diagram with Stravinsky's self-characterisations quoted above, it acquires a definite meaning, for all its schematic character. To continue the analogy, it is possible to visualise his music as developing on flat planes, but with breaks and jerks in the movement. At the same time different planes, each with its own level of development, merge into each other, forming 'volumes' of sonorities.

In speaking of musical structure, and following Stravinsky himself, we have involuntarily found ourselves using a spatial imagery of planes, volumes, parallel lines and their intersection. This is only logical, since movement takes place not only in time but in space. The realisation of spatial conceptions in music presents another complicated problem that we must now consider.

10

>-

Space

Time and space are inseparable categories. As G. Orlov has correctly observed, 'Nothing, either in the world of physical objects or in the world of subjective ideas, exists in space without existing also in time or in time without also existing in space.' Working from this indisputable premiss, scholars today speak of 'perceptual time' (the sense of time) as applied to the visual arts and 'perceptual space' as applied to music. Jozsef Uifaldussy says more precisely that 'musical space is possible, potential space, and time in the visual arts is possible, potential time'.

A number of different writers have discussed the application of spatial conceptions to music.[1] The role played by spatial factors not only in listening, but also in composing music has been pointed out – 'the succession of sonorities being perceived as *movement*, a transference to an imagined spatial plane, dynamic levels are then perceived as shifting planes of sonorous *perspective*, or correlatives in a vertical dimension'. It has also been pointed out that in imagining the process of music, which in fact takes place in time, we mentally divide it up in spatial terms. The generally accepted theoretical analysis of music rests in fact on analogies and metaphors of this kind, so does much of the terminology of music; as for instance when in speaking of music scientifically we use the expression 'sonorous space' (*Klangraum*).

These and similar considerations are fruitful, because they deepen our understanding of the ontological characteristics of music, of its expressive potentialities and the areas of its psycho-physiological action. Hitherto the historical method has not been applied to the study of this problem. The significance of spatial factors in music is beyond question, but what has been their semantic function in the different historical stages of musical evolution? The idea of 'artistic time', of speed, of duration and concentration as applied to 'events' in the musical process – all these are different in different historical epochs. 'Perceptual space' also changes according to differences in style between one composition and another, as we have already mentioned. What we must now ask ourselves is whether it is possible to discover any direct mutual interdependence in these matters. What is certainly true is that, with the modifications of general musical practice determining the artist's methods of modelling reality, the function of spatial ideas in music also changes: these ideas have a new qualitative content and evoke a new layer of associations.

In order to confirm this let us first turn to the Baroque period. Baroque composers, basing themselves on the artistic experience of their predecessors, elaborated a musical symbolism of their own, founded on the suggestion, by association, of external movements – rising and falling, upward and downward pull etc. An imagery of this kind based on spatial conceptions is universal in the music of J. S. Bach. When we listen to his music much of the sense of his imagery eludes us, because Bach's contemporaries took it for granted that any reference in the text to 'rising' or 'going upwards' would be reflected by an upward movement, just as any reference to the Fall of Man would mean a downward movement in the melodic line etc.[2] Furthermore, these spatial associations were used to express Bach's spiritual view of the world – hence the similarity between the musical imagery used to express night, darkness, shadows, depth or 'the pit' and feelings of suffering, grief and pain, or at the other extreme the associations of joy, peace, triumph with height or the sky. This naively rationalistic use of spatial imagery is combined in Bach's music with a concrete-objective conception of these images repeatedly asserted in his instrumental as well as his vocal music.

Now let us take a quite different example – Claude Debussy. Bach followed the fashion of his day in understanding space in a spiritual sense, and this changed completely when nineteenth-century Romanticism aroused an interest in description and illustration. The sensory now replaced the spiritual, and spatial–sonorous effects began to be employed not as symbols of something represented but as actual likenesses, perceptible analogies with visual sensations.

Debussy was a master of the out-of-doors, and he explored the possibilities of communicating in music different planes of breadth and depth, nearness and distance, tension and relaxation. Many nineteenth-century composers had produced 'scenes from nature', of course, from Beethoven and Berlioz to Wagner and Rimsky-Korsakov. It has often been pointed out, as an important feature, that Debussy introduced fine shades of chiaroscuro into his out-of-door scenes, and these have been compared to similar features in Impressionist painting. This, however, is only part of Debussy's contribution to the renaissance in twentieth-century music. The roots of his innovations lie deeper.

In the years between 1890 and 1910, when Debussy was at the height of his powers as a composer, European artists were discovering, or rediscovering, the graphic arts of non-European peoples and earlier ages – Japanese painting and African sculpture, and Russo-Byzantine ikon-painting. These non-European arts deeply impressed the imagination of artists by their conventional treatment of artistic space, conventions quite unfamiliar to nineteenth-century artists: and these provided an important stimulus to Van Gogh, Gauguin and Picasso in their search for a new style. Each had his own interpretation, and it was Japanese prints and Russian ikons that particularly struck Debussy's imagination. In the early years of the present century a number of discoveries were made in the realm of physics, such as Einstein's theory of relativity and quantum mechanics; and these often refuted hitherto received opinions about the space–time continuum. Such discoveries proved to be the beginning of a scientific–technical revolution on a huge scale, and they forced artists, too, to review their relationship to the world of physical appearances.[3]

We must take into account this whole complex of new ideas if we are to understand and estimate the growing importance of spatial phenomena in Debussy's music. His out-of-door effects are fundamentally different from those of his immediate predecessors, Wagner and Rimsky-Korsakov. Spatial effects in Debussy's music are obtained not by purely imitative, illustrative means but by the juxtaposition and confrontation of different planes and volumes of sonority. He links together different dynamics and textures in vertical layers, and these evoke an association with nearness and distance, with the extension and the volume of the object portrayed, while at the same time its other planes 'appear'. The same effect is achieved by the alternating functions of line and background – at one moment the melodic line occupies the more important role, at the next it merges into the background, thus producing a sensation of breadth and depth. In the same way sensations of tension and relaxation are emphasised by thickness or thinness of texture and the juxtaposition of registers, timbres etc.

Among Debussy's younger contemporaries none came so near to him in understanding this new handling of 'perceptual space' as Stravinsky. Other composers adopted Debussy's modal system, his harmonic structures and his orchestral colours, but Stravinsky was chiefly attracted, it seems to me, by the spatial character of his music. He guessed the secret of Debussy's achievements in this field and further developed the principles underlying them: what Debussy felt intuitively, Stravinsky elaborated consciously and with conviction. This seemed to be his vocation; for unlike Debussy, whose personal inclinations were towards the Symbolist poets rather than the Impressionist painters, Stravinsky possessed the clear vision of the visual artist, as we have seen, and his interest in contemporary painting and his creative contacts with contemporary painters continued for many years.

In his article 'What I wished to express in *The Rite of Spring*' (1913) he wrote that 'the material of music is growing, swelling, expanding. Each instrument in this work is like a bud on the bark of an ancient trunk.'[4] This visual imagery of a bud growing, swelling, expanding on the bark of a tree-trunk is very characteristic of the composer, who was antagonistic to all 'tone-painting' in music and rejected illustration because he thought either in terms of sonorous volume or, if he thought in terms of line, in geometrical figures. This explains the frequency in his writings about music of such terms as the 'distribution' of musical material or the 'expansion' or 'filling' of sonorous space.

Not long before he published this article, in the summer of 1912, Stravinsky began the composition of the *Three Japanese Lyrics* for voice and chamber ensemble, which he finished in January 1913.

What he says in *Chronicle* about this work is so significant that I shall quote it in full:

While putting the finishing touches to the orchestration of the *Sacre*, I was busy with another composition which was very close to my heart. In the summer I had read a little anthology of Japanese lyrics – short poems of a few lines each, selected from the old poets. The impression which they made on me was exactly like that made by Japanese paintings and engravings. *The graphic solution of problems of perspective and space shown by their art incited me to find something analogous in music* . . . I gave myself up to the task, and succeeded by a metrical and rhythmical process too complex to be explained here.[5]

In the sentence which I have italicised Stravinsky alludes to his interest in problems of perspective and space. In his *Three Japanese Lyrics* he solved these by the varying accentuation of the tonic stress in the vocal line, which forestalls the accompaniment by roughly a quarter of a bar, thus creating an original two-tiered effect in establishing the sonorous perspective. We need go into no further detail, as the importance lies in the composer's own observation.

He spoke in greater detail on this subject in the essay published in connection with the first performance of the *Octet* in 1923 and already referred to (see p. 89). It will be remembered that in that article Stravinsky speaks of the 'fullness', 'weight', and 'volume' of different sonorities. These sonorities, he says, as they move through time, have a certain weight and occupy a definite place in space; and he speaks of a 'play of volumes', as an element on which the 'action of the musical text' of the *Octet* is based. But for the circumstance that the writer of this manifesto is in fact a musician, we might well suppose that it is a Cubist painter speaking.

There is in fact a striking similarity to the theories and, indeed, to the pictures of the Cubist painters. They too assumed that volumes are created by the combination of different planes, and a two-dimensional canvas could thus aim at suggesting the idea of three-dimensional space. The object is seen, as it were, in different foreshortenings simultaneously. Cubism was, in fact, a stage in the development of many artists, including its one-time protagonist Picasso; and even in his late, post-Cubist portraits we find the 'voluminous' piling-up of planes 'the combination of full-face and profile – a simplified profile outline cutting across a full-face portrait or, vice versa, a profile in which the eyes and mouth are shown full-face . . . an asymmetrical displacement of features'.[6] It is interesting that Paul Klee, who had a number of contacts with Cubism, spoke of his pictures as 'polyphonic', of the presence in them of a multi-dimensional simultaneity (*mehrdimensionale Gleichzeitigkeit*). We can hardly be surprised therefore that Stravinsky's music has often been called 'Cubistic'.

Like all analogies between the different arts, this is of course no more than approximate. Moreover, Stravinsky's style changed, and the parallels with Cubism to be found in the works which he wrote between 1910 and the early 1920's cannot be pressed when examining his later works. If Picasso's work continued to show traces of his early Cubism, the same may be said of Stravinsky, whose music continued to show an affinity with Cubism in the multiplicity of its planes and angles of vision. Before examining this I should like to emphasise that the 'spatial' vocabulary used by the composer in his writing about *The Rite of Spring* and the *Octet* was later to prove an essential, one might almost say organic, feature of his personality, as any careful reader of his conversations with Craft must discover. I quote a handful of instances. In speaking of *Apollo Musagetes* Stravinsky says that this was 'my first attempt to compose a large-scale work in which contrasts of volume replace contrasts of instrumental colours'.[7] On another occasion he suggests replacing the traditional term 'harmony', which is no longer relevant when talking about contemporary music, by the word 'density'. And he uses similar language when speaking of Varèse: 'he was among the first composers to plot the intensities of a composition, the highs and lows in pitch, speed, density, rhythmic movement. As Webern is associated with small volumes, so Varese is identified with large ones.'[8]

For the painter, perspective is the very heart of composition – the reference-point establishing the horizon of his picture and determining the levels of his vision, the different planes on which objects are distributed and the relationships and proportions of those objects. Perspective has been an essential feature of European painting from the earliest times to the present day; but it has been treated differently at different periods. These changes have been discussed at length and in detail by modern art-historians, who distinguish two historical types of perspective – linear and reverse.

Linear is what we call 'normal' or 'real' perspective, the perspective which helps us to establish spatial dimensions. Imaginary lines are drawn, as in a geometrical figure, from each point of an object to our eye, and their intersection establishes the 'perspective'. They also intersect on the artist's two-dimensional canvas giving a life-like illusion of depth and volume. We commonly see our surroundings from a single, unmoving point, to which there corresponds a single vanishing-point lying on the horizon. But suppose this point to be not motionless but shifting, thus giving the object under observation a kind of rotatory movement, and the whole hierarchy of dimensions in what is depicted will then be destroyed – so that for example an object imagined in the background will appear larger than one in the foreground and concave will appear convex. In that case we shall have, instead of an illusion of similarity, a different, conventional, 'noumenal' reality. This is in fact what is called 'reverse' perspective, though the term is inexact. It was first introduced by O. Wulff,[9] and his supporters attempt to explain the deformation of objects seen in this perspective by the fact that the artist is looking as it were from the inside of the picture, as though he were behind it and on its 'reverse' side. It is difficult to imagine such a position, and D. Likhachev has pointed to another possible explanation of artists trying to destroy the illusion of the lifelike. 'There has quite simply never existed a picture composed throughout from a single viewpoint. In fact one part of the composition is always seen from one viewpoint, another part from another.'[10] It is not, of course, simply a question of terminology but connected with the characteristics of a definite artistic method. B. Uspensky explains it thus:

The system of reverse perspective arises from the viewer's (i.e. the artist's) adopting a number of different positions. That is to say, it is connected with the dynamic of the viewer's gaze and consequent total impression obtained ... In this total view the dynamic of the viewer's position is transferred to the representation, with the result that deformations arise that belong specifically to the forms of reverse perspective ... Thus the opposition between linear and reverse perspective can be connected with either the immobility or, on the other hand, with the dynamism of the viewer's position.[11]

The formulation proposed by P. A. Florensky gives a precise and laconic definition of the differences of these two 'systems'. 'Linear perspective', he says, 'is unicentral, reverse perspective is multi-central.'[12]

Linear perspective has been understood for centuries and the ancient Greeks, for example, used it in their decorative designs.

Mediaeval art (including that of the Russian ikon-painters), on the other hand, was based entirely on reverse perspective. The influence of the decorative forms used in the mystery-plays probably played a part in Giotto's use of linear perspective, which was finally adopted by the artists of the Renaissance, although Raphael, El Greco, Veronese, Rubens, Dürer and other artists of the fifteenth and early sixteenth centuries on occasion rejected it. It was the nineteenth century that established the primacy of linear perspective, while our own century is again trying to destroy that primacy. According to L. Zhegin there have been three historical phases in the treatment of spatial depth in a picture:

1. the conventional 'flat' treatment which we find from the earliest times up to the Middle Ages, when a turning point occurred in the middle of the fifteenth century
2. the treatment of comparatively great depth in space (seventeenth and eighteenth centuries)
3. the treatment of unlimited depth (nineteenth century).[13]

To this I should add for my own part that the return to the comparatively 'flat' handling of space began with Gauguin and Matisse and has since become more marked.

One further essential point is made by Uspensky (p. 193). Like linear, so-called reverse perspective is a conventional system of conveying the spatial characteristics of the real world on a flat surface. The choice between methods of distortion is a matter of convention, but the presence of distortion of one kind or another is unavoidable.

'Deformation' of this kind, that is to say some deviation from the 'normal', can be seen not only in the relationship between the levels of a horizon and the proportions of the objects represented, but also in the lighting of a picture. This, too, is regulated by accepted rules, since the outlines of distant objects appear less distinct and less brightly coloured compared with those of objects nearer to the spectator. In reverse perspective these rules are not observed, but Rembrandt did not always observe them either, often surreptitiously modifying the position of the light-source in his pictures and thus producing further evidence of the relative, conventional character of linear perspective.

The reader may well ask what all this has to do with music. Direct parallels drawn between arts so different in their matter as painting and music are always open to question. Parallels in this case however are legitimate because 'the ear is the organ by which we actually perceive space' and it is therefore permissible, when speaking of music, to touch on problems analogous to those of spatial dimensions in painting, namely perspective. Can we, however, use the term 'perspective' when speaking of sound? Is there such a thing as 'sonorous perspective'?

It is by sensory analogy that we can see most clearly how close music and painting lie to one another. Like the eye, the ear is aware of spatial gradations – of 'nearer' and 'farther'. According to its intensity ('loudness'), an individual sound or complex of sounds is felt to be closer or further away. Composers have made great use of this fact in representing a concrete 'object' thought of as moving. Obvious instances are 'Bydlo' from Mussorgsky's *Pictures from an Exhibition* and 'In the hall of the Mountain King' from Grieg's *Peer Gynt* music. There are a host of instances in operatic and orchestral music – the Soldiers' Marches in Gounod's *Faust* and in Berg's *Wozzeck*, Berlioz's use of the Rakoczy March in the *Damnation of Faust*, the march-episode in Debussy's *Fêtes*. In each of these cases – and there are hundreds of others – it is not the object itself that concerns the composer so much as the fact of its being in motion, something which music is most fitted to convey, as we have seen in an earlier chapter.

The list of such things is endless, and music is full of 'representations' of pursuits, galloping horses, battle-sounds coming nearer and then retreating, storms, hurricanes, rough seas and so forth. Obvious examples of objects moving towards the listener are Honegger's *Pacific 231* and the finale of his Third Symphony, the development section in the first movement of Shostakovich's Seventh Symphony and the Scherzo of his Eighth. Ravel's *Bolero* is another, though in this case the 'object' does not move and it is only the latent energy inherent in it that expands into the final, as it were frontal, modulation to E major. The modulation from E flat to A major at the end of the variations in the development section of the first movement of Shostakovich's Seventh Symphony is equally abrupt; and these 'turning-points' are designed to give an additional force to what is being 'represented', which is moving towards us and suddenly seems to be approaching us from another angle.

The effect in music is the same whether the composer is concerned with the objective realities of the external world – the movements of a crowd, say, or of an engine such as *Pacific 231* – or the mounting flood of interior emotion, a 'storm' in the individual rather than in the natural world. In each case it is spatial categories that are involved – a 'mounting' or 'growth', which we experience as a movement towards us.

Space

The sensation of space is obtained in music by degrees of loudness or by contrasting different dynamic planes. But distance – 'nearer' and 'farther' – is also established in music by the character of the sonority concerned, its density or thinness; and these depend before all else on the juxtaposition of different sound-complexes, whether monophonic or polyphonic. This method was quite familiar to the old masters. Couplings on the lower manual of harpsichord or organ were contrasted with the more refined sonorities of the upper manual, on the principle of solo and tutti. And indeed these possibilities are in fact familiar to all musicians – an open fifth, for instance, compared with a full chord sounded at the same dynamic level, seems not only 'emptier' but also more distant – the 'weight' of the mass of different sounds tells. On the other hand, 'weight' may be defined by timbre and pitch, so that in isolation a flute playing forte in a high register sounds 'further away' than a tuba playing a low note at the same dynamic level. The dramatic orchestration of the ragamuffins' chorus in Act 1 of *Carmen* is founded on this fact. Bizet's dynamic markings, which range from *ppp* to *ff*, emphasise the effect, and in the orchestra we hear first two piccolos, then the strings and finally the brass. The sense of distance or extended, prolonged space, can also be created by the juxtaposition of extreme and middle registers, forming different planes in a vertical sense – spare or concentrated, according to the size of the intervals forming the chord. Finally, there is often a 'colour' effect in the relationship 'nearer–farther': an open fifth is more 'transparent' than a thick chord, just as the flute is more 'transparent' than the tuba. It is significant, too, that colours appear fainter at a distance than close to, and this is why, at the beginning of the march in *Wozzeck*, Berg uses the hollow sounds of the lower bass instruments. Bizet's instrumentation of the ragamuffins' chorus is more symbolical (flutes are not clearly distinguishable at a distance!) whereas Berg is more logical in creating the illusion of real life. Berlioz's use of muted timpani in the *Scène aux champs* to suggest distant thunder provides an analogous instance. In the same way an aerial perspective can be created by music, and this was in fact an effect that Debussy excelled in producing.

These are some of the analogies that present themselves if we compare visual and auditory perspective on the basis of our sensory experience. Analogies can be continued in the field of construction also, but there they are of a more speculative character and must therefore be drawn with great care. If, for instance, we take the vanishing point as equivalent to the tonic or basic tonality of a work, from which all the 'rays' originate, penetrating the form of the whole or at least of a section, we must then allow 'sonorous' or auditory perspective an organising significance analogous to geometrical perspective in painting – and in fact gravitation, the 'pull' that exists between sounds, does indeed provide the chief coordinate in the system of expressive means at the composer's disposal. By gravitation we mean the different principles of musical organisation – the modal, tonal, modulatory, harmonic etc. In the broader sense all music, even so-called 'atonal' music, is in some sense 'tonal', though the function of the tonic may be assigned to some definite sonorous complex or parameter – pitch or dynamics, timbre or register etc.

Paul Hindemith interprets the idea of tonality in a more restricted sense. For him the sensation of spatial depth, or 'sound-perspective', is obtained by the distance from, or the return to, a basic tonal point; and he goes on to compare the 'harmonic pulls to the fundamental tone' to the force of the earth's gravity. He calls tonality 'the subtlest form of the earth's gravity', and contrasts 'the power of tonal gravitation' with atonal music which, he believes, causes in the listener a sensation not unlike that of vertigo or seasickness.[14] This appears to me more convincing, though the illusory, purely conventional proportions of perspective are not equivalent to the unambiguous physical reality of gravity, and the two can be only metaphorically equated. With respect to the pulls within tonality, therefore, it is advisable – if only for the sake of terminological accuracy – to compare them to the dimensions of the gravitational field rather than to perspective. Quite apart from questions of terminology, however, in studying the laws of musical construction, we shall find ourselves somehow abandoning any direct analogy with painting and laying greater stress on the category of time rather than that of space in our analysis of sound-relationships, though the two are in the last instance inseparable.

With this reservation, the overall climax of a musical work may be said, metaphorically, to resemble the vanishing-point to which the alternating tensions are directed as they rise and fall. A composition of this kind may be called 'unicentral': it is, as it were, conceived from a single viewpoint. Let us take a single example – a classical sonata movement. In itself, of course, the form has no real interest: the interest lies in the use the individual makes of it. There are nevertheless characteristics that are typical of the form and these constitute the 'ideal' sonata movement. If we examine these characteristics, we shall discover that the form is essentially unicentral. There is a relationship of a dialectical kind between the main and the subsidiary sections, which are regulated by tonal relationships assimilated in the recapitulation: and the main sections, with the repeat of the exposition and the caesura or formal break at the transition to the recapitulation, are marked by dynamic waves – these and other hallmarks of the classical sonata allegro reveal premisses analogous to those of the unicentral system in painting. These are complicated questions which demand considerably more theoretical development, and I have only been able to touch on them in passing. We must now return to Stravinsky, the exact nature of whose innovations prompted this short excursus.

Stravinsky followed a line initiated by his friend Souvchinsky in his attempt to distinguish two kinds of music – chronoametric (or 'Romantic') and chronometric: or, in Wölfflin's terminology, atectonic and tectonic. The first is characterised by alternate rising and falling, the second by ordered articulation: the first by contrast, the second by variations of a single identity: the first by a continuing process of development, the second by separate 'numbers'. We must here support what we have already said on this subject by some new considerations. The continuing process of development is now replaced in Stravinsky's work by the mutual relating of different planes and volumes; the single vanishing-point by a multiplicity of independent 'horizon-levels'; unicentral, object-centred composition by multicentral.

Stravinsky was not the only twentieth-century composer to enrich music by innovations of this kind, but, although he had a forerunner in Debussy, Stravinsky developed these innovations more consistently than other composers. It was at the end of the 1920's and the beginning of the 1930's that he made his discoveries of the spatial factors in music, and his note on the *Octet* served as a kind of manifesto. It was his new contact with the 'world classics' that intensified his researches in this field, and the works of his neoclassical period provide many evidences of these researches. Let us now examine each of the contrasts involved, beginning with the antithesis between 'continuous development' and closed 'numbers'. We have already observed in our analysis of his method of composing, and in his attitudes to the theatre, Stravinsky's opposition to the principles of development and are therefore better able to understand his hostility towards Wagner and the Wagnerian elements persisting in contemporary music. He often insisted on the necessity of replacing *unendliche Melodie*, or the 'continuous stream' of sounds, by 'discreet' order; the 'symphonisation' of opera and ballet by a return to self-contained 'numbers'; emotional self-expression by strict 'versification'; and in his polemical writings he even introduced the idea of 'anti-development'.

The principle of continuous development is based on the uninterrupted alternation and accumulation of dynamic waves, to which Stravinsky opposed the idea of layered or 'terraced' dynamics, replacing the smooth transitions of *crescendo* and *diminuendo* by the establishment of different dynamic planes comparable in some ways to the different horizon-levels in painting. As in the music of the Baroque, these interruptions in the dynamics of a work are determined by syntactic articulations, and they thus assume a formal significance.

Debussy's simultaneous linking of layers of different consistency does not resemble linear development so much as the relating of the planes forming the outlines of different masses. Stravinsky went further and shifted these outlines; and by these shiftings, breaks and interruptions he 'up-ended' the process of continuous development. Metaphorically speaking, he replaced the single viewpoint and the single, given position of the 'spectator' by the totality of impressions obtained from multiple points of vision. This can be seen most clearly in the rhythmic organisation of his music, in which the measurements and groupings of metrical counting often do not coincide with the length of the motif itself, whose accentuation varies. A complex rhythmic – or polyrhythmic – network is established, in which there appear different angles of varying measurement, or 'points of vision', whose multiplicity also makes itself felt in the failure of melodic structures to coincide with harmonic functions. This is particularly noticeable in his grotesque deformations of banal musical material. Discussing the Royal March in *The Soldier's Tale* Asafiev has pointed to 'the confusion, the zigzagging alternation, in the regular relationship between strong and weak beats in the bar'. There are similar zigzaggings in other areas of the music, including the relationship between melodic line and accompaniment.

It was Rudolf Reti who introduced the useful concept of a 'polyphony of groups', by which he meant a polyphony not of single lines, or 'voices', but of whole musical units living their own interior harmonic and contrapuntal life. He rightly observed that 'the polyphony of Schoenberg and his followers remains a polyphony of single lines, however much it may surpass previous methods of formation in relation to harmonic thinking and phrasing'.[15] On the other hand Reti failed to appreciate Stravinsky's part in the development of this 'polyphony of groups', giving Charles Ives the honour of being the first to use it. In fact Stravinsky can claim the honour of introducing into contemporary music the idea of 'collision', the deliberate use of 'non-coordination' resulting from the simultaneous combination of different layers in the texture of the music. Indeed this formed the link between his music and Cubist painting.

It was Stravinsky, too, who first recognized the problem of the 'density' of sounds as being one of capital importance, explaining that 'vertical construction' is the basis of all variation and permutation techniques. Indeed, the 'variation and permutation' of sound-masses is one of the specific traits of Stravinsky's individual style; and this brings us back to the contrast between unicentral and multicentral composition.

Many students of Stravinsky's music have commented on the synchronisation of the different elements of development. Robert Siohan, for instance, has compared the combination of different planes in *Les Noces* to the art of the Byzantine ikon painters 'to whom perspective was unknown'.

The composer himself has pointed to 'the simultaneous scraps of conversation without any connecting thread of discourse' in *Les Noces* and the resulting superimposition of individual words and even whole remarks. He also observes that 'although the bride and bridegroom are always on the stage, the guests can speak of them as though they were not there', and draws an analogy with the Japanese Kabuki theatre in which events are combined which in real life happen separately.[16] The events on the stage are, as it were, made applicable to the events in the music. Stravinsky constructed his musical forms by means of interlacings and correspondences, of rhythm and attack, creating 'arches' of sound and shifting, changing and varying them. His compositions owe their dynamic power to the relentless movement of blocks or masses of sonorities, and their static character to the complex intersection of these vaulted arches. The four scenes of *Les Noces*, for instance, are as it were bolted together by arches of this kind. In accordance with the marriage ritual there are clear correspondences between scenes 2 and 3, in which we see the ritual farewells first of the bridegroom and then of the bride. The action in the two scenes is parallel – blessing, invocation and farewell – and the same song is used ('Pod na svad'bu' – Down to the wedding). At the same time there are thematic connections with Scene 1 in the exchanges between the soloists, while Scene 4 sums up the whole occasion. The linking of the scenes is achieved by identity, repetition, by cross-references and parallelisms, all of which are features of Stravinsky's multicentral works and particularly noticeable in cyclic works belonging to mixed forms, whether these are designed for the theatre or the concert-hall.

Speaking of the creation of *Symphony of Psalms* Stravinsky wrote 'As in the case of my sonata, I wanted to create an organic whole without conforming to the various models adopted by custom, but still retaining the periodic order by which the *Symphony* is distinguished from the *Suite*, the latter being simply a succession of pieces varying in character.'[17] Stravinsky maintained that there could be no form without 'identity of some sort'. This becomes apparent in the composer's choice among the means of expression, a choice depending on the era in which he lives and his own personality. Stravinsky's own 'special kind of identity' is to be found first and foremost in rhythm, for in every one of his works the movement is organised and directed by rhythm. Other factors make their appearance at different times in his career – motivic construction, timbre, *facture*, euphony (in the Russian period), tonality (in the neo-classical years); and tonality, as the composer himself observed, plays an essential part in his scores for the ballet, because the language of the dance demands more or less precise cadences. In *Conversations* we find him giving a guarded answer to Craft's question as to whether he foresaw the possibility of abandoning this 'tonal identification': 'Possibly. We can still create a sense of return to exactly the same place without tonality: musical rhyme can accomplish the same thing as poetic rhyme. But form cannot exist without identity of some sort.'[18]

Identity appears in repetition – a repetition that is neither complete nor exact, in fact 'parallelism'. Thus we come to the important theoretical conclusion which Stravinsky formulated by saying that 'the composer must avoid symmetry, but he can construct in parallelisms'.

There is no absolute symmetry in nature, where there are always some deviations, however small, some insignificant infringements of the proportions. To be absolutely symmetrical, as the composer himself said, is to be absolutely dead. A. V. Shubnikov[19] has introduced the supplementary concept of 'dissymmetry' or 'asymmetrical symmetry', i.e. proportions in which there are partial infringements or confusions of styles, or kinds, of symmetry, e.g. a square in a circle.

Stravinsky himself quotes the mosaics of the *Last Judgment* at Torcello as an example of 'asymmetrical symmetry':

Their subject is division – division, moreover, into two halves suggesting equal halves. But in fact each is the other's complement, not its equal or its mirror, and the dividing-line itself is not a perfect perpendicular. On the one side skulls with, in the sockets, lightning-shaped snakes . . . and on the other Eternal Life . . . The sizes and proportions, movements and rests, darks and lights, of the two sides are always varied.[20]

This was his credo as an artist, and he remained faithful to it from the early works of his Russian period to the end of his life.

It will perhaps be as well to say a little more on this subject. Symmetry means commensurate proportions, and proportions were defined by Vitruvius as 'analogies'. An artistic structure is balanced by a clearly defined rhythmic system in the disposition of its proportions. Departures from precise symmetry are conditioned by these proportions being in a dynamic relationship to each other; and this is clearly what Stravinsky had in mind when he spoke of 'imperceptible parallelisms'.

Parallelism is of course a geometrical concept, supposing the variation and displacement of a single identity on different levels of perceptual space; and this concept corresponds exactly to the mutual relationship of planes and volumes in Stravinsky's music. If we bear this in mind, the following words of Stravinsky's will be easier to understand: 'Music is far closer to mathematics than to literature – not perhaps to mathematics itself, but certainly to something like mathematical thinking and mathematical relationships.'[21] It was in relationships of this kind that Stravinsky was dealing when he established difference within similarity, combined apparent opposites and introduced the principle of order into various forms of synchronicity and asynchronicity. This, in fact, is the fundamental meaning of unicentral composition.

An additional reason for the importance of dissymmetry and parallelism in Stravinsky's music lies in the fact that these served him as a means of checking the dynamic pressure. He had never thought it possible to cultivate dynamics for their own sake. We have only to recall his favourite expression of 'dynamic rest' to understand that a strong system of organic connections was one of the most important factors in assuring the precise regulation of the degrees of explosive power in his music. He instanced *Wozzeck* as representing the diametrical opposite of his own attitudes, pointing out that it was possible to convey passionate emotion by very different means, and within the most 'limiting' conventions.

The Timurid miniaturists, for example, were forbidden to portray facial expression. In one moving scene, from the life of an early Zoroastrian king, the artist shows a group of totally blank faces. The dramatic tension is in the way the ladies of the Court are shown eavesdropping and in the slightly discordant gesture of one of the principal figures. In another of these miniatures, two lovers confront each other with stony looks, but the man unconsciously touches his fingers to his lips, and this packs the picture with, for me, as much passion as the *crescendo molto* in *Wozzeck*.[22]

Stravinsky was eighty at the time of this conversation with Craft and he was regarding in what is in many ways a new light the course both of his own life and of contemporary art. His words have a profound meaning and convey the essence of his personality; and they also give us a glimpse of what concerned him during the last fifteen years of his life.

11

▶▶▶

'Torniamo all'antico . . .'[1]

Most writers discussing Stravinsky's final period devote their chief attention to his sudden, and at first sight inexplicable, adoption of serial methods of composition. This was all the more unexpected by contemporaries because for many years Stravinsky and Schoenberg were regarded as opposite extremes among composers, and with good reason, Schoenberg being the convinced champion of atonality and Stravinsky – especially in his neo-classical period – of a tonality which, though non-traditional, expanded and sophisticated, was still rooted in the diatonic system. An important consideration in assessing their fundamental aesthetic differences is the fact that throughout his creative career Schoenberg was a follower and a leading exponent of the Expressionist school, while Stravinsky remained for many years faithful to the ideal of neo-classicism. By the middle of the century they represented irreconcilable, mutually exclusive aesthetic attitudes, and this was in fact how they appeared to contemporaries.

There can be no doubt of the fascination exercised by Schoenberg's personality and opinions, and we find even a composer as remote from Schoenberg in musical character as Maurice Ravel writing of his 'great sympathy with the Schoenberg school . . . which is both Romantic and strict, Romantic because it is in opposition to what is old, and strict in its promulgation of new laws', and he adds 'I myself learned from Schoenberg when I wrote *Poèmes de Mallarmé* and *Chansons madécasses* which, like *Pierrot lunaire*, are based on very strict counterpoint.'[2] Bartók, too, acknowledged Schoenberg's influence in, as he says, the 'free and equal employment of each of the twelve notes of the chromatic scale, both vertically and horizontally'.[3]

Stravinsky never made any acknowledgments of this kind: 'In 1920 or 1921 I heard *Pierrot* in Paris, conducted by Darius Milhaud . . . After that, incredibly, I did not hear another note until the *Suite* op.29 in Venice in 1937, and the *Prelude to Genesis* in Hollywood in November, 1945.' Nor was he interested in the music of Schoenberg's pupils and associates Berg and Webern. He knew nothing of Webern's music until 1952 and 'had no recollection of meeting him' at dinner in Schoenberg's house in November 1912 after the première of *Pierrot lunaire*.[4] He may well have heard *Wozzeck* in Berlin about 1930, but he seems to have made no comment on it. (*Oedipus Rex* and *Wozzeck* are complete opposites, both in musical language and in musico-dramatic conception.) 'When I met Berg in Venice in September 1934, at the concert in which I conducted my *Capriccio* and Scherchen *Der Wein* . . . we did not mention an earlier meeting. Someone told me that after hearing the *Capriccio* Berg said he wished he could write such light-hearted music.' Coming from an Expressionist composer, this sounds condescending, ironical rather than laudatory.

For many years Stravinsky avoided mentioning Schoenberg's name. The reference to *Pierrot lunaire* in *Chronicle* is critical, in *Poetics of Music* cold but respectful. Was this simply the enmity of rivals in search of recognition? In Stravinsky's case it is impossible to speak of such a search: by the middle of the century he enjoyed a unique reputation among contemporary composers, whereas Schoenberg's music never in his lifetime attracted the attention of a large public, although it interested professional musicians and often aroused bitter controversy. The bitterness between the two camps was increased by the followers of each, who did much to widen the gulf between the two, very much as in the case of Wagner and Brahms, with Schoenberg adopting the same uncompromising attitude as Wagner and acknowledging no authority but his own.

Stravinsky was later to make a passing reference to the public cause of the quarrel: 'In 1925 Schoenberg wrote a very nasty verse about me (though I almost forgive him, for setting it to such a remarkable mirror canon).'[5] This was the text of the second of the *Three Satires* op.28 for mixed chorus, which is entitled *Vielseitigkeit*:

Ja, wer tommerlt denn da?	Who's that drumming away there?
das ist ja der kleine Modernsky!	why, it's little Modernsky!
hat sich ein Bubizopf schneiden lassen;	he's got himself a pigtail,
sieht ganz gut aus!	suits him quite well!
wie echt falsches Haar!	like real false hair!
wie eine Perücke,	like a wig,
ganz (wie sich der kleine Modernsky vorstellt)	just (as little Modernsky imagines)
ganz der Papa Bach!	just like old Bach.

This of course was only the pretext of the quarrel, and the real contradictions between the two men were more profound. The 'New Viennese School' and its followers accepted neither the 'folk-lore' nor the neo-classical elements in Stravinsky's music, as is very clear from the writings of the Schoenbergian musicologist Theodor Adorno; and it is small wonder therefore that the personal relations of Stravinsky and Schoenberg were catastrophically unsuccessful. They did not meet even in California when they lived only fifteen kilometres away from each other; and mutual friends or acquaintances, like Thomas Mann and Franz Werfel, were aware that one composer's name must not be mentioned in the other's presence. Stravinsky himself records[6]

When I came to Los Angeles in 1935, Klemperer and other mutual friends tried to bring us together, but only after 1948 did a meeting seem possible. I saw Schoenberg for the last time in 1949 . . . Two days after Schoenberg's death I happened to visit Mrs Mahler-Werfel's home and to see there Schoenberg's not-yet-dry death-mask.

The turning-point in Stravinsky's attitude to the music of the New Viennese School came at the beginning of the fifties, though possibly (according to Robert Craft) earlier when, in writing the Agnus Dei of the *Mass* he had the idea of using a 'series'.[7] Craft also tells us that when, after twelve years absence, Stravinsky returned to Europe for the first time in 1951 for the production of *The Rake's Progress*, he was impressed by discovering that a number of young, and indeed not-so-young, composers were using dodecaphonic methods, in Italy especially, where Luigi Dallapiccola had been a Stravinskian neo-classicist before the war. This visit to Europe took place between August and November, and it is worth noting the fact that it was immediately after Schoenberg's death, which occurred on July 13. Stravinsky visited Europe again during April and May, 1952 and it was at this time that he became acquainted with a number of

Webern's works. Craft specifies the Quartet op.22 which deeply impressed Stravinsky early in 1952.

The turning-point had been reached. In the composer's own hallowed phrase quoted by Craft, *'Rake's Progress* was the end of a trend.' There was an abrupt change in Stravinsky's stylistic manner: he wrote first the *Cantata* on old English texts (1951–2) and then the *Septet*, in which he experimented for the first time with the use of a series. From now onwards his whole attitude to the New Viennese School was different, and he was ready and anxious to talk at length on the subject.

What had in fact happened? Had Schoenberg's death had such a deep effect on him? Had he in fact wished to study dodecaphonic methods earlier and been embarrassed by the existence of a rival whose death alone could liberate him from this inhibition? There is no answer to a psychological question of this kind; but there is one supposition that must be categorically rejected.

People sometimes talk as though Craft were a kind of 'tempter' in Stravinsky's life, the man who 'converted' him to the serialist faith. This is manifest nonsense. When Craft first met Stravinsky, who was already a world-famous composer, he was twenty-four years old. He was gradually to become the composer's indispensable assistant, his travelling-companion, a not unbiassed witness and correspondent of Stravinsky's last years, a kind of Eckermann to his Goethe, though a much more enterprising and masterful personality than Eckermann. We have no means of verifying anything that Craft has already written, or may in the future write, on the subject of Stravinsky; nor do we need to concern ourselves with the crescendo of conflicting opinions that arose after the composer's death.[8] But can anyone seriously suppose that a composer who all his conscious life had composed in accordance with an inner artistic law which he had deliberately imposed on himself, who was spontaneous and impulsive in his creative life and therefore changeable in his aesthetic tastes – that such a man would be untrue to his own character and allow himself to be persuaded by a young man who had not as yet in any way proved himself as an artist? Assistance must not be confused with influence. Craft could help Stravinsky to become better acquainted with the works and the methods of the New Viennese School, with which he was very familiar, but he could not, of course, direct or control the spiritual interests of a composer of genius. On the contrary, he became necessary to Stravinsky precisely because he penetrated those interests and became so familiar with them that he was eventually an *alter ego*. Let us therefore be fair to Craft. If Stravinsky was to conceive a passion for the New Viennese School, it was with Craft's help that he was able in a short time to satisfy that passion and, once having satisfied it, to discover himself in a new 'manner'. I can only repeat that Stravinsky was always susceptible to the attractions of different musical styles, past and present, and some of these proved to be passing influences, while others persisted. But the enthusiastic tone which he adopted when he first spoke of each of these discoveries was later replaced by a more reserved, sometimes even critical attitude, once the delight of making a new artistic discovery had worn off. It was so on this occasion, also, when he made his discovery of the New Viennese composers in the fifties.

They attracted him before all else by the moral integrity of their personalities. He himself was a favourite of fortune's, and these men's spiritual independence, their non-conformist attitude to life impressed him. He never spoke of his contemporaries, even close friends, with the warmth and the very uncharacteristic elevation with which he spoke of Berg and Webern, whose photographs hung above his writing-table – 'great musicians, two pure souls, two noble human beings', as he called them.

His response to their music was more guarded. Berg was plainly less close to him than Webern, and Stravinsky could not accept 'the radically alien emotional climate of his music', particularly *Wozzeck*, which he nevertheless spoke of as a masterpiece. He did not deny that *Lulu* had a certain fascination, but made no bones about its 'immense decadence'.

He was incomparably more interested as a composer by the rare, esoteric world of Webern's music. He imagined Webern 'standing there in the quiet, looking to the mountains',[9] and his imagination was captivated by this world set quite apart from the prototypes of human existence, the very antithesis of the world of his own 'factual', 'seen' music with its essential muscular energy and intense activity. For that very reason he concentrated all his attention on the crystalline sonorities of Webern's music; and their precision of structure, the extreme fineness of their detail and their laconic, aphoristic manner answered his own fanatical desire for 'order' in art. When he first became acquainted with this music it seemed to him a kind of Pentecost, the composer himself a kind of Messiah. After the first wave of enthusiasm, however, his language was more reserved, though he still retained his admiration for the man. In a long and interesting interview given in 1965 Stravinsky spoke of his temperament as incompatible with Webern's and said that he now

found Webern's *molto ritenuto* and *molto espressivo* markings and
dying-away phrase-endings tedious. In the vocal music he sensed a
'touch of charmingness' that he did not like and there were
'commonplace harmonies' and 'little variety of form'[10] in a number
of episodes before the end of the *First Cantata* and passages in
parallel intervals in Part 5 of the *Second Cantata*.

Stravinsky's attitude to Schoenberg was more complex. It can
hardly be doubted that he found the 'emotional climate' of
Schoenberg's music quite as alien as that of Berg's, if not more so.
This can sometimes be felt reading between the lines of some of his
analyses of Schoenberg's works, and is sometimes stated openly. Of
the *Violin Concerto*, for instance, he said that 'its pathos belongs to
the nineteenth century, and since pathos is rooted in language, the
musical language of the concerto also belongs to that century. A few
erasures in the harmonisation of the second movement "à la
Brahms", and the theme easily returns to its historical frame.'[11] In
that case, we may well ask, why did Stravinsky speak with such
respect and devotion – such *pietas* – of Schoenberg? There were, I
believe, two reasons.

In the first place he was attracted by Schoenberg's personality, his
rock-like conviction, his inflexible will. He probably regretted the
abrupt parting of their ways and would have been prepared to forget
old injuries for the sheer interest of a meeting. To repair this mistake
he humbly bowed his head before Schoenberg. But there is, I believe,
a second reason, and that lies in Stravinsky's quarrels with the avant-
garde, which began as an attitude of mere suspicion but became
increasingly open and sarcastic. The avant-garde rejected Schoenberg, relegating him to the past ('Schoenberg is dead', as Boulez
entitled one of his articles), and it was in answer to this attitude that
Stravinsky extolled Schoenberg, and with increasing insistence as the
quarrel became fiercer.

It is no simple matter to unravel so tight a skein of contradictions,
and let us therefore leave the subject and turn to the music. But we
must first come to an understanding. Stravinsky's change of
'manner' in the third phase of his career as a composer was neither
fortuitous nor, it goes without saying, a simple following of musical
'fashion' – after all, how is it possible to speak of fashion when the
first serial works of the Viennese composers date from the beginning
of the twenties? No, this change was an organic need of the artist's
and part of his responsible attitude to his work. At the same time we
must not forget that Stravinsky was then entering his eighth decade.

Shall we in fact be able to penetrate the true causes of this particular change of attitude? We must make the attempt, though bearing in mind that complex psychological questions of this kind do not permit a single direct answer.

The question of ageing and its effect on the psychophysiology of the creative artist has not yet been studied. Music, it seems to me, is a field in which this effect is particularly clear, perhaps because of all the arts music exercises the most direct power of emotional influence. The emotions of the old, and indeed the whole element of *espressivo* in the works of an artist whose vital powers are waning with age, differ from those of an artist in the years of his maturity. Thanks to the power of memory there is no direct break between the two, but the emotions of maturity take on a different quality, the specific quality of old age. It is of course impossible to say exactly when old age begins and where the border separating it from maturity lies. This varies greatly with the individual. For example, we feel that Beethoven was an old man at fifty, but the same is not true of Verdi, who was seventy-four when he wrote *Otello*. Verdi, however, as we have seen earlier, was an exception, and what follows does not apply to him. Although the borderline is variable, there is an elusive, hitherto undefined pattern in the first appearance and the manifestation of a 'late style' in Beethoven, Brahms, J. S. Bach (*The Musical Offering* and the *Art of Fugue*), Wagner (*Götterdämmerung* and *Parsifal*), Liszt (*Valse oubliée* and *Csardas macabre*) and in many other composers. If we leave aside individual differences, what is common to all 'late' styles?

The feature most affected by the onset of old age seems to me to be richness of melodic invention, that is to say the quality of maximum emotional immediacy. But the loss of one quality is balanced by the gain of another, in this case an increase in the significance of thematic contrapuntal skill and other structural factors. Metaphorically speaking, as muscular power diminishes the sinews supporting the muscles stand out more clearly, and the breathing-rhythm becomes more staccato, deep chest-breathing being replaced by a close succession of short breaths. The patterning of the texture and its graphic character, the detailing of the main outline, a chamber-music quality and an inclination to speculative, abstract thinking – all these seem to be marks of a 'late' style. The chief overall feature is an intellectualisation of the emotions and it is this, however vague the expression may be, that seems to mark the characteristics of a late style such as I have tried to suggest.

Artistic creation in old age is not a longing for vanished vital powers and for passions that have in fact grown cold. Great artists recognise their vocation and neither strive for rejuvenation nor adapt themselves to the young. The old have one undeniable advantage over the young, and that is experience; and this preserves them from temptations and makes them consider more responsibly their place in art and the place of art itself in human life. The spiritual range of the old is wider and they direct their gaze towards greater depths within themselves, and do so with greater concentration. In the cases of Bach, Beethoven, Wagner and – as we shall see – Stravinsky, another characteristic feature appears: the artist directs his gaze to the art of the remote past in order to comprehend the historical process and his own place in it. Thus Bach turned to what seemed to be the obsolete form of the ricercar, Beethoven gave new life to the fugue and Wagner dreamed of resurrecting the style of Palestrina in the Graal scenes of *Parsifal*.

All that I have said above is simply a preliminary to the elucidation of some characteristics of Stravinsky's late style. The development of these characteristics was latent and it was only at the beginning of the fifties that they began to appear more distinctly.

The end of the war marked the end of Stravinsky's years of spiritual isolation, the years in which he failed to make contact with the milieu in which he was then forced to live. His journeys to Europe became more frequent, but Europe had changed and no longer resembled that of the pre-war years to which he had become so accustomed. He was at a crossroads and could apply to himself the lines of T. S. Eliot:

> So here I am, in the middle way, having had twenty years –
> Twenty years largely wasted, the years of *l'entre deux guerres* –
> Trying to learn to use new words, and every attempt
> Is a wholly new start, and a different kind of failure
>
> (*Four Quartets*, East Coker)

Not all of that can be applied literally to Stravinsky, but the bitter thought behind the passage may well have been not far from his mind at that time. There was no other escape from the impasse in which he found himself except to make a clean break with the style whose resources he had exhausted, to learn a new language and make a fresh start.

A number of works written in the forties – the cantata *Babel* and the *Mass* for example – had already indicated the direction in which he was moving. When these works first appeared, they seemed 'sports', inexplicable departures from his general style, and they (especially the *Mass*) were not valued at their true worth, either for themselves or as straws in the wind. Why should a composer who, in

Symphony in Three Movements had regained his former Dionysian afflatus and even flirted occasionally with the muse of Broadway, suddenly interest himself in examples of ancient European culture, in Gregorian chant, mediaeval *faux bourdon* and the technique of the Ars Nova – 'pre-harmonic' music, as he called it?

These proved to be no passing interests, moreover, but persisted and grew stronger. Stravinsky was increasingly attracted to the music of Bach, the Netherlanders and the Italian madrigalists who were Shakespeare's contemporaries, to Tallis and Byrd, and the earliest composers of the Renaissance such as Guillaume de Machaut. And, as on earlier occasions, he was not content simply to 'stylise' *à l'ancienne*, but extracted from this early music means of expression and stylistic peculiarities which could enrich his own modern musical language.

Parallel to this interest was an interest in the subject-matter of these early composers, and he was drawn to texts taken from the Old and the New Testament and from the age-old liturgy of the Catholic Church, the universal heritage of European culture. These form the most important element in Stravinsky's third and last period, in which intensity and economy of expression replace the widely extended interests of the preceding period.

If we regard his evolution from this point of view, we shall be able to understand it and to distinguish between cause and effect.

Serial composition did not interest Stravinsky as such, as a method of organising total chromaticism. Atonality was, and remained, fundamentally alien to him. At every stage of his development as a composer, his thinking was, overtly or covertly, diatonic. He approached serialism not from contemporary, but from ancient music. As one of the great twentieth-century experts in counterpoint, he discovered in the musical archives of the West a great variety of polyphonic devices and, with his marvellous ear, he sought out and adopted ways of transforming intervallic structures.

In his Russian period, when he was working with old folk-tunes, Stravinsky selected as typical various intervallic structures which I have defined as 'formulary' themes. Now, in his last period, he did the same with European music of the past. It is as though these two periods were telescoped, one appearing as an extension of the other. In each case it was vocal music that played the most important part. During his Russian period it was the play of speech-accents in folk-song that had helped him to elaborate his method of motivic variation. Now it was the concept of 'sonorous space' and the technique of rotating and inverting motifs and combining them contrapuntally etc. In short, the methods of composition during the period which culminated in *Les Noces* might theoretically be called 'serial'. Though it was far removed from Schoenberg's serialism in that it rejected the atonality on which Schoenberg's serial practice was based, Stravinsky's serialism was similar in that there was a serial principle in what the composer called the 'pull-idea' which, as it were, 'pre-fabricated' the development of the music, only in a much freer manner and without the severe restrictions of Schoenberg's method.

In this last stage of his musical career Stravinsky, enriched by the experience of a lifetime, revived some of the features of his former method of composing. Once again he found inspiration in the intonations and the actual phonetic sounds of vocal speech, only the texts which he chose to set were no longer Russian but Latin, English and (in *Abraham and Isaac*) ancient Hebrew. However hard he studied these languages, they could not inspire him as his native tongue had done. I have already quoted his own admission that even at the end of his life he still thought in Russian and mentally translated from Russian whatever foreign language he spoke. But if he found in the phonetic sounds of these languages no inspiration comparable in freshness and directness to that which he found in the Russian language, he found other methods of formalising speech in intervallic structure and its various modifications. Serial technique, which provides a rich supply of such methods, was a help to Stravinsky in this matter.

The contrapuntal methods of serialism are borrowed from those of classical polyphony, in which an initial idea, now called the row (O) is heard in different permutations – reversed or crabwise (R) inverted (I) and with the crab reversion inverted (RI). Stravinsky used these methods in a number of works – the fugue in Part 2 of *Symphony of Psalms*, the finale of the *Concerto for Two Pianos* and the Scherzo of the *Symphony in C* are obvious examples. In the finale of *Orpheus* and in the *Mass* he employed the strict counterpoint of the old masters, and the formal significance of these combinations revealed itself all the more forcibly. In the *Cantata* on old English texts, as we shall see, he followed Bach and resuscitated the ricercar. At the same time he gave a new importance to the canon, a form in which identity is preserved while the parts move and combine in different ways. Ricercar II in the *Cantata* demonstrates Stravinsky's great contrapuntal skill. The theme, entrusted to the tenor soloist, is marked in the old way *cantus cancrizans*, i.e. crab-form melody, and this melody in its various permutations forms a continuous musical proposition, or strophe, in which the sequence O–R–I–R–I is maintained. Later in

Igor Stravinsky

the piece motifs branch out from this strophe and these give rise to a series of canons. In the *Septet* the polyphonic texture becomes even thicker: there is a fugato in the development of the first movement, the following Passacaglia contains a number of canons, and in the final Gigue four fugues – the last of which is a double fugue – are closely knit together. In the whole *Septet* the 'sonorous space' of the music is subordinated to the theme of the first movement whose first five notes in transposition provide the theme of the Passacaglia which in its turn predetermines the thematic material of the Gigue. This highly complex counterpoint, often in six or seven parts, assumes a major significance in the *Septet*, which was the composer's first experiment with serial technique.

His free handling of that technique earned him the disapproval of orthodox serialists. In the first place his series contained an arbitrary number of notes, rather than the obligatory twelve. The series of the Passacaglia contains sixteen notes, eight of which are not repeated: the series of *Three Songs from William Shakespeare* has a four-note series. In addition to this he used the series horizontally, for the most part ignoring its vertical aspect. Finally, he on occasion combined tonal and serial music in a single work. Thus the horizontal statement of the series and its modifications remotely recall the conduct of the cantus firmus in the 'voices' of a fugue, while the vertical statement is based on the simultaneous statement of the series in all parts. The outer of the five movements of *Canticum sacrum* are tonal, and in *Agon* the first third of the music is tonal while the remaining two thirds are serial.

From the end of the fifties – from *Threni* onwards, that is to say – Stravinsky was stricter in his observance of serial rules; and the question naturally arises whether he was not at first simply a clumsy pupil who could not immediately master the new technique. Even if one can use such an expression of a great master, we must still formulate the question differently: he was not so much a clumsy as a refractory pupil. Neither at the beginning of the fifties nor at any other time did Stravinsky surrender his position – he was and always remained a tonal composer, adopting serialism and at the same time quarrelling with it, using some of its methods while rejecting its atonal essence.

The territory occupied by his music is chromatic dodecaphony based on tonal foundations. The formula may be altered because, although its sense remains unchanged, the emphasis may shift – it may be described as tonal music based on the experience of total chromaticism. Stravinsky himself provided an even shorter descrip-

148

tion when he spoke of 'triadic atonality'.[12] Towards the end of his life he never tired of repeating 'I think harmonically . . . my series have a tonal pull' and, elsewhere, 'My pieces are composed in the tonal system . . . my system.' In fact he was so convinced that tonality is the unshakable foundation of music that in 1959 he said that he heard even Webern's music more tonally than he had twenty years earlier. Nor was he indulging in polemics in saying this. If this is how he heard Webern's music, how much more did he construct his own on tonal principles!

We have seen that in his first serial works he ignored some of the laws that determine the atonal character of serial music. In the *Septet*, for instance, the chief theme of the first part clearly belongs to the sphere of A major, while in the series of the Passacaglia the two poles are E and A. The four-note series in *Three Songs from William Shakespeare* is polytonal, formed by a major and a minor third linked by an intermediate tone (B–G–A–B flat). In the cantata *In Memoriam Dylan Thomas* the series (E–E flat–C–C sharp–D) reveals a tonal centre (E), from which spring the cadential turns with their 'pull' towards C major etc.

Here his quarrel with serialism was, as it were, an external one, but later it was to become internal. While accepting serial prescriptions, he still preserved his own manner as a composer; so that listening to *Threni*, for instance, one is aware the whole time of these tonal supporting-points and indeed of the basically triadic nature of the music, as the composer himself insisted, who said that every bar of *Threni* contained a hint of simple triadic harmony. Another striking example is the penultimate number of *Requiem Canticles*, and there are many others.

While accepting the laws of serial composition, Stravinsky worked out his own technique, using two levels or planes of composition, one controlled by diatonic principles and the other by serial counterpoint. These two levels are related differently in different works, and in works composed of several movements the influence of each often varies between movements. The prime consideration in every case is melodic, intervallic construction of the original idea, the point of departure. In this he was nearer to Webern than to Schoenberg, whose series are thematic,[13] though in another way Stravinsky was diametrically opposed to Webern, who was even more attached to total chromaticism than Schoenberg.

In *Poetics of Music*, that is to say long before Stravinsky entered his third period, he maintained that tonality in the old sense was obsolete. What interested him was the latent polarity of a single note, an interval or a whole complex of sounds. This polarity, he said, was at the very root of his own work; and he saw the function of his music as the ordering of notes in their intervallic relationships.

In his new phase Stravinsky narrowed his sphere of action and concentrated even more exclusively on this idea. The catalysts were old (mediaeval and Renaissance) music and serialism, but he never became either a styliser of the past or an orthodox serialist. In fact he never lost his unique individuality: he simply discovered new facets of it.

After these general considerations we need hardly trace the works written during the last fifteen years of his life in chronological order. Let us rather try to classify them and examine them in groups according to their different marks of identity at different levels.

The prevalence of vocal music clearly distinguishes this period from that which immediately preceded it. In these vocal works the instrumental element plays a varying part. In some only a few instruments are used, while in others the number is increased as though to recall the 'full' orchestra. Stravinsky, however, always avoids any standard specification and remains wholly individual. It would be a misnomer to speak of the instruments 'accompanying' the voices in these pieces, as both the solo and the choral parts are closely interwoven with the instrumental. The technique of this interweaving deserves special investigation.

Three Songs from William Shakespeare for mezzo-soprano, flute, clarinet and viola belongs to a group of strictly chamber works for the voice. These were the first songs of Stravinsky's for more than thirty years, since his Russian period in fact. They came after the *Cantata* on anonymous English texts of the fifteenth and sixteenth centuries, in which Stravinsky used a tenor as well as a soprano voice, four winds (two flutes, oboe, cor anglais) and a single cello as well as a chorus of women's voices. Although the *Cantata*, unlike *Three Songs*, is not serial though it is strictly contrapuntal, the two works have a number of points in common. Both contain echoes of the 'bell-sonorities' of the Russian period which I have mentioned earlier.[14] These echoes are significant, because at this time the composer was making new versions of a number of vocal miniatures written between 1910 and 1920, in which the piano is replaced by a chamber ensemble. For example, in the new version of the Balmont settings the piano was replaced by two flutes, two clarinets, piano and string quartet, and in the Russian songs by flute, harp and string quartet.

Thus new and old are interwoven in Stravinsky's music, and we find an antiphonal lay-out – another reminder of his old manner – in a number of these pieces, such as the dirge-canons *In Memoriam Dylan Thomas* for tenor voice, four trombones and string quartet, where the canons for the winds, set against the strings, frame the vocal 'Threnody' of the middle movement. Two further examples are to be found in *Elegy for J.F.K.* for baritone and three clarinets (1964) – a chamber miniature like the Japanese *hokku* – and the solo cantata-ballad *Abraham and Isaac* for baritone and chamber orchestra (1962–3), in which the organic interpenetration of the vocal and instrumental parts is particularly remarkable.

Before continuing our survey of these late works I should like to say something more about the *Cantata*, not only on account of its artistic qualities but because it comes at the very beginning of a new period and anticipates many of its features.

Stravinsky's turn to the past is quite clear from his choice of fifteenth- and sixteenth-century English texts, in which the secular and the religious are strangely alternated. To suit these texts he revived the old technique of ricercar and old contrapuntal methods. This same technique – based on Willaert, Frescobaldi and other sixteenth- and seventeenth-century masters – was later to serve as the foundation for the cantata *Threni*, in which he made a virtuoso use of canon. At the same time the secular character of some sections of the cantata suggested a melodic style more like the neo-classical, particularly in the lyrical Prelude for women's voices which is heard on three further occasions – in the two Interludes and the Postlude.

The *Cantata* is in seven sections, and although this is essentially a chamber work it is one of the longest of Stravinsky's late pieces, lasting thirty minutes. Its form is interesting as an example of the composer's method of 'constructing in parallelisms' on the basis of dissymmetry. The cycle is braced together by parallel cross-connections, and although there is symmetry in the composition, it is perpetually destroyed.

Thus the opening Song, partly varied, is repeated in the first, third, fifth and seventh numbers, i.e. the odd numbers. The even numbers, i.e. Ricercar I (soprano aria), Ricercar II (the tenor *Cantus cancrizans* referred to above, with canons added) and the song 'Westron Wind' (duet for soprano and tenor), recur in the second, fourth and sixth parts. In the centre of the cycle Ricercar II appears with the title 'Sacred History', developed at length and with much counterpointing. After three appearances in various permutations the *Cantus cancrizans* is followed by nine canons in different combinations, with eleven *ritornelli*. The bass figure of the Prelude appears in Ricercar I and again in the *ritornello* of Ricercar II and forms the basis of the duet of 'Westron Wind'. The characteristics described further emphasise the significance of Ricercar II as the central point of the work. Its characteristics suggest a concentric or – to use concrete, spatial terms – conical form. We shall speak in greater detail about this form in connection with the other important vocal–instrumental works, to which we must now turn our attention after a preliminary observation.

Stravinsky now gave an important place to choral works, which had hitherto been used episodically and were more frequent during the composer's Russian than during his neo-classical period. Now, however, they appear systematically, though the chorus is rarely used without instrumental accompaniment. [15] In the large-scale cycles the choral sections are combined with solos.

Leaving aside works based on the music of Bach and Gesualdo, let us turn our attention for a moment to the *Introitus* in memory of T. S. Eliot, for male-voice choir and instrumental ensemble (1965). 'Introitus' is the introductory section of the Catholic Requiem Mass, and Schütz also uses the word for the opening movement of his Passions. Stravinsky had originally intended to write a Requiem Mass in memory of his friend, but a year later he carried out his plan in connection with another mourning occasion. *Introitus* is characterised by low-lying sonorities which sound muffled in both voices and instruments (piano, harp, two timpani, two bass drums, solo viola and double bass). The colour of the music is dark and enigmatic, with a suggestion of Dante's *Inferno*, and in fact Stravinsky exhibits in this short piece truly inexhaustible resources of sonorous imagination.

Remarkable on a different plane is the cantata *A Sermon, a Narrative and a Prayer* for reader, two soloists (mezzo-soprano and tenor), chorus and orchestra (1960–1) with English text. The character of each movement is suggested by its title. The broad choral lines of the first movement are replaced by a high degree of tension in the second, which is a kind of dramatic *scena*, while the choral writing in the third looks forward to a number of passages in *Requiem Canticles*. This variety of character introduces an operatic note.

Three works stand out among the pieces written during these last fifteen years – *Canticum sacrum* (1955–6), *Threni* (1957–8) and *Requiem Canticles* (1965–6). Each of these is in several movements forming a cycle, and employs chorus, orchestra and soloists. The texts are Latin and are taken chiefly from the Gospels (*Canticum Sacrum*), the Old Testament (*Threni*, where Stravinsky chose texts that had been set by many of the old masters, including Palestrina,

Victoria, Lassus, Couperin and in our own day, before Stravinsky, by Křenek) and the Catholic liturgy (*Requiem Canticles*). None of these pieces was meant for liturgical use, but the spirit of the music is nevertheless that of the liturgy, and this fact needs some further explanation.

We have already commented on Stravinsky's preference for religious themes during this last period, and have mentioned the most important examples, to which we should add *The Flood*. The large number of works of this kind is explained not only by Stravinsky's being a religious man, but also by his wish to give expression to universal human feelings, to what is common spiritual property and supra-personal. There are many different nuances of this – some more subjective in tone (*In Memoriam Dylan Thomas, Introitus*), some dramatic (*Abraham and Isaac*), some for stage presentation (*The Flood*) and so forth. In a special class of their own are the liturgical works, in which the composer's long-standing interest in rites and ceremonies finds expression. In connection with the Latin text of *Oedipus Rex* he had observed that 'an older, even an imperfectly remembered language must contain an incantatory element that could be exploited in music'.[16] After *Oedipus* he used Latin for its 'incantatory' power in *Symphony of Psalms*, and then in the *Mass* and other works that we have discussed. But both in the *Mass* and other works a new element enters, a direct or indirect link with Catholicism.

Stravinsky explained his use of Catholic liturgical texts by the fact that instrumental music is forbidden in the Orthodox rite and that he cannot himself imagine vocal music without instruments. There were, however, other more important reasons. The more deeply he penetrated the world of 'pre-harmonic' music, the greater the interest he naturally felt in the music of the Catholic Church, the institution which has preserved in its archives the universal artistic models of the remote past. It was not an interest in Catholic doctrine but a wish to sample these models and to verify the continuing power of their ritual significance that caused Stravinsky to write these works, which we must now examine.

They vary greatly in content and in the means employed. The role of the chorus is most important in *Threni*, which is also the most extended of these late works. The musical colouring of *Threni* is severe, in accordance with the biblical text. The archaic character of the work is emphasised by the 'allusions to simple triads', and by the nature of the vocal writing which includes monody, heterophony and rhythmically uniform recitation (chanting), as well as by the sonorities of the orchestra, which in correlation with the vocal parts often fulfils the function of a harmonic foundation. Support is provided by the brass, which includes a number of instruments rarely used today (four horns, three trombones, trumpet, sarrusophone and flügelhorn), with two flutes, two oboes, three clarinets – including bass clarinet and a normal string section with the piano, harp, celesta and bass drum commonly used by Stravinsky in these late works. Despite the potential weight of such an orchestra there are very few tutti, and the instruments appear in alternate groupings, another trait common to these last works.

There are six soloists – soprano, alto, two tenors and two basses – but there is little solo-singing in the ordinary sense of the word, no arias or arioso passages. The soloists are in fact no more than protagonists of the chorus, and their entries simply thin out the choral texture and form points of support in the continuous development of the music. These points may be passages of monody or structurally independent instrumental fragments (short duets in the first part, series of canons in the second). There is a marked preference for men's voices.

The texture of the music is dense with counterpoint, and indeed *Threni* occupies in Stravinsky's oeuvre a position similar to that occupied by the *Art of Fugue* in Bach's. In this work, though, he does not use fugue but much earlier forms such as ricercar, canzone, isorhythmic motet and so forth. The result is not classical polyphony – a matter of broad strata of sound – but a minutely worked interlinking of mutually connected fragments. Beside the points of support formed by the solo passages there are other short choral passages which fulfil the same purpose and also announce each new idea in the text. In the Bible these are headed by letters of the old Hebrew alphabet (aleph, beth, heth, lamed etc). Stravinsky preserves the unusual sounds of these letters in the body of the Latin text and makes them dividing-points in the music.

Threni is in three movements and opens with the words 'Here beginneth the lamentation of the prophet Jeremiah.' This is one of those solemn, festive openings that Stravinsky often used in his theatrical works, and we find similar passages at the beginning of *Canticum Sacrum*, *Requiem Canticles*, *Agon* and *The Flood*. The first movement is narrative and begins with the words 'How solitary she sits, the city once so populous but now like unto a widow . . . Nightlong she weeps and her cheeks are covered with tears . . . Behold, Lord, and see how I am brought low.' The music enhances the dramatic character of the text but with rigid objectivity and brevity.

In the extensive second movement complaint, despair, anger, doubt, prayer and humility alternate with each other. There are three main sections headed respectively 'plaint', 'feeling of hope' and 'recompense'. The first section contains the most highly worked counterpoint and the composer has suggested the 'trials of sorrow' mentioned in the text by a persistent succession of increasingly complicated canons. The second section is powerfully developed, the polyphonic lines take on a wider span, tension increases and with it the dynamic level of the music, particularly at the words 'We have done evil and provoked Thy wrath . . . Thou hast made us as outcasts and an abomination among the peoples.' In the third section there are moments when a wild joy explodes, moments such as are frequent in Stravinsky's music, beginning with *Symphony of Psalms*. There are echoes of this joy in the dialogue between the two basses at the beginning of the final Prayer, a short movement which ends peacefully.

As this analysis shows, although *Threni* is in three movements, it is in fact a work in five sections, the centre of which is formed – as in a conical figure – by the middle section of the second movement. In the same way in the seven-movement *Cantata* of 1952 the central fourth movement (Ricercar II, tenor aria) forms the point of the cone, framed by the wide circles of Ricercar I (soprano aria) and 'Westron Wind' (soprano and tenor duet). Similarly in the five-movement *Mass* the third movement (Credo) stands out both by its dimensions and also by employing different means of expression from those in Gloria and Sanctus which flank it. This concentric form of composition is even more marked in *Canticum Sacrum*, where it is founded on a system of musical symbolism.

Canticum Sacrum was composed in honour of Saint Mark, as the opening Dedicatio announces, and was designed for performance in the Basilica di San Marco in Venice. The basilica has five porticoes and there are correspondingly five sections in the *Canticum*. The outer movements are similar, the fifth being the *cancrizans* of the first, and the texts chosen form a hymn to the word 'revelation'. Two middle movements flank the third movement, which forms the centrepiece; they are 'asymmetrically symmetrical' and are the only solo numbers of the five. The second movement is a tenor solo to a text from the *Song of Solomon*, with soft colouring and Byzantine patterning. The fourth movement, for baritone and chorus, is severe and economical in character and the text is from the Gospels: 'Lord, I believe! Help thou mine unbelief!' The third and most fully developed of the five movements is a hymn to the virtues of faith, hope and charity. The middle of the three (Hope) also consists of five fragments. Consequently the form of *Canticum Sacrum* expressed in graphic terms is conical, but in a double sense, i.e. a large cone with a small cone (the third movement) on top of it, like one box inside another. In this way the musical form mirrors the architectural form of the basilica.

This symbolism is of course so deeply embedded in the music that the listener does not feel it to be in any sense forcibly imposed, and this in fact was Stravinsky's great art, to develop intellectually ideas conceived with great clarity and immediacy.

Compared with *Threni*, *Canticum Sacrum* is more decorative in character and therefore more easily accessible, though less unified in style. The outer movements have the same impetuous energy as is to be found in *Symphony of Psalms*. These are tonal movements resting on the polarisation of the D–A area and the adjacent B flat–G area, polytonally sharpened (e.g. the simultaneous combination B flat major/B minor). The chorus's three announcements are framed by orchestral intermezzi. In contrast to the severe, astringent quality of these choral pieces the tenor aria has a delicate refinement corresponding to the tender character of the text from the *Song of Solomon*: 'Awake, North wind: and come thou South! blow upon my garden that the spices thereof may flow. Let my beloved come into his garden and eat his pleasant fruits . . . Eat, friends, drink and drink abundantly!' The tenor announces the series in the opening bars of the aria, and this series has tonal associations in the pull between the fifths A–E and A flat–E flat. As in other series of Stravinsky's, there is a pull towards polytonality as well as towards tonality.

The music of the third movement is more speculative in character. At the opening of each section the organ announces the series as though it were a subject for debate, recalling Stravinsky's observation on the subject of musical form, as being 'the result of the "logical discussion" of the musical material selected'. Thus in the present movement the series and its transformations are, as it were, discussed. Contrapuntally the most complicated of the sections is the second, which forms the 'tip' of the cone. The laconic tension of the fourth movement is in strong contrast with the teleological speculation of the third. The transition to the finale, with its trumpet fanfares, sounds entirely natural and sums up the cycle as a whole. Despite the weaknesses mentioned, the work in its entirety gives the impression of completeness, conclusiveness and integrity.

Stravinsky's greatest achievement is his Requiem – *Requiem Canticles*, written when he was eighty-four and marked by true artistic insight. The musical language is clearer and more graphic, and it has greater emotional variety; and he has left behind the eclecticism of *Canticum Sacrum* and the uniform archaic austerity of *Threni*. *Requiem Canticles* is a summation of Stravinsky's work, not only because it is his last major piece but because so much of the composer's past artistic experience is here absorbed, synthesised and generalised. In this music the sap of life, its very 'material', is the fundamental factor. Stravinsky takes the imagery and ideas of the Catholic Requiem Mass and treats them in his own way, a twentieth-century way. This explains the significance of the stormy passage for piano and strings in the 'Dies irae', the trumpet call in the 'Tuba mirum', the terror-stricken trembling of the flutes and strings in the 'Rex tremendae', the lamenting tone of the 'Lacrymosa', the chorale of the 'Libera me' and the funeral sonorities of the Postlude for celesta, bells and vibraphone. These, in fact, are the concrete 'material' touches mentioned above. There is no trace of stylisation in this music: it is wholly inspired by the composer's resourceful imagination. Each piece has its own, unique colour. The exposition is extremely brief, and this preference for exposition rather than development is justified by the clarity of the musical imagery.

There are nine movements. Three orchestral pieces form the vaults on which the work rests – an unexpectedly violent Prelude for strings, an Interlude for winds, in which the choral 'Dies irae' of the third movement is developed, and a funereal-sounding Postlude, which differs from the previous orchestral numbers by its static quality and by being for strings only.

Thus the work is framed by two strongly contrasted pieces: the strings are contrasted with the percussion, and the impetuous energy of the even semi-quaver movement with the frozen, static quality of the many-tiered chords. The Prelude begins and ends with the note F in the cellos. In the Postlude the chord complexes rest on the horns' sustained bass, but the development – as the composer says – is here as always in his music, concentrated round the bass, which fulfils the function of harmonic foundation. The horn sounds the notes F,G sharp, B sharp in succession – an F minor triad, in fact. The last, upward-straining chord of the work is based on the horn's low F. At the end of the Prelude the double basses' F is marked *sf staccato* but here it is a long sustained note in the wind. This is a characteristic instance of 'construction by parallelisms'.

157

Equally characteristic of his favourite conical forms is the placing of the Interlude (no.5) as the centre of this nine-movement work. The transition to the Interlude – which is for winds, as you will remember – is prepared by a dramatic piece of scoring. In the previous number ('Tuba mirum') the trombone is the soloist, with the horns, and in the following number ('Rex tremendae') the trombone is again the soloist, with the trumpet, and the flutes join the strings. In the number following this (no.7) the chief role is played by flutes with a single double bass and harp, and this is the solo contralto aria ('Lacrymosa') which forms the lyrical heart of the work. Another bridge in its turn links this with another solo aria (no.4 for bass, 'Tuba mirum'). Thus by means of arch-like connections and dissymmetry the Interlude is encircled by two circular frames; it is connected thematically with the 'Dies irae', and, if the 'Lacrymosa' is the lyrical heart of the work, the Interlude is its dramatic centre.

I spoke of parallelisms a moment ago and should like to draw attention to some other instances. First of all, in the field of timbre. The sixth and seventh numbers are connected by flute with strings or harp, and in the same way flutes with harp and piano form the clusters of chords in the Postlude. Or take the field of style – the second number ('Exaudi') is a choral prayer ('Hear my prayer') and the seventh number ('Libera me') is also a choral prayer resembling an Orthodox chant in character. Here the chorus is divided, one group singing in four parts and supported by four horns and the other chanting in a soft *parlando*, which makes a most impressive effect.

The harmonic structure of the chorale prepares the listener for the static character of the Postlude, with its sequence of polymorphic, or many-layered, chords. At the same time there is a real contrast, since these chords are not compact like those of the chorale, but rarified. This may seem a strange way of describing chords consisting of as many as seven, eight, nine or even twelve notes, but thanks to Stravinsky's orchestration, to wide spacing and the upward movement of these chords, the clusters have a fascinatingly remote, unearthly quality. Polymorphic chords of this kind become increasingly frequent in Stravinsky's late works. *Introitus*, in which chords of eight and nine notes are given a dark, enigmatic character, provides a further instance, and there is yet another in the *Variations* in memory of Aldous Huxley, written rather later. As opposed to the dark colour and thick texture of *Introitus*, the colouring of these separate variations is compared by the composer to 'splinters of sound', like the breaking of a very thin piece of glass. The ephemeral nature of timbres of this kind recalls the chordal combinations of *Requiem*

Canticles – dense in quantity (texture) and disembodied, or rarified, in quality (sonority).

At this point, as it seems to me, there was a kind of break in Stravinsky's style. He once observed that the history of harmony was brilliant but short, and yet for all that did he not experience a nostalgia for harmony after his long commitment to counterpoint? This would explain the fact that during his long and exhausting final illness, he took to listening to Debussy, and especially *Pelléas et Mélisande*. This is naturally no more than a guess and needs to be confirmed, but there is certainly no doubt that since Scriabin no Russian composer has produced such unusual, complex yet crystalline-sounding chordal complexes – not based on the interval of the third – as those that fascinate us in these late works of Stravinsky's.

One further remark in connection with *Requiem Canticles*, which is dedicated to the memory of Ellen Seegers. Stravinsky at this time wrote a number of such memorial pieces – epitaphs, in effect, like the *tombeaux* written by French composers in the past. These were generally very short instrumental pieces, mostly canons or miniature vocal pieces, though some were larger. Earlier works were written in memory of Rimsky-Korsakov, Debussy and Natalie Koussevitzky; late *in memoriam* works were dedicated to Dylan Thomas, T. S. Eliot, Aldous Huxley, Raoul Dufy, Alphonse Annou, J. F. Kennedy, Egon von Fürsenberg. Helen Buchanan Seeger's *Requiem Canticles* was the last of the series.

I shall speak only briefly of the remaining works of this last period. They fall into two groups – the one theatrical and the other for the concert-hall. To the first group belong *Agon* and *The Flood* and to the second *Septet*, *Movements* and *Variations* for orchestra. There are stylistic parallels between these two groups and the distinction between them is therefore not absolute.

The *Septet* stands on its own. Harsh in sonority, this piece has already been mentioned in different contexts. It marked the opening of Stravinsky's last period, in which the distinguishing feature of his music was concentration of expression, and so it is in the *Septet* whose three movements last about eleven minutes. Originally the first movement was entitled 'Sonata allegro' but the title was later removed. It is symptomatic that his interest in sonata form began with the *Octet* in 1922 and ended with the *Symphony* (1945) or the chamber *Concerto in D*. During the fifteen years after the *Septet* of 1953, Stravinsky never returned to sonata form nor was his music ever again so deliberately harsh in character.

The remaining works I should describe as belonging to the 'decorative' category of which there are so many brilliant examples from his neo-classical period. The play-element is still dominant, as it was then, but the 'decoration' is more finely patterned and more *recherché*. 'Sweetness' has been almost entirely eliminated, and though colouring is rich, emotions have been intellectualised. The note of 'art for art's sake' elegance creeps in at times, and then mere prettinness replaces genuine beauty.

Let us now examine the theatre works. *Agon* is an abstract ballet. Its title is taken from the Greek word for contest, or place of contest.[17] In the ballet there are eight ballerinas, four male dancers and the instruments of the orchestra.

The orchestra is of normal dimensions, the same as Stravinsky had used for *Symphony in Three Movements*; but there are virtually no tutti, and individual instruments, or groups of instruments, appear in different relationships to each other. The orchestral colour of the work is influenced by the fact that the second of the three scenes is based on fifteenth- and sixteenth-century dances. In addition, therefore, to the piano and harp obligatory in all these late works, Stravinsky includes mandoline, xylophone, castanets and three bass drums, and these at times give the music a slightly exotic character.

The first sketches for *Agon* date from December 1953 and include the C-major fanfares for two trumpets with polytonal chromaticisms, and more than a third of the ballet is in Stravinsky's earlier, pre-serial manner. Work on *Agon* was interrupted by the death of Dylan Thomas, which put an end to Stravinsky's plans for collaborating with him in an opera based on the Odyssey. Instead, he wrote the dirge-canons *In Memoriam Dylan Thomas*, putting *Agon* on one side, and then devoted the year 1955 to writing *Canticum Sacrum*. It was only after this that he returned to *Agon*, so that the position was not unlike that of *The Nightingale* at the beginning of his career, when for similar reasons there was a stylistic break between the first scene and those written later. This time, however, the composer, having completed the ballet for his seventy-fifth birthday, revised the music of the first third though without altering its essentially tonal character. The result is a work in a kind of *genre mixte*, but it has a stylistic unity nonetheless.

The most remarkable feature of *Agon* is the prevalence of fast tempi, and the immediate impression that it makes on the listener is one of lively activity, a pleasant exception among Stravinsky's last works. Rhythmic energy is the distinguishing feature of the first movement, which is a kind of dancers' 'exposition' – a quartet in the first section, a double quartet in the second and a triple quartet in the third. The second movement, or scene, is preceded by a Prelude based on two types of movement – one bravura in character and the other flowing – and the music of the Prelude is repeated to form a link between the three sections into which the scene falls. The first of these consists of a heroic 'saraband-step' (solo violin, xylophone and trombone), a stately *gailliarde* (with harp and mandolin) and a lively 'fluttering' coda (solo part for violin). The second section comprises a *bransle simple* (two trumpets as soloists), a *bransle gay* (flutes and castanets) and a *bransle de Poitou* – the dance from which the minuet developed – (violins and brass). The third section consists of an Adagio with two variations and a coda (solo parts for violin, as is customary for a choreographic Adagio, and later horn and piano).

Dramatically this second scene moves from the stately and heroic through the subtle colouring of the *bransles* to its lyrical centre in the Adagio. The third scene is marked by·a return to the musical character of the first – four duos, four trios and a coda, in which we hear the opening fanfares again.

This scheme reveals the importance of the *concertante* principle in *Agon*, one of those works of Stravinsky's in which the play-element is a decisive factor.

The same element is present in *The Flood*, which dates from 1961–2, though here the composer had set himself a different task – an actual 'play' of 'real' life, in the primitive allegorical sense. His model was the mediaeval miracle-play, with its naive faith and rough buffooneries, as they seem to us, an ambivalent unity combining the lofty and the commonplace, the devout and the vulgar. Naturally the modern composer is not in a position to penetrate the spirit of these mediaeval pieces: he can only stylise them, and Stravinsky was not wholly successful in this experiment.

In *Agon* the abstraction from real life in no way impoverished the vital colours of the music, whereas in *The Flood* the kaleidoscopic succession of 'objectified' situations gives the music a kind of sham, illusory character. Descriptive imagery – generally rare in Stravinsky's music – plays an important part, and *The Flood* is in fact the most 'visual' of all his works.

Once we accept the 'rules of the game' as laid down by the composer, it is easy to discover a number of witty *trouvailles* and some powerful moments in the score. What we have is some twenty minutes of highly variegated music, a succession of episodes in which the serious alternates with the comic, the sacred with the profane; scenes of action are followed by static episodes and instrumental and vocal passages are interrupted by the spoken word. This richly episodic character is not wholly unlike the paintings of Hieronymus Bosch, in which scenes of the most diverse character are combined on different planes or levels of the canvas. The voice of God and Noah's quarrel with his wife, the choral chants and the catalogue of the 'two times seven' pairs of 'clean' and 'unclean' animals, Lucifer's caricatured tenor and the endless ostinato of the downpouring deluge – these are examples of the ambivalent musico-dramatic action of *The Flood* in which a reader, solo singers, a chorus, dancers and orchestra all take part. The visual element in the work is further emphasised by the inclusion in the score of a number of exotic instruments – three bass drums, xylophone-marimba, cymbals, big drum, as well as the piano, harp and celesta obligatory in these late works of Stravinsky's.

The action is introduced by a Prelude or *intrada*, and we then hear 'Te Deum' (soprano, alto, tenor), a melodrama (Narrator, in the orchestra), the voice of God (two basses), Lucifer's aria, another melodrama (the seducing of Eve) and again the voice of God. This completes the first, introductory part of the action. The second part contains four numbers and is framed by two large choreographic scenes – Noah's building of the Ark, and the Flood. The third part recounts the story of man's repentance and God's forgiveness; and here the constituents of the first part reappear in a slightly different order and with changed significance (voice of God, melodrama, repeat of the instrumental Prelude, aria of Satan, Sanctus). Thus the whole work is arranged dissymmetrically, with the highlighting of the second, central part by reason of its proportions in relation to the rest.

Stravinsky's last purely instrumental compositions derive from *Agon* rather than from *The Flood*. They consist of a piano concerto entitled *Movements* (1959) and orchestral *Variations* (1963–4). Both these works exhibit the quality of laconic brevity associated with Webern, whose influence is more noticeable in the five-movement concerto. Originally Stravinsky meant to entitle the work 'for piano and groups of instruments', thus emphasising his new approach to orchestral writing. In actual fact the *concertante* principle permeates not only the soloists' music but all the other orchestral parts as well. In the *Variations*, on the other hand, the strings play the most significant role and the string section is augmented (twelve violins, ten violas, eight cellos, four double basses). In both these works there is a clear preference for airy, disembodied sonorities, which sparkle like diamond facets; and it was this path that led to the final *Requiem Canticles*.

It is not our intention to analyse the many smaller, often occasional, works of these last years, none of which modifies the general characterisation of the composer's stylistic tendencies and other interests. During this whole period of fifteen years his creative activity never flagged, and the works that we have examined testify to the continuing intensity of his spiritual life. Taking into account the fact that he continued to appear in concerts all over the world until the age of eighty-five, Stravinsky's old age may well be said to have been unimaginably rich and fruitful.

12

Far and near

This chapter is a kind of supplement to the last, in that it is still concerned with 'late Stravinsky'; but the subject of our investigation is now the composer's musical taste. Since his own 'manners' of composing changed so frequently, it is hardly to be wondered at that he expressed different opinions about the composers of the past at different stages of his own evolution. In the early years, and particularly in *Chronicle*, he spoke of his contemporaries with a studied politeness in which condescension made little distinction of merit. In his conversations with Craft the tone is more personal and the opinions are more clearly subjective. His own individuality was very marked and he now spoke openly and directly, avoiding the commonplace and any show of false piety towards generally accepted ideas. 'I am wrong, of course,' he observed ironically, 'to question what "everyone knows".'[1] But Stravinsky never attempted to make his views objective. He was neither an historian nor a theorist of music, but a practical musician, and he made his judgments of the 'authorities', great and small, from his own angle of vision, that of the composer. This must be borne in mind if we are to avoid entering into useless disputes with him. After all we do not quarrel with Dostoevsky for failing to appreciate Tolstoy (and vice versa) nor with Tolstoy for rejecting Turgenev, blame Wagner for holding Brahms small or Taneev and Tchaikovsky for not accepting Mussorgsky. These were, of course, disagreements between contemporaries, whereas Stravinsky's criticism of Beethoven's Ninth Symphony was an attack on a great classical tradition. Even so, this was not without

163

Stravinsky with his son, Theodore, 1970

precedent either, if we think of Rimsky-Korsakov's indifference to Haydn and Bach, Debussy's indifference to Schubert, and Wagner's extolling Gluck at the expense of Mozart.

Composers always champion what they feel to be close to them personally, whether it be in conversation or in print. There was therefore nothing strange in Stravinsky feeling disinclined to enter into raptures over Beethoven's Ninth Symphony – after all, nobody is shocked by Tchaikovsky's critical attitude towards late Beethoven. What is strange is his wish to argue his criticisms, as he does in his conversations with Craft; and we must try to look at his criticisms in a different way, to realise that, right or wrong, these criticisms are a great aid to our understanding of Stravinsky's own methods of work. Both his sympathies and his antipathies were dictated by a single consideration: he quite simply welcomed anything that confirmed his own 'manner' of composing and, more broadly speaking, his own artistic ideal, and rejected anything that contradicted either of these. Regarded from this angle it is precisely the prejudiced, subjective nature of his judgments that give them their value. If we pay careful attention to them, we shall be in a better position to understand his enthusiasms during these last years of his life. The conversations with Craft provide ample material.

We have already spoken at length of Stravinsky's attitude to the classics of Russian music and of his enduring love for Tchaikovsky, and there is no need to return to this. It must, however, be admitted with regret that, with the possible exception of Prokofiev,[2] the work of Soviet composers was very little known to him. Moreover, until his visit to Russia in 1962 his ideas on the subject were mistaken. They found expression in the fifth chapter of *Poetics of Music*. There are, in fact, grounds for believing that Stravinsky was not the author of this chapter and that it was written by some ill-intentioned émigré with little knowledge of musical matters. Stravinsky unconditionally condemned this chapter in 1962, and there is therefore no point in going back over these earlier misunderstandings. Let us rather concentrate our attention on his attitude to non-Russian music, limiting ourselves to factual information, to actual quotations and, if necessary, to commenting on these.

From the end of the fifties – Craft pinpoints the year 1957 – until his death Stravinsky's chief listening was Bach, whom he idolised, speaking of him as beautiful, wise, 'indispensable'. In Handel, he said, one never experiences 'the wonderful jolts, the sudden modulations, the unexpected harmonic changes, the deceptive cadences that are the joy of every Bach cantata'.[3] He was impressed by the conciseness of the *Two-Part Inventions*; and, although he was in principle opposed to the expression 'technique of composition', he nevertheless maintained that – in whatever sense it might be used – Bach possessed this technique to a higher degree than any other composer.

Stravinsky also admired Beethoven's 'technique', though his attitude to Beethoven contained elements of repulsion as well as attraction – as, for different stylistic reasons, was surely true of Chopin's attitude to Beethoven. In the Ninth Symphony the rhythmic regularity of the music and its lack of variety irritated Stravinsky, though he comments on the musical 'riches' of the *Allegro energico* in the finale. The Eighth Symphony, on the other hand, he called 'a miracle of growth and development',[4] and he felt both the Second and Fourth Symphonies particularly 'close' to him. If the odd numbers among the symphonies attracted him less, it was probably on account of their rhythmic regularity, that 'squareness of phrase' to which he referred in another connection. In fact it was for the 'different length of its sentences', its rhythmic inventiveness and dissymmetrical construction that he so much admired Haydn's music. He spoke of Beethoven as the 'greatest of all masters of orchestration' and regarded the quartets, the piano sonatas and the symphonies mentioned above as 'immaculately fresh and entrancing'.[5] Moreover in 'Thoughts of an Octogenarian' he declared

At eighty I have found new joy in Beethoven, and the Great Fugue now seems to me – it was not always so – a perfect miracle. How right Beethoven's friends were when they convinced him to detach it from opus 130, for it must stand by itself, this absolutely contemporary piece of music that will be contemporary for ever . . . Hardly birthmarked by its age, the Great Fugue is as rhythm alone more subtle than any music composed in my own century . . . It is pure interval music, this fugue, and I love it beyond any other.[6]

The interest in experimenting with different intervallic structures is characteristic of Stravinsky in his last period, and this explains his intense concern with the music of Bach's contemporaries and immediate predecessors, who were virtuosos in this field. In 1959 he spoke of 'playing the English virginalists with never-failing delight . . . Couperin, too, and Bach cantatas too many to specify, an even greater number of Italian madrigals, Schütz's *Sinfoniae Sacrae* and the Masses of Josquin, Okeghem, Obrecht and others'.

Seventeenth-century music also interested him, for another additional reason. The dark, stormy, enigmatic age of the Baroque witnessed the shift from modality to tonality, and the intense emotions of the age demanded new means of expression, of which chromaticism was one.

Stravinsky was deeply interested in these questions, which he discusses with all the penetration of a genuine scholar,[7] observing incidentally, 'I prefer to use chromatic in a limited sense, and in relation to diatonic.' This remark, which dates from 1960, when he had already fully mastered serial technique, is a help to understanding his own use of tonality. '"Chromaticism" means something different to each and every composer today', he added in the same conversation. He particularly mentions Schubert's Fourth Symphony as 'far surpassing later composers in the ripeness of its chromatic idiom' and goes on to praise the chromaticisms in Mozart.

The rhythmic problems solved by the old composers also continued to fascinate him. 'Gesualdo's riches are more obvious in the domain of harmony than in rhythm', he observed,[8] 'though there are some madrigals which exhibit a mastery both in the phrase-construction, in the motivic development, the intervallic construction and the variations of rhythm.' Gesualdo and Monteverdi were the two Italian masters of the sixteenth–seventeenth centuries of whom Stravinsky spoke with the greatest warmth and admiration. What struck him most in Monteverdi was the 'unprecedented scale of his musical thinking'. He was also attracted by Monteverdi's personality, which he found 'amazingly modern and, if one can say such a thing, near to me in spirit'. And he goes on: 'If I am primarily attracted by Monteverdi's rhythmic invention, it is chiefly because in fact I myself have been working all my life in the same direction. Thus his theory of rhythm forms part of my own creed as a composer.' The relationship between modality and tonality, diatonicism and chromaticism, regularity and irregularity – these things attracted him to Gabrieli, Cipriano and Willaert as well as to Gesualdo and Monteverdi. They all belong to a period remote from our own but an important turning-point in the history of European music, a period when the struggle between the old and the new found expression in a contradictory unity. Stravinsky may well have seen a parallel between the aims of composers in the Baroque period and those in our own day, another harsh and deeply disturbed era in which different artistic systems dispute yet influence each other, while he – the partisan of order in art – tried to reveal their common legitimacy and to synthesise them.

Stravinsky returned to his 'composer's creed' when analysing the works of the Venetian School. 'When will musicians learn that the performance depends on Gabrieli's music rhythm, not harmony? when will they stop trying to make mass choral effects out of simple harmonic changes and bring out, articulate, those marvellous rhythmic inventions? Gabrieli is rhythmic polyphony.'[9] And on another occasion he acknowledged that he 'had studied all the church music of Palestrina, Tallis and Byrd'.

It is hardly necessary to give any further evidence of Stravinsky's extraordinary musical erudition, almost unique among twentieth-century composers. This erudition was both the foundation and at the same time the consequence of the transformations that his style underwent during the last years of his life.

His attitude to music since the age of Beethoven was more selective and at times sceptical. Chopin he found alien and avoided speaking about him, as he did about Liszt. He categorically rejected Berlioz, Wagner and Richard Strauss in whose works, he believed, the literary element disturbed logical development and bred arbitrariness that is fatal to musical order.[10] Against them he championed those composers of the Romantic Age – and chief among them Schubert, whose music charmed him by the immediacy of its purely musical invention. Even as a boy he had loved the Schubert song-cycles, and later he came to love the instrumental works; and he could never forgive Scriabin for describing 'the marvellous F minor Fantasia for four hands' as 'la musique pour les jeunes demoiselles'.[11] Of the Fourth Symphony he said that here 'Schubert's feeling for the largest-extending tonality relationships, his harmonic skill, his powers of development, are to be compared only to those of Beethoven',[12] and he ridicules those who claim that Schubert could do no more than string together song-forms, maintaining that in this respect Schubert was 'infinitely richer' than other Romantic composers. What he had to say about later Romantics can be summed up in a number of short quotations.

Schumann is a composer for whom I have a personal weakness, but the symphony is not his domain. If I compare, say, the D minor which I have just heard, with the Schubert Fourth . . . the Schumann seems not to be a symphony at all, in the Beethoven sense . . .[13]

My *Scherzo Fantastique* owes much more to Mendelssohn by way of Tchaikovsky than to Rimsky-Korsakov . . . My appreciation of Weber did not come until the 1920's, with a performance of *Der Freischütz* in Prague conducted by Alexander von Zemlinsky. I acquainted myself with all of Weber's piano music after that *Freischütz*, with the result that his piano sonatas may have exercised a spell over me at the time I composed my *Capriccio*; a specific rhythmic device in the *Capriccio* may be traced to Weber, at any rate. The Weber of the *Invitation to the Dance*, the overtures, the *Konzertstück* and the Mendelssohn of the 'Italian' Symphony, the *Octet*, the *Rondo Capriccioso* and other piano pieces, the *Midsummer Night's Dream* overture – these are the Beau Brummells of music.[14]

It was probably similar qualities of 'elegance' that captivated Stravinsky in a number of French composers, including some operetta-composers like Lecocq.

As for Gounod, I was once greatly attracted by his melodic gifts, but I did not mean to condone his insipidity. Gounod blinded me to Bizet in my Russian years . . . In the cold war of Tchaikovsky vs. Rimsky-Korsakov, *Carmen* was admired more by the Muscovite than by the Petersburg school.[15]

Like a good Rimsky pupil, therefore, Stravinsky originally rated Gounod higher than Bizet; and although half a century later he corrected his mistake, he still had reserves about *Carmen*. He also corrected his earlier view of Verdi's late works, expressed in *Poetics of Music*, in discussion with Craft. 'Verdi's gift is pure; but even more remarkable than the gift itself is the strength with which he developed it from *Rigoletto* to *Falstaff*, to name the two operas I love best.'[16] Having so long and close a connection with Paris, Stravinsky was naturally very well acquainted with contemporary French music, but to judge from the Craft conversations and other interviews during his last years, it seems to have left him strangely indifferent. The exception to this was, of course, Debussy who played such an important part in the formation of Stravinsky's own artistic ideals. He parted company with Ravel, with whom he was on very friendly terms immediately before the war of 1914–18, and later spoke sympathetically but with a certain scepticism of his music. In fact he couples Ravel's name with those of Berlioz and Rimsky-Korsakov as composers in whose works 'the first thing we remark is the instrumentation'. This, he says, is 'not generally a good sign' and these 'are not the best composers'.[17] Of Satie he speaks sympathetically,[18] of Messiaen with a certain sarcasm. The members of 'Les Six' are not mentioned, and we can only guess the reason for this silence.

During his 'last' period Stravinsky preferred to talk about his early, Russian years rather than the neo-classical period of his life. It was of course in France that he developed his neo-classical ideas, and these were taken up by a large number of French composers, including Poulenc and Milhaud. Now that he was a fervent admirer of the New Viennese School he turned away from these composers. As well as Bach, for whom his enthusiasm continued to grow, and Bach's predecessors, his other discoveries included Bruckner. 'I still have not learned to like Bruckner, but I have come to respect him, and I think that the Adagio of the Ninth Symphony must be accounted one of the most truly inspired of all works in symphonic form.'[19] Such a *volte-face*, away from the Latin music which had earlier captured his imagination to the German, deserves our closer inspection, and this may help us to understand some puzzling remarks which occur in his discussion of *Oedipus Rex* with Robert Craft: 'I know that I relate only from an angle to the German stem (Bach–Haydn–Mozart–Beethoven–Schubert–Brahms–Wagner–Mahler–Schoenberg)... but an angle may be an advantage.'[20] Even with the reservation quoted here, it is not easy to imagine the composer of *Pulcinella*, *The Fairy's Kiss* and *Persephone* using such language in the twenties or thirties!

His attachment to the 'German stem' also showed itself, of course, in his attitude to the New Viennese School, of which we have already spoken, pointing out the many contradictions in his attitude to Schoenberg, both as a man and as an artist. His relations with the so-called avant-garde during the fifties and sixties proved no less complex.

With his insatiable curiosity, Stravinsky originally showed great interest in avant-garde experiments, speaking with respect of Pierre Boulez and with rather more reserve of Karlheinz Stockhausen. Having broken with neo-classicism, he wished to establish links with the young composers, but no mutual comprehension was established and as time went on his criticisms betrayed an increasing exasperation. He had always been hostile to sensationalism, to *bruitisme* and to any innovations which represented an irresponsible breaking with tradition. As early as 1934, in *Chronicle*, he had described the people 'whose greatest fear was lest they should appear to be behind the times' as 'the publicity-mongers of what was once the advance guard; and he had condemned Diaghilev's policy of 'modernism at all costs', that search for sensation that gave rise to 'an uncertainty in choosing the path to be followed in the future'.[21] Ten years later he was to use much the same language in *Poetics of Music*, where he speaks with ruthless sarcasm of the 'snobs' whom he calls 'representatives of *pompiérisme*'. He expresses indignation at the foolish habit of 'judging all new works by the scale of their modernity, that is to say by a non-existent scale of values'. Finally he proclaimed himself, with some polemical exaggeration, 'as much an academic as a modernist, and as much a modernist as a conservative'.[22]

Twenty years later, in his conversations with Craft, he expressed himself even more clearly and decisively: 'What is most new in new music dies quickest, and that which makes it live is all that is oldest and most tried. To contrast the new and the old is a *reductio ad absurdum*, and sectarian "new music" is the blight of contemporaneity.'

'Musical teddy-boys', who have no right to do so, try to adopt the heritage of Webern and – in a burst of anger – 'there is a whole world between me and the musical modernists, between me and the sectarians'. He goes on to criticise works in which 'each moment is organised to create movement, but the result often gives the impression of a statistical extract'. He raged against today's 'Dadaists', whom he called the parasites of art. To him experimentation was pointless without creative imagination.

What about the infinity of possibilities in connection with the new art material of electronically produced sound? With a few exceptions 'infinite possibilities' has meant collages of organ burbling, rubber suction noises, machine-gunning and other – this is curious – representational and associative noises more appropriate to Mr Disney's musical mimicries. Not the fact of possibilities, of course, but choice is the beginning of art . . . The most nearly perfect musical machine, a Stradivarius or an electronic synthesiser, is useless until joined to a man with musical skill and imagination. The stained-glass artists of Chartres had few colours, and the stained-glass artists of today have hundreds of colours but no Chartres. Organs, too, have more stops now than ever before, but no Bach. Not enlarged resources, then, but men and what they believe.[23]

Writing on another occasion he said

How much we miss, in the so-called post-Webern period, that grandiose emotional machinery that Beethoven had at his disposition, let alone the sense of harmony etc. . . . . I no longer have the patience to listen to music which not only lacks any singing or dancing quality but is simply concerned with reproducing the sound of different technical processes.[24]

As time went on Stravinsky's rejection of avant-garde music became increasingly direct. He found Stockhausen's works 'more boring than the most boring eighteenth-century music', 'unnecessary, useless and uninteresting'. They show no advance. '"Conformism" lies so heavily on the mass-produced works of the avant-garde that the concepts of forward-looking and reactionary succeed each other with astonishing speed.' He was merciless towards the young composers who adopted a disdainful attitude to the musical past. 'Some composers have proclaimed their repudiation of all music before their own. They probably do this because they are well aware that any comparison of their works with those of the past would be a major disaster for them.'

Stravinsky saw similar distortions inherent in the commercial development of the music industry in capitalist countries; and he never tired of exposing the realities of bourgeois life, though without of course touching on its basic social and political character. Yet one thing was quite clear – that he felt specifically American conditions of life and American culture wholly alien, admitting with an ache of nostalgia that he tried to avoid everything but conversation with Russian-speakers. We have already mentioned his regret at the gradual disappearance of the old habits and ceremonies of Russian life, and he spoke even more openly of his own sense of spiritual isolation:

Although I do not feel bitter at not belonging to any contemporary musical movement, and though there is no demand – commercial or otherwise – for the music I am writing now, I should still like to exchange something more than a casual word with my colleagues. But nowadays I have no one to talk to who looks at the world with the same eyes as I do.[25]

He spoke with open dislike and biting sarcasm of 'the American way of life' in an interview which he gave in New York on 24 April 1969.

Inexhaustibly curious and indefatigable in his desire to live *con tempo*, Stravinsky nevertheless ended his life in solitude, and his nostalgia for Russia increased all the more. According to Lilian Libman, he curtly interrupted Nicholas Nabokov's account of his visit to Leningrad in 1968 with the words 'The time will come when I shall be there alongside my father.'[26] Nevertheless during these final years his artistic position became more clearly defined than before. His artistic taste became more severe, more selective but also broader and more profound, while his judgments though more subjective were better considered and wiser.

His achievements both as a man and an artist were great, as were his occasional mistakes, when he was untrue to himself and failed to find the right solutions to the problems that faced him during his periods of artistic crisis. These mistakes, however, often serve as guides to students of his personality, since they were the cause of the abrupt changes in his style and 'manner'. At eighty-five, when he had finished the *Requiem*, he said that this work transformed the whole panorama of his life. To continue the metaphor, we might say that the panorama of Stravinsky's whole life as a creative artist was clearly reflected in the best of his last compositions and in his acute judgments of music, whether sympathetic or alien to him personally.

13

Instead of a conclusion

When in 1968 Stravinsky described his *Requiem* as a panorama of his quest as an artist, he added 'And here I am now, summoning up my strength to make still another change in this "finished" picture.' That, however, was something that he was never to achieve. After the *Requiem* he wrote *The Owl and the Pussycat*, a miniature for voice and piano to Edward Lear's words (1966); and two years later he completed the orchestral arrangement of two religious songs from Wolf's *Spanisches Liederbuch*. But he never carried out his long-standing plan to orchestrate the piano part of Mussorgsky's *Sunless* songs.

In 1969 his health seriously deteriorated and only his persistently beating heart prolonged the last flickers of life. Ravel's last years, he once said, were cruel: 'He was gradually losing his memory and some of his coordinating powers, and, he was, of course, quite aware of it. Gogol died screaming and Diaghilev died laughing (and singing *La Bohème* which he loved genuinely and as much as any music), but Ravel died gradually. That is the worst.'[1] Fate proved unkind and Stravinsky, too, died gradually. The date of his death was 6 April 1971, when he was within two months of his eighty-ninth birthday.

When an artist of his stature dies, it is only natural to attempt to sum up the artistic achievement of his life, but in Stravinsky's case this is difficult, since his life was intrinsically many-sided and packed with great accomplishments. Nevertheless it is important to remember as of primary importance that in all the various phases of his artistic career he never lost the feeling of 'modernity'.

Contempo: 'with the times'. Con-tempo music is the most interesting music that has ever been written, and the present moment is the most exciting in music history. It always has been . . . Modern: *modernus, modo*: 'just now'. But, also, *modus*, 'manner', whence 'up-to-date', 'fashionable'. A more complex word, and evidently of urban origin . . . Let us use contempo, then, not technically, in the sense that Schoenberg and Chaminade lived at the same time, but in my meaning 'with the times'.[2]

To Stravinsky 'belonging to one's times' is not determined by any formal chronology, still less by fashion, but by the sphere of one's emotional and intellectual interests, the level of one's understanding, one's *Weltanschauung*. At this level the past and the present are thought of as indissolubly one, and Bach or Beethoven, Gesualdo or Monteverdi are more 'contemporary' than either Chaminade or those members of the avant-garde who reject all connection with universal artistic tradition. On the other hand Stravinsky also maintained that 'unless he has a comprehensive and lively feeling for the present and consciously participates in the life around him, nobody is in a position to grasp fully the art of a bygone period. Only those who are essentially alive can discover the real life of the "dead".'[3]

Elsewhere Stravinsky explains that by 'modern' or 'contemporary' we should understand 'new susceptibilities, new emotions, new feelings'. In this sense 'contemporary' is not a matter of style or, primarily, of novelty, although a new style and its innovatory features do of course enter into the meaning. The basic criterion is the 'time of vital experience', and the object is a 'dynamic passage through time'.[4] This was something of which Stravinsky never lost sight. The final sentences of *Chronicle* are significant: 'I live neither in the past nor in the future. I am in the present. I cannot know what tomorrow will bring forth. I can only know what the truth is for me to-day. That is what I am called upon to serve, and I serve it in all lucidity.'[5] 'Today's truth' is an expression that embodies a great idea, a truth that Stravinsky discovered for himself in his work. 'I love whatever I am now doing and with each new work I feel that I have at last found the way, have just begun to compose.'[6]

He lamented that many people's way of thinking was sub-musical.[7] The motto of his own life was 'to love music for its own sake', and he was scrupulously and devoutly true to it.

This love of music made him demanding towards both himself and his work, and from this followed his cult of craftsmanship. He had every right to be proud of his own achievements in this field, and from the height of that achievement he rejected all slipshod work, all amateurishness. George Balanchine quotes a remark of Stravinsky's while they were collaborating on the ballet *Orpheus*: 'Don't say "approximately" – there is no such thing. Am I to write two minutes' music, two minutes fifteen seconds', two minutes thirty seconds' – or other fractions of seconds? Tell me the precise timing and I will do my best to provide the right amount of music.'[8] Or take another example from much earlier in Stravinsky's career. When Arthur Honegger[9] was commissioned to write *Le Roi David*, he was bold enough to turn to Stravinsky for advice – how should he write for a chorus of 100 voices with only 17 players in the orchestra? 'Quite simple', replied

Stravinsky. 'Work as though you had chosen these numbers yourself and write an oratorio for 100 voices and 17 instruments.' There are many other similar instances, some of them from Stravinsky's own experience as a composer.

Stravinsky had a strong sense of responsibility towards his chosen profession of musician, and he knew how to inspire this in all those with whom he associated. Moreover he set a standard for our times in the importance that he attached to professionalism. Honegger bears impressive witness to this: 'As a master of the musician's craft, Stravinsky defended and continually fought for the moral qualities of his "estate", demanding the highest degree of precision on the creative plane, and of executants a perfect embodiment in sound of his ideas . . . He conferred a new dignity on the whole profession of music.' [10]

'Master of the musician's craft' is a high title, and Stravinsky defended it jealously throughout his long career. As a master who loved his profession, he was continually perfecting it, and this 'dynamic passage through time' provides the explanation of his changing artistic 'manners'. These changes were not simply personal whims: they were precise reactions to changes in 'the time of vital experience'. It is true that, by disassociating himself from great popular movements and from the life of revolutionary socialism, Stravinsky deprived himself of the possibility of catching what Blok called 'the hum of time', its 'unique musical pressure'. Even so, an artist with such rare gifts of observation and of such exceptional sensibility could not fail to feel the catastrophic instability of the world that surrounded him, and he suffered – as he himself said – 'from the impossibility of accepting the world as it is'. After sixty years of hard work even he, the favourite of fortune, could not avoid suffering from 'time's mutability'. His quite extraordinary sense of the fullness of existence enabled him to reject everything that was detrimental either to his art or his life.

A full-blooded view of the world – this perhaps is the clearest definition of the artistic reality that stamps his music – and fullness both includes the joyful affirmation of life, with its dramatic and tragic elements, and at the same time excludes everything pretentious, everything neurasthenic, everything spiritually perverted, warped or decadent. Each of his works is a refutation of any charge of decadence, and a refutation made with all the warmth of his temperament and his sarcastic turn of mind.

His natural love of classicism was rooted in the same qualities, as were his intolerance of vagueness, of all that was not clearly stated, all that lacked order. Alexander Blok compared Romanticism to 'a solemn moment of repose'. But, as he pointed out, 'the moment that state of repose becomes a "lasting" state, classicism becomes degenerate, i.e. pseudo-classicism, and perishes beneath the pressure of the elements'. That moment of repose reminded the poet of 'the moment at which the sun set, suddenly illuminating with a tranquil light the tops of oaks and pines. A moment later night falls and during the night the storm clears the air.'[11] Blok was not speaking of Stravinsky, but several of Blok's ideas and metaphors seem to me applicable to Stravinsky, who stood on the threshold of such moments. His music contains both 'the great repose that finds itself' and a presentiment of 'the pressure of the elements'. Therein lies Stravinsky's strength and the lasting value of his music. At the same time there are psuedo-classical as well as classical things in his music – precisely when, as it seemed, the storm must break.

It is clear that Stravinsky's actual personality contained a number of contradictions. Sometimes he got the upper hand of these contradictions, and then his music has an indestructible integrity. At other times he was tormented by them, like the Furies of Greek mythology, and then he tried to conceal his suffering by adopting an aesthetic pose.

In one way or another Stravinsky cultivated the whole length and breadth of contemporary music. Some of the seeds that he sowed yielded a rich harvest, while others plainly withered; nor could he prevent tares from springing up. The consequences of his work have been various and are not yet clearly defined, so that it is too early for us to make a full and final estimate of his various achievements, though not to come to some preliminary conclusions.

There are many possible reactions to this most important composer of our time. We may, and sometimes should, disagree with his ideas, and criticise his social attitudes, genius though he was. On the other hand there can be no doubt that his best works will retain their active musical power, for the very good reason that this music carries the deep imprint not only of the personal contradictions in the composer's character but also of the modern world in all its many manifestations.

Notes

Preface by Theodore Strawinsky

1 In 1948 I myself wrote *Le Message d'Igor Strawinsky*, a new edition of which appeared in 1980, Lausanne.

Author's preface

1 Somerset Maugham, *The Summing Up* (New York, 1938), p. 6.

1 *Preliminary portrait*

1 *Chronicle*, p. 39.
2 *Chronicle*, p. 107.
3 *Dialogues and a Diary* (referred to in future simply as *Dialogues*), p. 62.
4 *Dialogues*, pp. 123–4.
5 'I wish to walk faster, but my unwilling partner will not execute the wish, and one immiment tomorrow will refuse to move at all' (*Dialogues*, p. 125). This, alas, happened in 1968.
6 *Chronicle*, p. 33.
7 *Chronicle*, p. 283.
8 Friedrich Schiller, *Über die aesthetische Erziehung der Menschen*, Letter 15, 1795.
9 Johan Huizinga, *Homo Ludens* (Haarlem, 1938). English translation partly by Huizinga (London, 1949), pp. 29–32.
10 N. Dmitrieva, *Picasso* (Moscow, 1971), p. 41.
11 Alexandre Tansman, *Igor Stravinsky* (Paris, 1948), pp. 23–5. English translation by Therese and Charles Bleefield (New York, 1949).
12 Huizinga, pp. 33–9.
13 *Poetics of Music*, p. 31.
14 *Chronicle*, p. 215.
15 Huizinga, p. 29.
16 *Poetics of Music*, p. 11.
17 Tansman, p. 219.
18 *Chronicle*, p. 31.
19 *Poetics of Music*, p. 76.
20 *Chronicle*, p. 277.
21 Dmitrieva, p. 113.
22 *Dialogues*, p. 22.
23 *Chronicle*, p. 164.
24 Theodore Strawinsky, *Le Message d'Igor Strawinsky* (Lausanne, 1948). English translation by Robert Craft and André Marion (London, 1953).

177

25 See Eric Walter White, *Stravinsky – the Composer and his Works* (Berkeley and Los Angeles, 1966; London, 1966), p. 389; and Roman Vlad, *Stravinsky* (London, 1960).

In his *Answers to Thirty-Five Questions* Stravinsky said 'I distinguish the Apollonian and Dionysian principles in my music. In Orpheus, for instance, the first scene is Apollonian, the second Dionysian.' He said that Apollonian features were stronger in *Persephone* and the *Symphony in C*, Dionysian in the *Concerto for Two Pianos* and the *Symphony in Three Movements*.

2   *Petersburg*

1 *Expositions and Developments*, p. 34.
2 *Expositions and Developments*, p. 31.
3 Yuri Tynyanov, *Collected Works*, vol. 1 (Moscow and Leningrad, 1959), p. 221.

Stravinsky also remembered (*Expositions and Developments*, p. 32) Petersburg as 'a city of large, open piazzas'. One of these, the Marsovoe Pol'e ('Champ de Mars') might well have been the scene of the Shrovetide festivities in *Petrushka*.
4 *Memories and Commentaries*, p. 95.
5 *Conversations*, p. 21.
6 *Chronicle*, p. 93.
7 B.I. Bursov, pp. 46 and 124 and chapter 2 (Pushkin and World Literature).
   Peculiarity of Russian Literature) (Leningrad, 1967), p. 23. 'Of all Russian artists Pushkin is in the highest degree European . . . Pushkin's Europeanness is only a form of Russianness.'

3   *Pushkin*

1 *Conversations*, p. 47.
2 *Conversations*, p. 33.
3 *Conversations*, p. 84.
4 *Chronicle*, pp. 159–60.
5 *Chronicle*, p. 162.
6 G. A. Gukovsky, *Pushkin i problemy realisticheskogo stilya* (Pushkin and the Problems of Realistic Style) (Moscow, 1957), p. 109.
7 B. I. Bursov, pp. 46 and 124 and chapter 2 (Pushkin and World Literature).
8 V. V. Vinogradov, *Stil Pushkina* (Pushkin's Style) (Moscow, 1941), pp. 485–9.
9 *Expositions and Developments*, p. 113.
10 *Chronicle*, p. 3€
11 *Chronicle*, p. 284.
12 Dmitrieva, p. 230.

13 *Dialogues*, pp. 107–8.
14 Vinogradov, p. 492.
15 Cf. *Chronicle*, p. 135 and White, pp. 532–3.

4 *Three stages*

1 *Chronicle*, pp. 285–6.
2 Vlad, p. 176.
3 *Expositions and Developments*, pp. 42–3.

5 *The Russian element*

1 This was probably the hall of the Reform Institute which was on the Moika.
2 *Memories and Commentaries*, p. 28.
3 N. Y. Myaskovsky, *Stat'i. Pis'ma. Vospominaniya* (Articles. Letters. Recollections), 2 vols. (Moscow, 1960), vol. 1, p. 72.
3a *Conversations*.
4 *Chronicle*, p. 44.
5 N. Rimsky-Korsakov, *Principles of Orchestration*. English translation by Edward Agate (New York, 1930). Author's Preface (1891), p. 2.
6 Igor Glebov, *Kniga o Stravinskom* (A Book about Stravinsky) (Leningrad, 1929), p. 100. I have omitted some considerations of the author's with which I do not agree. Igor Glebov was Asafiev's pen-name.
7 *Conversations*, p. 44.
8 *Chronicle*, p. 36.
9 The first Petersburg performance of *Prélude à l'après-midi d'un faune* was in 1905, followed in 1907 by *Nocturnes*.
10 Cf. V. V. Yastrebtsev, *N. A. Rimsky-Korsakov. Vospominaniya* (Recollections), 2 vols. (Leningrad, 1960).
11 *Conversations*, p. 54.
12 *Expositions and Developments*, p. 138.
13 *Expositions and Developments*, p. 37.
14 'Everyone who notes down a folksong – whether by ear or from a recording – distorts it in his own way, adapts it to his own level of understanding' – these, or approximately these, were the words used by Stravinsky in a conversation with the author in 1962.
15 Other possible instances are the 'factory-song' in *Les Noces* (though why Stravinsky called it a factory-song is hard to understand, as it is not one) and the opening bassoon theme in *The Rite of Spring*, borrowed from a folk-song collection (*Memories and Commentaries*, p. 98). Asafiev wrote that 'Russian melody is Stravinsky's living language, not "material" for quotation', p. 10.
16 *Chronicle*, p. 45.
17 *Chronicle*, p. 43.
18 Glebov, p. 85.
19 *Conversations*, p. 51.
20 *Chronicle*, p. 55.

21 *Chronicle*, p. 57.
22 Stravinsky himself drew attention to this by comparing the three chords after figure ⟨173⟩ in *The Rite* with figure ⟨22⟩ in *Renard* and with bars 69–71 of the first movement of *Symphony in Three Movements*.
23 He first had in mind a large orchestra like that of *The Rite*. In the second version the instrumentation corresponded roughly to that of *Renard* – 3 violins, 2 violas, 2 cellos, 1 double bass, 1 clarinet, 2 flutes, 1 oboe (cor anglais), 2 bassoons, 2 horns, drums, cymbals. The decision to use 4 pianos dates from 1921. The vocal parts remained virtually unchanged in each version.
24 *Expositions and Developments*, p. 118.
25 See 'Stravinsky on Russian Music and Musicians', in *America*, 1963, no. 76, p. 26.
26 Glebov, p. 237.
27 Glebov, p. 143. 'I consider these three laconic pieces in the highest degree significant in Stravinsky's oeuvre.' The author could not possibly have known the importance that the composer himself attached to them.
28 In 1952 Stravinsky was to produce a version of the *Concertino* entirely different in sonority, with ten wind instruments, a violin and cello.
29 *Chronicle*, pp. 156–7.
30 Eric Walter White, *Stravinsky – the Composer and his Works* (Berkeley and Los Angeles, 1966; London, 1966), p. 274.
31 Robert Craft, *Igor Stravinsky* (Munich, 1958), p. 25.
32 *Dialogues*, p. 46.
33 *Dialogues*, p. 46.
34 In the magazine *America*, 1967, no. 123, p. 46.
35 Glebov, pp. 109, 119.
36 Glebov, pp. 30, 36.
37 *Dialogues*, p. 46.

6 *The theatre*

1 *Brecht on Theatre*, ed. John Willett. Reprinted in London, 1964, pp. 33–42.
2 See V. Krasovskaya, *Russkii baletny teatr nachala xx veka* (Russian Ballet in the Early Twentieth Century), 1. Choreographers (Leningrad, 1972), pp. 507–8.
3 *Dialogues*, p. 23.
4 *Expositions and Developments*, p. 117.
5 Cf. Debussy's piano prelude 'General Lavine-eccentric'. It was under the impression made by Little Tich's performance that Stravinsky wrote the second of the *Three Pieces for String Quartet*. When he arranged these for orchestra, he in fact gave this movement the title 'Eccentric'.
6 Tristan Rémy, *Entrées clownesques*, Paris, 1962.
7 *Dialogues*, p. 107.
8 *Chronicle*, p. 164.
9 Huizinga, p. 189.
10 *Stravinsky and the Dance* (New York, 1962).

11 Quoted by Tansman, pp. 136–7.
12 *Memories and Commentaries*, p. 37.
13 See Krasovskaya, pp. 429–32.
14 K. Rudnitsky, *Rezhisser Meierkhold* (Meyerhold as Producer) (Moscow, 1969), p. 122.
15 *Musical Poetics*, p. 62.
16 *Memories and Commentaries*, p. 60.
17 Vlad (p. 45) sees the influence of Mussorgsky's *Sunless* songs in a number of vocal passages in *The Nightingale*.
18 Meyerhold, *Stat'i, Pis'ma, Rechi, Besedy* (Essays, Letters, Speeches, Conversations), p. 125. The poet M. Kuzmin also wrote on the 'theatre of immobility' in an essay entitled 'Uslovnosti v iskusstve' (Conventions in Art) (Leningrad, 1923), pp. 57–8.
19 *Dialogues*, p. 24.
20 Meyerhold's ideas were developed along individual lines by Paul Claudel and later by T. S. Eliot.
21 *Chronicle*, p. 90.
22 *Memories and Commentaries*, p. 92.
23 White, p. 227.

7 *Neo-classicism*

1 Stravinsky himself disliked the word, but applied it to Hindemith and Schoenberg as well as to himself. Adorno and the followers of the Second Viennese School considered Stravinsky responsible for introducing the temptation of neo-classicism into twentieth-century music.
2 *Chronicle*, p. 150.
3 *Poetics of Music*, pp. 56–7.
4 Dmitrieva, p. 107.
5 Vinogradov, p. 486.
6 *Memories and Commentaries*, p. 30.

8 *World classics*

1 *Poetics of Music*, p. 40.
2 *Expositions and Developments*, p. 114.
3 See Stravinsky's article in *Muzyka*, 1913, no. 141, p. 490.
4 Quoted in Helmut Kirchmeyer, *Strawinsky – Zeitgeschichte in Persönlichkeit* (Stravinsky – a Modern Personality) (Regensburg, 1958), pp. 240–1.
5 *The Arts*, January, 1924 – full text in White, pp. 528–30.
6 Exceptions are *Piano-Rag-Music*, *Four Russian Songs* and isolated episodes in *Capriccio*, *Threni* etc.
7 The ornamentation of Oedipus's music in Part 1, like that of the tenor aria in the second section of *Canticum Sacrum*, is ecclesiastical and represents the Byzantine streak in Stravinsky's music.
8 *Chronicle*, p. 243.

9 *Dialogues*, p. 34.
10 *Chronicle*, p. 222.
11 See White, pp. 316, 334–5.
12 Robert Siohan, *Stravinsky* (Paris, 1959), p. 123.
13 *Dialogues*, pp. 45–6.
14 See Robert W. Nelson, 'Stravinsky's Concept of Variations', in *Stravinsky – a New Appraisal of his Work*, ed. Paul Henry Lang (New York, 1963), pp. 61–73.
15 *Memories and Commentaries*, p. 112.
16 *Dialogues*, pp. 49–50.

9 *Movement*

1 *Chronicle*, p. 219.
1a The information in this paragraph comes from *Conversations*.
2 For the artists concerned with the first productions of Stravinsky's ballets and operas see *Strawinsky – Wirklichkeit und Wirkung* (Stravinsky – Personal Characteristics and Influence), *Music der Zeit*, new series, vol. 1 (Bonn and London, 1958), pp. 45–50. Other well-known artists not mentioned above include Matisse, De Chirico and Izami Noguki.
3 *Memories and Commentaries*, p. 154.
4 *Chronicle*, pp. 122–3.
5 *Conversations*, pp. 118–19.
6 Thomas Mann, *Der Zauberberg* (Berlin, 1924). English translation by H. T. Lowe-Porter, *The Magic Mountain* (London, 1928), pp. 102–5, 344.
7 Pierre Souvchinsky, 'La notion de temps et la musique', in *Revue Musicale* (Paris, 1939, mai-juin).
8 *Conversations*, p. 108.

10 *Space*

1 See Ernst Kurt, *Musikpsychologie*, vol. 2, 'Das musikalische Raumphänomen' (Berne, 1930).
2 See M. Druskin, *Passiony I.-S. Bacha* (The Passions of J. S. Bach) (Leningrad, 1972), pp. 34–9.
3 For a more detailed handling of this, see my article 'At the turning-point of the century' at the beginning of the collection *O zapadnoevropeiskoi muzyke xx veka* (Western European Music in the Twentieth Century) (Moscow, 1973).
4 *Muzyka* (Moscow, 1913), no. 141, p. 490.
5 *Chronicle*, p. 78.
6 Dmitrieva, p. 64.
7 *Dialogues*, p. 34.
8 *Dialogues*, p. 110.
9 O. Wulff, *Die umgekehrte Perspektive* (Reverse Perspective) (Leipzig, 1907).
10 D. Likhachev, *Poetika drevnirusskoi literatury* (The Poetics of Early Russian Literature) (Leningrad, 1967), pp. 328–9.
11 B.A. Uspensky, *Semiotika ikony* (The Semiotics of the Ikon) (Tartu, 1971).

12 P. A. Florensky, *Obratnaya perspektiva* (Reverse Perspective) (Tartu, 1967), p. 402.
13 L. F. Zhegin, *Yazyk zhivopisnogo proizvedeniya* (The Language of Painting) (Moscow, 1970), p. 36.
14 See Paul Hindemith, *Der Komponist in seiner Welt* (Mainz, 1959). *A Composer's World: Horizons and Limitations*, Charles Eliot Norton Lectures, 1949–50 (Cambridge, Mass., 1952).
15 Rudolf Reti, *Tonality–Atonality–Pantonality* (London, 1958), pp. 33–41.
16 *Expositions and Developments*, p. 116.
17 *Chronicle*, p. 262.
18 *Conversations*, p. 24.
19 A. V. Shubnikov and V. A. Koptsik, *Simmetria v nauke i iskusstve* (Symmetry in Science and Art) (Moscow, 1972), p. 90.
20 *Conversations*, p. 19.
21 *Conversations*, p. 20.
22 *Dialogues*, pp. 124–5.

11 *'Torniamo all'antico . . .'*

1 'Torniamo all'antico e sarà un progresso' ('Let us return to the old: it will be an advance'). Verdi wrote these words in a letter refusing an invitation to become the Director of the Naples Conservatory, in January 1871.
2 Quoted in Paul Collaer, *Geschichte der modernen Musik* (Stuttgart, 1963), pp. 45, 198.
3 Bela Bartók, 'Probleme der neuen Musik', in *Melos* (Berlin, 1920), no. 16, April, pp. 647–8.
4 *Dialogues*, pp. 105–6.
5 *Conversations*, p. 69.
6 *Dialogues*, p. 106.
7 Robert Craft, *Igor Stravinsky* (Munich, 1958), pp. 47–9. The first book devoted to the analysis of dodecaphonic technique, René Leibowitz's *Schoenberg et son école*, appeared in Paris in 1947 and two years later in English translation (New York, 1949).
8 These are partially reflected in the book by Stravinsky's personal secretary: Lilian Libman, *And Music at the Close – Stravinsky's Last Years* (New York, 1972).
9 *Conversations*, p. 74.
10 Anton Webern, *Perspectives* (Seattle and London, 1966), pp. xix–xxvii.
11 Craft, p. 45.
12 *Expositions and Developments*, p. 107.
13 In Webern the series is divided into motivic cells in which the piece is pre-fabricated, as it were, and this constitutes a relative similarity to Stravinsky.
14 Ariel's song from *The Tempest* is preceded by fourths and fifths in the instruments, which recall Byrd's *Bells*. In Ricercar II in the *Cantata* there is also a suggestion of bell-sonorities in the repeated syncopated accents of oboes and cello (a fifth with its fourth).

15 Exceptions to this are to be found in the short hymn to a text by Eliot, *The Dove Descending* (1962), and the re-workings of Gesualdo, *Tres Sacrae Cantiones* (1957–9).
16 *Dialogues*, p. 21, and *Chronicle*, p. 205.
17 Cf. Huizinga, p. 49.

12   Far and near

1 *Dialogues*, p. 113.
2 In 1964 Stravinsky spoke of Prokofiev's *The Fiery Angel* as one of the best operas of the twentieth century.
3 *Expositions and Developments*, p. 64.
4 *Dialogues*, pp. 112–13.
5 Cf. *Chronicle*, p. 190. 'In all his immense pianistic work, it is the "instrumental" side which is characteristic of him and makes him infinitely precious to me.'
6 *Dialogues*, p. 124.
7 See e.g. *Memories and Commentaries*, pp. 115–16, and *Expositions and Developments*, pp. 104–6.
8 Reprinted in *Za rubezhom* (Abroad), 1968, no. 20 (413), 10–16 May, p. 30.
9 *Conversations*, pp. 76–7.
10 At a meeting with Leningrad musicians, Stravinsky alluded to Rimsky-Korsakov's speaking of Berlioz's 'clumsy basses' – 'and he was quite right', he added emphatically. He returned to this point in conversation with Craft.
11 *Memories and Commentaries*, p. 64.
12 *Dialogues*, p. 116.
13 *Dialogues*, p. 116.
14 *Conversations*, p. 41 n.
15 *Dialogues*, p. 117.
16 *Conversations*, p. 75.
17 *Conversations*, p. 28.
18 *Dialogues*, p. 41.
19 *Expositions and Developments*, p. 61 n.
20 *Dialogues*, p. 30.
21 *Chronicle*, p. 183.
22 *Poetics of Music*, p. 85.
23 *Dialogues*, pp. 119, 136.
24 This and the following quotations are taken from *Sovietskaya Muzyka*, 1966, no. 12, p. 131, and 1968, no. 10, p. 141.
25 See *America*, 1967, no. 123, p. 46.
26 Libman, p. 32.

13   Instead of a conclusion

1 *Conversations*, p. 63.
2 *Dialogues*, p. 119.

3 *Chronicle*, p. 127.
4 *Dialogues*, p. 127.
5 *Chronicle*, p. 286.
6 *Dialogues*, p. 129.
7 *Chronicle*, pp. 248–50.
8 See 'Das tänzerische Element', in the collection *Strawinsky in Amerika: das compositorische Werk von 1939 bis 1955* (Bonn, 1955), p. 24.
9 See Collaer, p. 134.
10 Quoted in *Strawinsky – Wirklichkeit und Wirkung*, p. 7.
11 Alexander Blok, *O romantike* (Romanticism) (1919).

Index

compiled by Frederick Smyth

Index

Index

Index

influence on Stravinsky **30–1**, 37, 51
Boris Godunov 16, 31, 34
Khovanshchina 31, 34
Pictures from an Exhibition 130
songs 34, 173
Muzyka (Polish journal, 1942) q.12
Myaskovsky, Nikolai 29

Nabokov, Nicholas 172
Napravnik, Eduard 34, 115
Nicholas II, Tsar of Russia 115
Nietzsche, Friedrich Wilhelm 121
Nijinskaya, Bronislava 58, 62
Nijinsky, Vatslav 62–3
Nouvel, V.F. 3, 33
Nurok, A.P. 3, 33

Obrecht, Jacob 166
Okeghem, Jean de 166
Onnou, André 159
Orff, Carl 88
Orlov, G. 122
Ostolopov 80
Ovid (Publius Ovidius Naso) 19

Palestrina, Giovanni Pierluigi da 145,
152, 168
parody, in art and music **80**
Pergolesi, Giovanni Battista 51, 85–8
Petersburg
Court orchestra 29
Maryinsky Theatre 2, 15, 56, 69, 115
Music School 28
Petipa, Marius 65
Petrenko, Miss 28
Picasso, Pablo 2, 16, 22, 76–7, 80, 115,
124
on art and artists q.5, q.12, q.21
characteristics 8
and Cubism 127
his décor for *Pulcinella* 58, 88
Kataev's opinion q.82
and Matisse 7
Demoiselles d'Avignon, Les (1906–7)
76
Guernica (1937) 76
Pirandello, Luigi 57
Pokrovsky 33
Polignac, Princesse Edmond de 3
Poulenc, Francis 3, 169
Prokofiev, Sergei 10, 66, q.79, 81, 165
Ivan the Terrible – film music 63
Love for Three Oranges 56
Symphony no.4 96
Puccini, Giacomo 110
La Bohème 173

Pushkin, Alexander 5, 25, 32, 47–8, 59,
70, 80, 82
his letter to Prince Vyazemsky q.73
his Petersburg 15–16, 69
on Rossini 110
on Russian character q.8
Stravinsky's admiration **17–22**, 50
on taste q.11

Quantz, Johann Joachim 119
Quarenghi, Giacomo 15

Rachmaninov, Serge, *Vespers* 111
Ramuz, C.F. 11
Raphael (Raffaello Sanzio) 129
Rastrelli, Bartolomeo Francesco 15
Ravel, Maurice 3, 10, 34, 47, 169, 173
on Schoenberg q.138–9
Bolero 130
Chansons madécasses 139
Daphnis et Chloé 66, 102
Piano Concerto for the left hand 7
Poèmes de Mallarmé 139
Valse, La 7, 66
Reger, Max 75
Rembrandt van Rijn 79–80
Remizov, Nikolai 115
Reti, Rudolf 134
Revue Musicale (Debussy number) 49
Richter, Nicholas 28
Rilke, Rainer Maria q.4, q.120
Rimsky-Korsakov, Andrei 42
Rimsky-Korsakov, Nikolai 26, 33, 124,
159, 169
his antipathy to Tchaikovsky 31, 169
compared with Debussy 125
death 33, 36
his indifference to Bach and Haydn
165
influence on Stravinsky 23, **29–30**,
31, **36–7**, 65, 168
as Stravinsky's teacher 11, 20, 27,
29–30, 76
Capriccio Espagnol 101
Golden Cockerel, The 29–30, 56, 69
Invisible City of Kitezh, The 29, 37
Kaschei the Immortal 29, 36
Mlada 29
Pan Voevoda 29
Sadko 37
Servilia 29
Sheherazade 101
Snow Maiden, The 30
Tsar Saltan 115
Roerich, Nicholas 36, q.64, 115
Romanov, Boris 62

189

Index

Index